THE TENDERNE

of

CONSCIENCE

African Renaissance and the
Spirituality of Politics

Dr Allan A Boesak

WILD GOOSE PUBLICATIONS
www.ionabooks.com

Copyright © Allan A. Boesak 2005

UK edition first published 2008 by
Wild Goose Publications
4th Floor, Savoy House, 140 Sauchiehall Street, Glasgow G2 3DH, UK
www.ionabooks.com
Wild Goose Publications is the publishing division of the Iona Community.
Scottish Charity No. SCO03794. Limited Company Reg. No. SCO96243.

ISBN 978-1-905010-51-6

We gratefully acknowledge the support of the Drummond Trust,
3 Pitt Terrace, Stirling, in the publication of this book

English-language edition originally published in 2005 as:
THE TENDERNESS OF CONSCIENCE – African Renaissance and the Spirituality of Politics
Copyright © 2005 AFRICAN SUN MeDIA, Stellenbosch, South Africa. All rights reserved.
Published by agreement with AFRICAN SUN MeDIA (Pty) Ltd

Cover design by Laura Oliver
Typesetting by Wikus van Zyl

The cover photograph was kindly provided by the Mapungubwe Museum, University of Pretoria.
This famous gold rhinoceros (circa 1220–1290 AD) was discovered in 1934 on Mapungubwe Hill in Limpopo Province
in a royal grave as part of a thousand year old collection of artifacts made of gold and other materials. The rhino has
come to symbolise the high culture of Mapungubwe, and along with this, that of Africa. As these artifacts were found
in the graves of royalty, they also symbolise leadership in Africa and are evidence of the existence of an African
civilisation long before colonisation.

A catalogue record for this book is available from the British Library.

Overseas distribution:
Australia: Willow Connection Pty Ltd, Unit 4A, 3–9 Kenneth Road, Manly Vale, NSW 2093
New Zealand: Pleroma, Higginson Street, Otane 4170, Central Hawkes Bay
Canada: Novalis/Bayard Publishing & Distribution, 10 Lower Spadina Ave., Suite 400, Toronto, Ontario M5V 2Z2

Printed by Bell & Bain, Thornliebank, Glasgow, UK

THE
TENDERNESS
of
CONSCIENCE

Also by Allan Boesak and published by Wild Goose:

The Fire Within: Sermons from the Edge of Exile

Dedicated to
Jan de Waal, for whom yesterday
has always been a foreign country;

and to
The faithful people of God, unheard of, unsung, unmentioned,
but everywhere;
without whom the struggle could never have been won,
and who, in having become heroes of the struggle
have always been heroes of the faith.

Tomorrow belongs to us.

Dr Allan Boesak, major national and international figure in South African struggle politics of the 70s, 80s and 90s, was United Democratic Front leader, ANC politician and human rights activist. He is the recipient of twelve honorary doctorates and several international awards, and author of several books on theology and politics. Theologian and pastor of a local church, he remains an acute political observer and cultural critic of South African life.

ACKNOWLEDGEMENTS

In a very real sense an author never writes a book alone. There are always others without whose help no book will ever see the light. I gratefully therefore make use of this opportunity to thank those who have helped to make this book possible.

The idea for this book was born in late 1995 when my family and I were privileged to spend some time in the United States as guests of the Presbyterian Church USA. It was a period that gave us the distance, solitude and time for reflection that were sorely needed. I am deeply grateful to the PCUSA's Stony Point Conference Centre, the people of Lafayette-Orinda Presbyterian Church, the American Baptist Seminary of the West in Berkeley, California, its students and staff, Dr J Alfred Smith and the people of Allen Temple Baptist Church in Oakland, California. I have learned much from discussions with friends and colleagues, especially Prof Nicholas Wolterstorff, recently retired from Yale Divinity School.

In South Africa deeply appreciated support came from my long time friend Rev Jan de Waal and Ms Sue Anderson of the New World Foundation under whose auspices the Institute for Theology and Public Life came into being. Especially Jan de Waal believed in this book and pushed hard for the completion of this project. It is with deep gratitude that this book is partly dedicated to him. The Institute afforded me the necessary time for study, research and writing, and without the support of our partner in the Netherlands, the Netherlands Protestant Church and its Department of Global Ministries this project would never have been possible. Prof Danny Titus of Unisa's College of Law has been helpful and supportive in his reading of the manuscript, and invaluable in his constant encouragement. The Institute for Reconciliation and Justice in Cape Town graciously opened the doors of their library for purposes of research, and the staff has been extremely helpful and professional. Thank you. I thank my publisher, and especially Ms Justa Niemand and Ms Hanli Nothnagel for making this work available to the public.

My greatest supporter in life and work, my inspiration for all good things in my life is my wife Elna. To her and our children I owe a great debt of gratitude. Their love, patience and support have been indispensable.

The years during which this book was written had not always been easy. But God is gracious and merciful, and it is true: "My grace is enough… my strength comes into its own in the hour of your weakness". To God be the glory.

CONTENTS

INTRODUCTION

Yesterday is a Foreign Country

When President Thabo Mbeki first proposed the idea of an African renaissance, it was like a breath of fresh air blowing through the windows of our mind. He announced it as more than just a political, social and economic programme. He spoke of it as a vision, a dream, an absolute necessity for an Africa "whose time had come". This vision, for our country and our continent, freed us from the isolationist thinking of the past, placed us without apology or equivocation, indeed with great pride, in the midst of Africa as *Africans*, challenging us to be done with the self-pitying moroseness and the self-justifying angers of yesterday, and to face with determination the challenges of the new age which has dawned upon, and for, us. Gladly taking up the cry of the young Afrikaners he met, he called on us all to affirm with them: "Yesterday is a foreign country, tomorrow belongs to us!"

This cry, I believe, was, and is not, an unseemly appeal to "get away" from the ugliness of yesterday's apartheid, cloaking oneself in the false innocence of "We did not know, we did not do it (our parents did) and we do not want to know". It was meant to express a genuine desire to say, "Yesterday's South Africa will never happen again, it must forever be changed – tomorrow's opportunities shall be grasped with both hands. And we, the new generation of the new South Africa, shall do it differently". This is surely how Thabo Mbeki understood it in his "Prologue", when he threw it down as a challenge to the participants of the first major conference on "The African Renaissance", the proceedings of which have been published in a book of the same title we shall have cause to return to again and again in this work. Mbeki then invited us to accept both the challenge and the spirit of the African renaissance, and to "make foreign" all things that hold us back – from "backwardness" to the commitment to change the lot and role of women, to the "disempowerment of the masses of our people". We must dedicate ourselves to make sure we succeed in the struggle to make the masses of the people their own liberators. What we must also "make foreign" is the "abuse of political power to gain material wealth by those who exercise that power foreign to our continent and systems of governance".

The president invites us to "insert ourselves" into the international debate on the issues of globalization and its impact on the lives of the people, and make our voice heard about what we and the rest of the world should do to achieve the development which is a "fundamental right" of the masses of our people. All of this is crucial to the renaissance of Africa as Mbeki envisages it, and none of it will come about on its own. The renaissance "will be victorious only as a result of a protracted struggle that we ourselves must wage". Therefore, says the President, "I address myself to those on our continent who are ready and willing to repeat after the Afrikaner youth that 'yesterday is a foreign country - tomorrow belongs to us!' I address myself to those who are ready to be rebels against tyranny, instability, corruption and backwardness".

These are words that reverberate in my own heart and I consider myself as one so addressed. The president's challenge has been accepted by intellectuals from a wide spectrum of disciplines and the debate has been both vigorous and stimulating. This book is a response to Thabo Mbeki's invitation from a Christian theological point of view. The same faith, the same Bible, the same theological tradition I come from and that have shaped irrevocably my participation in the struggle for liberation, inspire me now to join this new struggle Thabo Mbeki has so accurately pinpointed. And I join this struggle with the same commitment that captivated me during the struggle against apartheid. I hope and pray some of that commitment will be apparent as the reader takes some familiar and some maybe less familiar paths with me through this book.

At that first "Renaissance" conference, Lesibo Teffo, professor of philosophy at the University of the North, posed a profoundly important question. "Where", he asked, "lies the anchor of this African renaissance? Arguably", he answers himself, "it lies in the moral renewal through African values. Politics and economics undoubtedly have a role to play. However, without a moral conscience, society is soulless". I am in complete agreement. It is perhaps for this reason Thabo Mbeki himself has talked of this project as "the search for the African soul".

When I read Prof. Teffo's words, it struck me forcefully how they resonated with what I myself understood at the beginning, in the middle of the nineties, when this book first began to form in my mind. I refer to Calvinism's "tenderness of conscience", which is the guiding theme throughout this book. What struck me also was the similarity of the insight from a thoroughly modern African philosopher and a sixteenth-century Christian reformer. It struck me with a sense of wonder and joy, of pride and humble gratitude how much I am the spiritual child of both: African and Reformed spirituality. If some of that becomes clear to the reader, as well as the ramifications of it, I shall be eternally grateful.

This book is a response to the invitation of Thabo Mbeki, and therefore, in a real sense, a conversation with him. But it is even more essentially an engagement with the idea, the dream, the necessity of Africa's renaissance itself, in the course of which it becomes an engagement with our own democratic project as well as global politics. Each of the issues the President has raised, and then one or two more, is discussed here. I believe, with Teffo, that without spirituality our politics is vain and our search for an African renaissance futile.

We begin this book with an overview of the African situation and we trace, as best one can in the scope of a single chapter, the development from Uhuru to Black power and their consequences for the African renaissance. Chapter Two is an attempt to understand, and respond to, Mbeki's concept of the African Renaissance. In chapter Three we "insert ourselves" into the realities of globalization, its impact on Africa's renaissance and on the lives of our people. Chapters Four, Five and Six bring our focus more to South Africa itself and our own struggles for authenticity as we lead the call for an African renaissance. Subsequently we give attention to the role of faith in our struggle against apartheid and for our freedom, the role of the church, especially in post-apartheid South Africa, and that most crucial of events in our recent history, the efforts at reconciliation and their meaning for South Africa's politics, transformation and future. The final chapter is an attempt to chart a possible course for a spirituality of politics without which, it is my firm conviction, we shall not succeed, and without which our country and the world are doomed.

This book is a contribution from a Christian theological point of view. It is not my intention to write broadly, which too often means vaguely, from a "religious" point of view. Our new democracy has given room to religious pluralism and one can only praise God for it. Without it my friend and colleague, Maulana Faried Essack, would not have felt as free to write and publish right here his very interesting book *On Being a Muslim,* and without it there would not have been the current robust debate on the validity of traditional African religions or indeed on the Africanisation of Christianity and Christian theology in South Africa. Likewise, my own views on Christian theology and the Bible did not find ready space for publication in South Africa in the past. Of some thirteen titles only two could be published in South Africa over some twenty years, even though some of them have appeared in as many as nine languages across the globe. No doubt we will see more and more contributions from specific religions to the discussion of the burning issues of our day.

The contribution from the Christian faith can only be meaningful and authentic if it is made from the heart of the Christian faith: the belief in the Lordship of Jesus Christ over all of life. It has always been my belief that Christian theology, if it is to be anything, is a *public* theology. It is public, because it is a theology of the Kingdom of God which is God's public claim on the world and the lives of God's people in the world. It is public because of Jesus of Nazareth, who took on public form when he became a human person, and because his life was lived in public servanthood and public vulnerability in obedience to God. It is public because He was crucified in public, for all to see. And it is public because He rose from the grave in the light of day and defied the power of death for all to see. Hence Christian theology is public, critical and prophetic in our cry to God; public, critical and prophetic in our struggle with God and in our stand against the godless powers of this world; and public, critical and prophetic in our hope in God.

This is not my discovery. It has been the sustenance and the rallying cry of the Calvinist reformation from its very beginning. This is the tradition of which I am a spiritual child, and this is the tradition in which I stand, and from whose wells I gratefully drink. And I have been pleasantly surprised to discover just how much the Reformed tradition has remained, and indeed has gained, theological and political potency in the new struggles we are called to wage. The tradition which gave the world its first "revolutionary saints" (Michael Walzer), which offered itself to the world as a "world-transforming" religion, (Nicholas Wolterstorff), and saw its spirituality as a "call to worldly holiness"(Richard

Mouw), is a tradition that has found in the call for justice and the cries of the poor the very voice of God.

So when Thabo Mbeki says, "As every revolution requires revolutionaries, so must the African renaissance have its militants and activists who will define the morrow that belongs to them in a way which will help restore our dignity", it is with *those* ears that I hear him. And it is in that spirit that this book is offered as a humble contribution to a crucial struggle in search of the morrow that makes yesterday a foreign country.

Allan Aubrey Boesak
Somerset West

CHAPTER ONE

FROM UHURU TO BLACK POWER
Dreams, Realities and the End of a Century

From Uhuru to Black Power

For the people of Africa the twentieth century was the century of their awakening. For four centuries Africa had been overrun, subdued and dominated by Europe; her civilizations wiped out, her kingdoms virtually destroyed.[1] The natural resources of the continent were wiped out or severely depleted, its cultural wealth plundered and Africa's people became slaves wherever white people opened up "new" lands and conquered indigenous peoples. The destruction of African civilizations did not mean the large-scale stripping of the continent's wealth only; it also meant that Africa's people were robbed of their dignity and their achievements past and present; it meant the denial and reversal of history on a scale not seen before or since. Henceforth Africa's civilizations would be relegated to the sphere of myth and legend, the industry of her people set in the service and enrichment of foreign powers. Of the African civilizations that "outstripped that of Europe"[2] there would be nothing left but empty shells devoid of the vision that made those very civilizations great and, in the battle to survive the unprecedented onslaught from Europe, they would neither survive nor stop the tide of self-destruction, an inevitable misery that always yokes with such historic disasters. "There can be little doubt", says WEB Du Bois, "that in the fourteenth century the level of culture in black Africa south of the Sudan was equal to that of Europe and was so recognized".[3] In the four centuries spanning the initial violation of the African continent, that reality was first destroyed and then it was denied that it ever existed.

The end of the slave trade and the abolition of slavery in the British colonies did not bring relief and the rape of Africa continued. The Arab slave trade did not end and, in fact, merely shifted more fully to the Arabs and formed the commercial basis of the trade in ivory. In a bitter irony the Arab trade in ivory led to a new and supplementary means of control, new explorations and eventual annexation of new lands under the pretence of attacking slavery. As ivory replaced the trade in human souls so Africa, scarcely given time to draw a second breath, was once again the field of plunder. By the

---

[1] Cf., for example, Basil Davidson, *Black Mother, A study of the pre-colonial connection between Africa and Europe* (London: Longman, 1970) and its bibliography. See also the monumental work of African scholar, Cheikh Anta Diop, *The African Origin of Civilization: Myth or Reality?* (New York: Lawrence and Hill, 1974).

[2] W E B Du Bois, *The World and Africa. An inquiry into the part which Africa has played in world history* (New York: International Publishers, 1946, 11th ed., 1980) 44.

[3] *Op. cit.*, 44-45. See also 79.

last half of the nineteenth century the West's appetite for ivory became voracious and its exploitation ruthless, wrote Du Bois. "Ivory became the scourge of central Africa".[4] The carnage wreaked in human terms is as incalculable as it is unspeakable.

The number of slaves abducted to Europe, the Americas and the Caribbean alone are set between 15 and 40 million persons, while more than 5 million died in the "middle passage", the crossing of the Atlantic Ocean. For Africans this was, says research specialist Bernard Makhosezwe Magubane, and he is right, "one of the greatest unnatural disasters of all time".[5] Furthermore, the abolition of slavery in the nineteenth century did not mean the end of colonization and the onrush of the industrial revolution left Africa largely behind, a cripple in a race too long and too fast on a field too unequal. This loss of human potential over 250 years is Africa's greatest impediment to full and meaningful participation in modern life.

The dawn of the twentieth century did not bring the progress and prosperity for Africa as it did for the industrializing world. Instead, the ongoing exploitation of Africa ensured, nurtured and fed the continuing prosperous development of the rich nations.[6] The rules of trade and the realities of the world economy set by the rich nations kept Africa economically dependent, poor and underdeveloped, and the dominant ideologies of the strong kept Africa politically subservient, while the full might of Western academic thought was mustered to keep Africans inferior, without merit, without a past and therefore without any measure of a humane future. There was no field of Western academic endeavour since the seventeenth century, whether science, philosophy, literature, art, and especially theology in which the dehumanisation of the African did not become the acid test of the superiority of both Western man and Western culture. The role of theology in Western thinking we have discussed elsewhere, but let us consider here, for example, Hegel, that great proponent of Western philosophical thought:

> If you want to understand [the Negro] rightly, you must abstract all elements of respect and morality and sensitivity [for] there is nothing remotely humanized in the Negro's character ... Africa proper, as far as history goes back, has remained for all purposes of connection with the rest of the world, shut up. It is ... the land of childhood, which lying beyond the days of self-conscious history, is enveloped in the dark mantle of Night ...

---

[4] *Op. cit.*, 68-72. See also Du Bois's withering critique of the "moral gap" in Europe concerning this issue, 74.

[5] Magubane, "The African Renaissance in Historical Perspective", in: *African Renaissance, The New Struggle* (Cape Town: Tafelberg, and Sandton: Mafube Publishing, 1999) 22. See also Magubane, *The Ties That Bind: African-American Consciousness of Africa* (Trenton: Africa World Press, 1987).

[6] See Walter Rodney, *How Europe Underdeveloped Africa* (Washington DC: Howard University Press). *The State of War and Peace Atlas, 3rd edition* (London: Penguin, 1997), 52 offers this insightful remark: "In the last twenty years of the nineteenth century, Europeans conquered 85% of Africa in a uniquely grandiose act of theft".

> In Negro life that consciousness has not yet reached the realization of any substantial objective existence - as for example God, or Law, in which the interest of man's volition is involved, and in which he realizes his own being [...] It is the essential principle of slavery that man has not yet attained self-consciousness of his freedom, and consequently sinks down to a mere Thing - an object of no value. Among Negroes moral sentiments are weak, or more strictly, non-existent.[7]

As far as Africa and the imperial project were concerned, academic thinking became an essential tool in the moral justification of slavery, the subjection of "inferior races", the theft of their lands as well as their souls, and ultimately in their extinction. Robert Knox's conclusion is maybe "chilling", as Magubane describes it, but it certainly is not shocking. The logic is too consistent, too relentless:

> What signify these races to us? Who cares particularly for the Negro, or Hottentot or the Kaffir? ... Destined by the nature of their race to run, like animals, a certain limited course of existence, it matters little how their extinction is brought about.[8]

This was also the logic that continued to underlie the colonialist era in Africa. It was the ultimate justification for the destruction of Africa and its peoples. But it was inevitable that there would come a point when the people of Africa would accept this no longer. They would rise up with pride, anger and determination, and take their stand on the soil of their motherland. They would raise their voices and shout with pride, courage and defiance the words that lifted Pixley Isaka Seme up from amongst his peers and made the world sit up and listen: *"I am an African!"* These are the words that now, a century later, inspired Thabo Mbeki to repeat it in lyrical and intensely moving terms seldom heard from a statesman. "I am an African!" exclaims Mbeki taking up Pixley's cry, "I am born of a people who would not tolerate oppression".[9] It was when the peoples of Africa realised this fundamental truth, looked with new eyes at their past and with renewed hope to their future, that the cry *"Uhuru!"* split the African skies. It was the cry for resistance against the racist oppression of Africa's people, against the economic exploitation that had gone on for too long, against the cultural diminishment of whole peoples, against the eroding legacy of slavery. It was a cry against the rape of a continent, against the injustices built into a world system in which Africa could hardly participate and over which it shared no control. It was a cry for the restoration of dignity and of justice. It was a cry for freedom. It was a cry from the heart of

---

[7] G W F Hegel, *The Philosophy of History* quoted in Magubane, *African Renaissance in Historical Perspective*, 24, 25. See also Robert Knox, *The Races of Mankind: A Philosophical Inquiry into the Influence of Race over the Destinies of Nations*, which Magubane calls "a must if one wants to understand the origins of scientific racism", *op. cit.*, 26.

[8] *African Renaissance*, 26.

[9] Thabo Mbeki, *Africa, the time has come* (Cape Town: Tafelberg & Mafube Publishers: 1998) 34

the people, given voice by leaders such as Kwame Nkrumah, Jomo Kenyatta, Amilcar Cabral, Patrice Lumumba, Julius Nyerere, Kenneth Kaunda.

In this part of the continent, the liberation movements took up the cry in their own struggles against the last bastions of colonialism. In South Africa, the African National Congress who had led the struggle since 1912 and had given admirable and sustained leadership to this country's masses became, together with the younger Pan Africanist Congress, a banned organization. But the foundations laid by decades of struggle remained strong and it is a tribute to the ANC that through many years of brutal suppression, imprisonment of leaders and the exile of thousands, the commitment of the people to the struggle for freedom and their loyalty to the ideals of the movement did not abate, but grew stronger.

By the end of the sixties, beginning of the seventies an important shift at three levels occurred that was destined to bring a completely new dynamic into the politics of struggle. First, the existing vacuum was filled by a new, youthful leadership, a militant, articulate generation who would remain rooted in the traditions of struggle, but would in many ways spell out a new vision, one more in accord with the changing dynamics within South Africa itself. Second, this vision was infused with an urgency that outstripped that of the older generation and would show an inclusivity the movement up till now did not display or understand, and the value of which was not realized. Third, the new struggle politics far better understood the importance of trans-national black solidarity and this had a more immediate impact than the sometimes hesitant internationalism that was part of the armoury of the pre-exilic generation. It was this reality that in South Africa found expression in a new phrase on the lips and in the actions of millions, especially those of young people and students. That phrase was Black Power. It set in motion an unprecedented wave of resistance after a long vacuum in the politics of resistance in South Africa that would not stop until the white minority regime finally had to give in to the pressure.

The Courage to be Black

For the youth involved in the struggle against racism and apartheid, *Black Power* carried with it more symbolism than any other political concept before it. First of all, it was the natural child of that other powerful cry, *Black Consciousness*. It was the realization by black people in South Africa that the racial and ethnic divisions so crucial to the successful workings of apartheid were crucial not just for *racist* reasons, but for reasons of *domination*. It meant the discovery of the brutal truth that under racism, colonialism and apartheid in all its guises, the black person has, in the words of Steve Biko, "become a shell, a shadow of a man, completely defeated, drowning in his own misery, a slave, an ox bearing the yoke of oppression with sheepish timidity".[10] We all knew that this

---

[10] Steve Biko, *I Write What I Like, A Selection of his Works* (Johannesburg: Ravan Press, 1996), 29.

was where we had to begin, with this "first truth, bitter as it may seem".[11] But that was the beginning.

Black Consciousness was also, and as a consequence, the affirmation of black personhood with an intensity that overcame centuries of mental and cultural domination and indoctrination. It became a unifying force amongst all oppressed people of South Africa overcoming ethnicity, race and cultural divisions. It was one of the most liberating experiences for young "coloured" persons ever, and brought a fundamental change in their thinking and political action such as no political philosophy could do before. Not to see ourselves as defined by the racist ideologies of oppression, not allowing our humanity to be prescribed and proscribed by apartheid was to have unlocked a door to political maturity and activism unknown before. It was the restoration of human dignity and pride, of a sense of purpose and togetherness, overcoming the divisions of race, culture and ethnicity. Indeed, recognizing their rich diversity as a source of inspiration and shared pride was a new experience for South Africa's oppressed people. It was, in short, the courage to be black.

Properly understood, Black Consciousness was the first truly non-racial experience for millions of South Africans. It was the indispensable requirement for the genuine non-racialism that was such an *essential* element of the struggle politics of the eighties and simultaneously so fundamental for the future of South Africa. Genuine non-racialism can only come about among equals, and without the affirmation of the human dignity of black people, it would have remained the meaningless theory white liberalism in South Africa has always meant for it to be, and which even today holds sway in liberal circles. Black Consciousness understood that the affirmation of black human dignity had personal, psychological, theological and political consequences. The new-found pride in their cognisance of "the deliberateness of God's plan in creating black people black", to continue Biko's argument, meant that "liberation, therefore, of is paramount importance in the concept of Black Consciousness".[12] Thus Black Consciousness became the impetus for a new phase in the liberation struggle at a time when it had become completely stagnated through the intransigence of the white minority regime, the dearth of leadership through oppression, imprisonment and exile, and the difficulty for the people to find a way out of the darkness of that particular age. And with it came Black Theology. Again Biko:

> Thus if Christianity in its *introduction* was corrupted by the inclusion of aspects which made it the ideal religion for the *colonisation* of people, nowadays in its *interpretation* it is the ideal religion for the maintenance of the *subjugation* of the same people.[13]

[11] *Op. cit.,* 29. The sexist language of the liberation movement, as in its philosophy, politics and theology even this late reflected the gaps in our own understanding of total liberation and proves how right women were, and are, in their insistence that without the liberation of women the liberation of the nation remains incomplete.

[12] *Op. cit.,* 49.

[13] *Op. cit.,* 57.

But this is where Steve Biko misunderstood and underestimated the power of the Christian message. Deeply embedded within the Christian message itself lies the indestructible seed of rebellion against inhumanity, injustice and oppression, and within it is the undeniable surge toward freedom, as African Americans have discovered, even though white Christianity has used the Bible for the justification of slavery and oppression over many centuries in the United States. As we now know, Black Theology – as liberation theology did elsewhere in the United States, Latin America and Asia – became the most powerful tool for oppressed Christians in South Africa to rediscover the gospel in its surge for justice, humanity and liberation. And *despite* its misuse for the subjugation of people, it became, to turn Biko's words around, the ideal religion for the *liberation* of the same people. We return to this discussion at a later stage.

So it is that Black Consciousness, Black Power and Black Theology merged and emerged as the key which unlocked the door to the future for the oppressed people of South Africa at a time when most of us thought that all was lost. It rekindled the almost decayed hope in the hearts of the downtrodden, reasserted the faith of the people in the liberation God of the Exodus, the prophets and of Jesus of Nazareth. It reclaimed the gospel for the poor and the oppressed; rediscovered, rewrote the vision and ran with it as the prophet Habakkuk enjoins us to do, unleashed the tremendous energies of a people who, long before Thabo Mbeki discovered it, knew that they were born of a people who would not tolerate oppression. It came at a most opportune time, a *kairos* moment, to put it biblically, and it paved the way for the decisive phase of the struggle during the eighties as it found expression in the United Democratic Front. It became a spiritual force without which resistance to apartheid would have remained singularly ineffectual.

What arises now, as a political curiosity of major proportions, is the fact that neither President Nelson Mandela, nor President Thabo Mbeki, nor any of the present leadership of the ANC have been willing to give any recognition to the fundamental role of Black Consciousness, Black Theology and Black Power in a crucial stage of the struggle against apartheid. In part I suppose it is understandable, now that the philosophical movement Biko started has solidified itself into a particularly unsuccessful political party (Azapo) to the "left" of the ANC, aligning itself more with the Pan Africanist Congress. But there is a difference between the philosophical movement of that time and party political politics after 1994, and the political situation ought not to be a hindrance to historical honesty.

While President Mbeki, surprisingly, in his writings does not refer to the Black Consciousness movement at all, President Mandela has, in an exhaustive piece written while he was still in prison, set out his views on the issue.[14] It will take us too far to give any detailed treatment of Mr Mandela's argumentation. One must say, however, that the most remarkable thing about that article is the dismissive tone Mr Mandela employs

---

[14]   Nelson Mandela, "Whither the Black Consciousness Movement? An Assessment", in: Mac Maharaj (Ed.): *Reflections in Prison* (Cape Town: Struik Publishers, Zebra Press & Robben Island Museum, 2001), 21-64.

toward the Black Consciousness movement and its proponents. In the course of his argument Mr Mandela, in my view, makes three fundamental mistakes.

Φ   He places all emphasis on the political groupings that came about as a result of the Black Consciousness philosophy and then proceeds to contrast them with the ANC in terms of the historical role of the ANC in South Africa. Of course they are bound to be weighed and found wanting. There is no political movement that can compete with the ANC in that regard. This means also that Mandela cannot conceive of any political initiative, successful or not, for which the ANC must not ultimately claim ownership. In his analysis, just about every initiative of the Black Consciousness generation is taken over and controlled by the ANC.

Φ   Mr Mandela shows no cognisance of the fact that Black Consciousness served as preparation for a whole new generation of political activists, not only to become politically active, but to become part of the historical movement of the oppressed in South Africa. For people like myself, and I daresay millions others, meaningful participation in the struggle under the banner of the ANC would not have been possible had we not secured for ourselves the fundamentals of the Black Consciousness philosophy. This flaw has proved to have all sorts of consequences for the way in which the ANC conceives itself, the people and the struggle after 1994.

Φ   There is no acknowledgement in the discussion of the *philosophy* of Black Consciousness, and therefore no need to respond to the philosophical challenges that philosophy posed to both the regime and the freedom movement, then as well as now.

This last point is proved most disturbingly when Mandela endeavours to respond to the criticism the Black Consciousness advocates had of Marxism, whose appropriateness and efficacy for the South African situation they strongly doubted. Mr Mandela begins by showing his disdain for Black Consciousness thinkers and advocates, whom he describes as "not serious" as "freedom fighters":

> No serious-minded freedom fighter would reject ideas in theoretical manuscripts that are a blueprint of the most advanced social order in world history, that have led to an unprecedented reconstruction of society and to the removal of all kinds of oppression for a third of mankind. Not even the most headstrong imperialist despises the socialist countries… Not only does scientific socialism bring security to all men in the form of a just distribution of the country's wealth and the removal of all sources of national and international friction, but the socialist countries are the best friends of those who fight for national liberation.[15]

---

[15]   Cf. 43

Even without becoming cynical about the ANC's turnabout on the "socialist revolution" after it had become the government in 1994, and about its resolute pursuit of neo-liberal, neo-capitalist economic policies at the moment, one has to wonder at the emotional tone from one who in the same article accuses the Black Consciousness movement of emotionalism in its affirmation that "Black is beautiful". Both in actual fact and with hindsight, Black Consciousness advocates were far closer to the truth than Nelson Mandela and the ANC, and it is not only the people of the former Soviet Union who would find Mandela's assertion that Marxism brought freedom from oppression "for a third of mankind", an extraordinarily romantic view of a system every bit as oppressive as fascist South Africa under apartheid – to say nothing of his belief that Marxism had removed "all sources of national and international friction".

But it is even more serious when Mr Mandela writes off as "a form of fanaticism" Black Consciousness's assertion that "race is a myth". This assertion came out of Black Consciousness's deep concern that the ethicising of South Africa's oppressed masses was one of the most powerful tools of our oppression in the apartheid arsenal, and that overcoming it was absolutely essential to our understanding of our own role, and the role of "race" in the struggle for freedom. Overcoming the divisions between "Bantus", "Coloureds" and "Indians" was one of the most significant and enduring victories of that phase of the struggle and without it, it is hard to imagine how apartheid would have been overcome. Black Consciousness, rather than feminism, created the historic instance when the political became the personal, and vice versa, with all the powerful ramifications of such a switch.[16] But Mr Mandela seems to have no understanding of this at all and in one fell swoop he dismisses not only the life-changing experiences of a whole generation of struggle activists, but a philosophical and psychological victory without which the struggle would not have gone forward at all.

> To say that race is a myth and that in our country there are no Africans, Coloureds and Indians, but only words, is to play with words. The main ethnological divisions of mankind are acknowledged by bourgeois and Marxist anthropologists and those from the so-called uncommitted world. People can observe them with the naked eye. Physical characteristics – the colour of the skin and the texture of the hair – can be observed by merely looking at a painting of Chaka and one of Napoleon, at Tambo and Dadoo, Kotane and Reggie September. In addition to the colour of their skins and the texture of their hair they differ in historical origins and in their culture and languages…But race as such exists in the world, and in our country there is nothing wrong with using the terms African, Coloured and Indian in appropriate cases.[17]

From a Christian point of view, departing from the essential oneness of the human race as created by God and the "new human" created through the reconciling work of Christ, of course race, as expounded by modern anthropology, is a myth. That argument can

---

[16] Contra Fay Weldon, *Godless in the Garden of Eden* (London: Flamingo Press, 2000), 33.
[17] *Reflections*, 49.

certainly be made. In the New Testament one of the most emphatic characteristics of the community of Jesus is its universality and its empowering inclusiveness. "From birth to death and in every moment between", writes US theologian Curtiss Paul DeYoung, "Jesus of Nazareth" (the One who relentlessly, joyfully and freely broke all barriers of race and class to draw all people unto himself and invited all from the east and west, from north and south, to eat in the Kingdom of God) "radiated a spirit of inclusiveness and reconciliation"[18], and it is that spirit that triumphs in Paul's ringing declaration in Galatians, that "there is no longer Jew or Greek, there is no longer slave or free, there is no longer male and female; for you are all one in Christ Jesus" (3:28-29). That is not just the rule for the church; its essence is the church's view of humanity in its oneness, diversity and its joyful reflection of the image of God.

It might be that theological arguments may not be enough. Modern sociology too, acknowledges that stereotypical anthropological assumptions were fundamentally flawed on this point. Racial awareness, and as a result racial prejudice, is in the culture, and we seem (even Mandela!) to acquire it without thinking and without knowing it. Race, says respected sociologist C. Eric Lincoln, is "a cultural fiction",

> An emotional crutch for people whose sense of personal adequacy is threatened. It is the joker in a deck stacked for personal advantage ina game of life where the dealer must always win to break even. But in the world of objective reality, the alleged pure and definable race does not exist... If race does not exist in reality, it exists with the *force* of reality and the *consequences* of reality in the minds of enough Americans to seriously qualify most orders of relationships between groups and among individuals.[19]

That is exactly the point Black Consciousness was trying to make. Lincoln speaks of the United States, but his point is aptly applicable to South Africa.

But that aside, it is not only the astounding ignorance of what Black Consciousness was all about and the painful struggles it had cost us to overcome the racial and ethnic divisions which were life-blood to apartheid that makes reading Nelson Mandela on this point so painful. Nor was it the fact that Mr Mandela sounded so like the apartheid apologists he had fought for so long without coming to understand one of the most deadly weapons in their arsenal. Neither was it the ease with which he simply accepted the views of "anthropologists", Marxist, bourgeois or otherwise, without showing an inkling of understanding of the battles we had to fight on the intellectual plane, following in the footsteps of black intellectual giants like Pixley Isaka Seme, WEB Du Bois, Cheik Anta Diop, Africanus Horton, Attoh Ahuma, Henry Sylvester Williams, Casely Hayford, Marc Kojo, Tovalou Houenou, Frantz Fanon, Leopold Senghor, James Baldwin, Es'kia Mphahlele and Robert Sobukwe, to name but a few.

---

[18] Curtiss Paul DeYoung, *Reconciliation, Our Greatest Challenge – Our only Hope* (Valley Forge: Judson Press, 1997), 54ff.
[19] Cited in DeYoung, *op. cit.,* 10.

It remains surprising how little understanding there still is of the value and power of the philosophy of Black Consciousness in ANC circles. Hence the dismissive way in which Mr Mandela relegated the hard-won victories over ethnic indoctrination in the struggle towards genuine non-racialism in South Africa to the trash heap of "fanaticism". Hence also the ease with which, after his release and the unbanning of the ANC, despite our most earnest pleadings and arguments, the ethnic terminology of apartheid was given legitimacy within the ANC and the country, to the eternal dismay of the many who had hoped that these divisive and senseless categories had been permanently overcome.

The dismay is genuine. Those who fought those battles not only know how difficult they had been, but also how crucial they were for this country's future. They know that it took the ANC until the early eighties to completely open the doors of its governing body to those who were not, in Mandela's definition, "Africans". They know that, unless the ANC can overcome ethnicity within it own ranks, the struggle for non-racialism in South Africa will remain a battle with little hope of success. It is no wonder that affirmative action, despite the sloganeering, has taken on such a tasteless, narrow ethnic hue, that the term "black" has become as ideologically loaded as the term "Bantu" or "Coloured" had been during apartheid, and that so many in the "coloured" community feel themselves disrespected, marginalised by the ANC, having been made to feel as "coloured", and therefore as excluded, as they had been during the years of apartheid. The disturbing signs of a nascent "coloured nationalism" here and there are a direct result of this. In fact "race" is becoming more and more a defining category in ways we could not have imagined, in general political discourse as well as within the ANC itself. Jokes about the ANC as "the Xhosa nostra" are the wilting flowers on the grave of the dignity of the struggle.

The one hopeful sign is that President Mbeki is quite explicit in his inclusive use of the term "African". What that means in terms of real political inclusiveness, as distinct from poetic usefulness, however, we shall have to wait and see. Another hopeful sign is the resilience of non-racialism that is to be found amongst our people rooted in the traditions of struggle.[20] Amongst ordinary South Africans there are many still who refuse to set aside the legacy of Black Consciousness and of the United Democratic Front. On this point it is a great disappointment that the ANC seems so unwilling to learn from the communal experiences of our people, especially as these found expression in the philosophy of Black Consciousness and the spirit of the UDF. It remains detrimental to the ANC also that it is so loathe to acknowledge the role of that movement during the struggle against apartheid and its lasting significance for us in this new era.

But all is not lost, it seems. In an apparent change of thinking Mr Mandela, at last, did recently give Black Consciousness the recognition it deserves.[21] Delivering the 5th Steve

---

[20] It is of great symbolic and political significance that I have been given the King Hintsa Bravery Award by the Xhosa Royal House. The relationship is both personal and political and public, setting an example in the tradition of non-racialism that goes beyond words.

[21] The text of this lecture, delivered on Friday September 10, 2004, is available from the Nelson Mandela Foundation, Johannesburg.

Biko Lecture in Cape Town, Mandela, in referring to his views "from Robben Island", did not openly renounce them. However, he clearly now has an appreciation for Black Consciousness he did not show before:

> The driving thrust of Black Consciousness was to forge pride and unity amongst all the oppressed, to foil the strategy of divide-and-rule, to engender pride amongst the mass of our people and confidence in their ability to throw off their oppression... And as we now increasingly speak of and work for an African Renaissance, the life, work, words, thoughts and example of Steve Biko assume a relevance and resonance as strong as in the time that he lived. His revolution had a simple but overwhelmingly powerful dimension in which it played itself out – that of radically changing the consciousness of people. The African Renaissance calls for and is situated in exactly such a fundamental change of consciousness: consciousness of ourselves, our place in the world, our capacity to shape history, and our relationship with each other and the rest of humanity.[22]

This is encouraging indeed. There is much in the philosophy of Black Consciousness that really cannot be set aside, both in our own transformation efforts and in the realisation of the dream of the African renaissance. But we must move on. To those who took to the battlefields against apartheid, Black Power was the answer to white, racist domination. It was an understanding that black people needed power to challenge the apartheid system, to confront the white power structure, and to bring about themselves the changes that were necessary. It understood, not instinctively but through careful analysis and bitter experience, that the solution to the problems facing the oppressed was not to simply shout at whites that they were devils, but to confront oppressive white power with another kind of power.[23] It was the power to challenge, but it was also the ability to suffer, to risk one's life in a just cause, namely the cause of freedom. It was an undaunted pride in blackness which was necessary to overcome the psychological ostracism and alienation that white domination brought and on which it thrived, and an unshakable faith that this battle for freedom would be won. Within the context of apartheid South Africa, it *was* absolutely wrong to continue to internalise the apartheid mentality by categorising ourselves in terms of the self-defeating definitions created by the oppressor.

---

[22] *Ibid.* It does not completely rhyme with the facts when Mandela asserts that "for its part the ANC welcomed Black Consciousness as part of the genuine forces of the revolution", but nevertheless the change is welcomed profoundly.

[23] This is not to deny the psychological power of the religious concept so masterfully manipulated by Malcolm X and the impact that it had on his audiences. But that particular theology did not to the same extent appeal to blacks in South Africa and did not resonate beyond a certain psychological satisfaction. We are speaking here of a *political* analysis that had to equip black people in South Africa deal with the realities of white power socially, politically and economically.

Also, Black Power was a most powerful expression of the transnational solidarity that black South Africans came to share with black Americans. It began with the resistance to slavery, continued with strong church and ecumenical relationships, the civil rights struggle and the enormous influence of Martin Luther King Jr. on a whole generation of young leaders, many of whom remained strongly committed to the ethic of non-violence. For others, the emotional resonance was with Malcolm X, that fiery preacher of the Nation of Islam, whose "eye for an eye" and "by all means necessary" ethic sounded a chord too real to ignore. Even though these two heroes of the Black American struggle have been contrasted, and quite severely so, there were those of us who found, despite the differences in belief and strategy, a fundamental commonality that refuses the easy option of a stark either/or choice between the two.[24] The call for Black Power made by Stokely Carmichael in Greenwood, Mississippi in 1966, and given theoretical foundation by Charles Hamilton was taken up by South Africa's Steve Biko in the late sixties and resonated with the new, militant generation. It was not a break with the traditions of the struggle in South Africa, but a new manifestation of those traditions. Young black South Africans were speaking the same language as their brothers and sisters in the United States and this solidarity would find its most meaningful expression in the anti-apartheid struggle in the United States itself, which had such a powerful impact on US policy vis-à-vis South Africa during the eighties. Now, with apartheid behind us, the challenge is how Africans in the Diaspora, along with all of us, could bring their enormous gifts and talents to bear in the realisation of the African Renaissance for the continent as a whole.

Those who criticized this new political expression or saw it as an "importation" or a mere emulation of "Black American ideology" failed to understand the power of a common understanding of Africanness, of the bonds forged through a common history of slavery, of the truly universal nature of racism and the struggle against it. They also failed to recognize the resonance of Pan Africanism as it found expression in the life and work of leaders such as WEB Du Bois, Marcus Garvey and Malcolm X in the United States, and Pixley Isaka Seme, Robert Sobukwe and a host of others in South Africa. There was, after all, a long tradition of contact and the sharing of ideas between black South African and black American intellectuals and a mutual beneficiation of their intellectual labour was normal. The critics failed, too, to understand the powerful appeal of the call for social justice in the Christian faith at whose heart universality lies. There is, after all, a reason why Black Consciousness and Black Power in South Africa found such strong expression among the students belonging to the Christian movement on university campuses.

Now, all of Africa is independent, albeit not yet totally free, South Africa is liberated from the death-grip of apartheid, Nelson Mandela emerged from prison to become one of the most respected statesmen in the world, and democracy, as expressed in

---

[24] See e.g. Allan Aubrey Boesak, *Coming In Out of the Wilderness, A Comparative Study of the Ethic of Malcolm X and Martin Luther King Jr* (Kampen: Kok, 1974). Cf. also James H Cone, *Martin and Malcolm and America: A Dream or a Nightmare.* (Maryknoll: Orbis, 1991).

"free and fair" elections, has become part of African political discourse. Recognition of human rights is now the measure of good government throughout the continent, even though at this point it is more an ideal than a reality. There are some who are trying to sound a word of caution to stem the somewhat rampant optimism regarding these developments. Says Prof. Jean Herskovits of the *Sub-Saharan Security Project*: "Elections were acclaimed the touchstone; few thought beyond them. Often hastily called, stamped with the international observers' 'free and fair' seal of approval. They would just be the beginning".[25] The warning is well taken: Africa still has a long way to go and both the election debacle of 2000 in the United States and the ongoing debate over campaign funding in that country are indications that we need to think deep and hard about what constitutes "democracy" in the world today. The struggle for democracy in Africa continues, and Robert Mugabe's Zimbabwe is not the only place we should be deeply concerned about. But even so, it is not too much to say that if the twentieth century was indeed the century of Africa's awakening, that awakening found voice in the two cries that embodied the changes we have seen: *Uhuru* and *Black Power*.

They said in no uncertain terms that "We are of a people that will not tolerate oppression". These words encapsulate the hopes and dreams of the continent's peoples as they saw their own take power in the hallowed places where strangers once sat, ruled their lands and decided upon their lives. Would the realities be the fulfilment of the dream? Many were certain they would be. "Africa is for the Africans", wrote Du Bois, giving voice to the expectations of millions,

> ... its land and labour, its natural wealth and resources; its mountains, lakes and rivers; its cultures and its Soul. Hereafter it will no longer be ruled by might or by power; by invading armies nor police, but by the Spirit of all its gods and the wisdom of its prophets...[26]

To Break Every Yoke

But Dr Du Bois's wishes would not be granted. In an address to the General Assembly of the All Africa Conference of Churches in Nairobi in 1981, I made the following statement:

> Africa is a wounded continent, and the wounds have not yet healed. Colonialism has been exchanged for newer, subtler forms of economic exploitation in which underdevelopment and dependency are both real and inescapable. Famine, hunger and starvation still claim their victims by the millions, and the truth is that these very often are not economic problems; they are *political* problems. Africa is torn by conflict and war.

[25] *Africans Solving African Problems: Militaries, Democracies and Security in West and Southern Africa*, Report of a Conference, the Sub-Saharan Security Project, New York: 1977.

[26] *Op. cit.*, 291.

> This is partly so because the continent has become the testing grounds for the ideologies of the super powers, the battlefield for their mad desire to rule the world. But it is also true that Africa knows too many iron-fisted rulers who have no respect for human rights. The colonial governor's mansion is now occupied by the representatives of new power elites that have as little concern for the people as did the colonialists. All too often 'independence' has not meant a new, meaningful life for the people, or a return to the values of African life that would have revitalized society. Values such as the wholeness of life, the meaning of human-beingness, and the relationship between human beings and nature have not been resuscitated in African life, because these values tend to subvert the economic interests of the new elite and their neo-colonial masters.[27]

It would be quite useful to ask just to what extent this rather dismal picture still reflects the truth.

By the end of the 1980s only five states in Africa could seriously claim to be democratically governed, which means they had held free elections with competing political parties: Botswana, Mauritius, The Gambia, Senegal and Zimbabwe. In 1994 there were sixteen countries with governments representing one single party or the military. Today, the situation is markedly different. Since 1990 twenty-seven multi-party elections have been held, in twenty-one cases for the first time. That is a remarkable improvement. There have been elections in Senegal and, notably, Nigeria has returned to democratic rule. Even though some point to the constant pressures on President Olusegun Obasanjo as a sign of the shakiness of the situation, conversely it may be said that the continuation of democracy despite the pressures in Nigeria is a sign of its resilience rather than of its weakness. In other places like the Democratic Republic of the Congo and Ivory Coast, for example, the slow but sure progress towards peace and accommodation of rival groups remains more encouraging than exasperating.

These are the results of the most recent phase in the struggle for democracy and human rights in Africa. The struggle for independence was not just a struggle against colonialism. For the many who rose to the call, it was also a struggle for democracy. Analysing Africa today, though, one must conclude that in many instances these struggles succeeded more in indigenising political control rather than in creating genuine democracy. In most cases African nations experienced a marked swing towards authoritarianism and the struggle for pro-democratic forces in these countries was not made any easier and sometimes immeasurably harder.

The current situation is less than promising. Oppression and the disregard for human rights abound. Rwanda, Liberia, Sierra Leone, Burundi and the Democratic Republic

---

[27] Allan Aubrey Boesak, "To Break Every Yoke: Liberation and the Churches of Africa", in: *Black and Reformed: Apartheid, Liberation and the Calvinist Tradition* (Maryknoll, New York: Orbis, 1984; Johannesburg: Skotaville, 1984).

of Congo still bleed from the wounds of their civil wars. Sudan is the greatest human disaster the continent has seen in a century. The Swazi king acts as if this were the Middle Ages. Things are just seeming to settle down in Lesotho, but Lesotho's turbulent history suggests, and we have been so warned, that unless fundamental constitutional changes are made in that country, it would be unwise to join the euphoria of the SADC-brokered solution after the South African invasion.[28]

One is forced to hold one's breath about Angola, where full-scale war has ended but the long trek to genuine peace has, in a real sense, only just begun. In Africa, Angola is perhaps the best example of the unpleasant truth that has plagued Africa, Latin America and the Third World in general for so long: that the anti-democratic forces created and propped up by superpowers like the United States and the Soviet Union remain a danger to the process of democratisation long after they have lost their usefulness to these superpowers. The Cold War is over, the intentions of both the US and Russia are thoroughly discredited. Ronald Reagan is long gone and Mikhail Gorbachev has brought Glasnost to the former Communist power. Bill Clinton has reached out to Africa like no other US president before him. Yet the effects of superpower policy in Africa since the Second World War continue in the destructive role played for so long by someone like Jonas Savimbi. The people of Angola continue to be ravaged and the chance to attain true democracy and genuine development remains an uphill battle.

In the once-promising Zimbabwe disaster has struck. "Democracy" has lost all meaning for the impoverished masses whose plight is totally ignored by the Mugabe government. Internal oppression has become a matter of course. There are almost daily clashes between the army and the trade unions; the elections were suspect and the new constitution no less so. What is presented as "land reform" has become common thievery. Spiralling prices and the scarcity of basic necessities stand in sharp and painful contrast with Zimbabwe's involvement in the war in the Congo. Not even the best intentions with the contentious land policies of the government can substitute for the damage done to the democratic ideal in Zimbabwe. And it all began, even if no one makes the fatal link, not with the tensions between the government and the judiciary, or with Mr Mugabe's alleged theft of the elections, but with his denial of the rights of ordinary, vulnerable citizens, for example, gays and lesbians, whom he has singled out for vicious persecution, attacking them publicly as "dogs" and "pigs", "not worthy" of human consideration.

Sadly, his poor example is being followed by President Sam Nujoma of Namibia. These are the really disturbing signs for those who have eyes to see: like the burning of the books and the "trial deaths" of Gypsies in Hitler's Germany. And as Hitler's abuses were carried out before the smoke started spiralling from the death camps, Mr Mugabe violated human rights long before any white farms were "expropriated". And

---

[28]   Cf. Kabhile Matlosa, "Lesotho's Political Turmoil and Prospects for the 1998 National Elections" in: *Africa Insight, Vol. 27, No. 4, 1997,* 240-246. According to Dr Matlosa, the constitution needs a "serious review".

inasmuch as the persecution of gay persons did not stir in the rest of the world the same indignant response and anger as does the land issue, the dismissal of a judge or trumped-up charges against the opposition leaders, it is a sure sign of what our democratic sensitivities world-wide are worth.

Black South Africans who accuse white South Africans of hypocrisy in their strident concern for whites in Zimbabwe, while never having showed an iota of that concern for blacks under apartheid, are right of course. Likewise those, on the flip side of that coin, who point to the contrast between the lamb-like silence toward P W Botha and the howls of indignation now directed at Robert Mugabe. But our (black) silence on the matter of the rights of gay persons condemns us as roundly. No wonder Mr Mugabe is so derisive of our protests. There is a lesson in this. Or biblically put, "Those who have an ear, listen to what the Spirit is saying to the churches". It is perhaps unnecessary to point out here that the issue is not so much that those so abominably treated by Mugabe are gay or lesbian, even though that too, is important. The issue is that in Mugabe's Zimbabwe they are *vulnerable,* and in their vulnerability targeted by the Mugabe regime. Their woundability is the call for our compassion and our search for justice and humanity on their behalf.

It behoves us, perhaps, while the land crisis in Zimbabwe is now full-blown with already such enormous consequences, to heed the words of Zimbabwean political observer Ibbo Mandaza. It may be, he suggests, that the current land war in Zimbabwe might be viewed as the desperate act of a government besieged by both an economic crisis and a decline in popularity, and therefore seeking to restore its legitimacy and image, especially in the light of what he calls the "overall failure of Mugabe's government in resolving this key question that underpins all else on the economic front". But Dr Mandaza gives us something else to think about in the complicated web of realities that face countries in Africa:

> In reality, however, it does demonstrate the political expediency that undergirded the policy of reconciliation at independence in Zimbabwe: the need to overlook in 1980 what Mugabe angrily described as 'colonial settler robbery' in 1997, in a reference to a pattern of land ownership in which almost 50 per cent of the agricultural land is still owned by less than 5 000 large commercial-scale farmers, mostly whites, while more than 8 million peasants are crowded in the remaining largely arid land".[29]

Mandaza touches on an issue we cannot ignore and shall have to address, namely the question of the impact of what he calls the "ideology of reconciliation" in the politics of Southern Africa. This is a sensitive issue for South Africans, in the light both of our

---

[29] Ibbo Mandaza, "Reconciliation and Social Justice in Southern Africa" in: *African Renaissance, The New Struggle*, Malegapuru William Makgoba, Thaninga Shope and Thami Mazwai (eds.) (Cape Town and Sandton: Tafelberg Publishers and Mafube Publishing, 1999), 86, 87.

recent political history, the importance of the issue and the theological significance of it for Christians. One of the great problems surrounding this matter is the profound lack of theological debate throughout the process of political reconciliation in South Africa, and the poor quality of theological participation by Christians in the process itself. As Christians, we will also want to engage Dr Mandaza on what we consider to be one of the central demands of our faith and his relegation of it to a mere political "ideology". But this is a matter for another chapter. Properly cautioned, however, we must nonetheless make the point that the Mugabe government's policies, aside from the "key question" of land distribution, have largely failed the poorest of the poor in Zimbabwe. They are paying the price for what is more than the failure of one policy issue, namely the failure of democracy itself.

In Zambia, hailed as a shining example of democracy only a few years ago, the father of that country's independence, Kenneth Kaunda, has been imprisoned and an attempt was made on his life, ostensibly to dissuade him from running as a presidential candidate. Generally, too, the democratically elected government of Mr Chaluba did not intend its democracy to include all Zambians and it is a good thing that the people of Zambia denied him his wish to change the constitution in order to grant him the right to run for a third term as president. Experience shows that once that door is opened, there is no guarantee that Zambia, like some other African countries, will not also embrace the "President-for-life" syndrome that has so persistently plagued politics in Africa and stifled so effectively the chances for democracy on the continent.

In Mozambique free elections have taken place, but this vital step towards democracy alone cannot guarantee economic development and the legacy of the civil war still proves to be as devastating as the war itself had been. Just the sheer costs alone, for example, of the land mines planted there during the war is enormous, both in denying the people access to their land and preventing proper agriculture, to say nothing of the deadly accidents that cost more lives on a daily basis. Removing these mines safely and efficiently is, of course, out of the question for such a poor country. As it is, Mozambique will have to hire and pay the very countries who manufactured and planted those mines now to remove them!

South Africa, with its "miracle" of 1994, and its concept of a "rainbow nation" seems to be one of the few beacons, if not the brightest beacon, of hope. Or so we are told. We shall have to see whether this is in fact so, and whether all the optimism generated by the South African situation is in fact justified.

In Sub-Saharan Africa, South Africa is indisputably the superpower. It is the strongest economically, has the best equipped military, as it should, since it is also by far the largest spender on arms on the continent. It has the best infrastructure and the most advanced bureaucracy. It has, in many ways, assumed for itself the mantle of leadership in the region. But the situation in the region is dire and the challenges daunting, and their impact on South Africa, vulnerable through its own painful transformation to democracy, is potentially devastating.

Who Pays the Price?

Professors Vale and Maseko ask a crucial question which we shall have cause to return to: "Who benefits from the African Renaissance?"[30] Here we shall have to ask the same question in different form: "Who pays the price if the African Renaissance fails?" These questions are not simply meant to introduce negativism into the discussion. They are meant to keep us focussed on the *human* reality which is at stake in our endeavours. These are the simple, yet crucial, questions which are inextricably linked to that other fundamental question which concerns this book: what is the spiritual quality of our politics? In Sub-Saharan Africa, so the 1996 UNDP report tells us, there is only one doctor for every 18 000 people, compared with one for every 390 in the industrialized countries. At primary and secondary levels more than 80 million boys and girls are still out of school - only about half the entrants at Grade 1 finish Grade 5. Nearly one third of the region's population (170 million) do not have enough to eat. During the past three decades the ratio of military to social spending increased, from 2% in 1960 to 43% in 1991. At the same time, about 33 million children remain malnourished. Yet another danger looms: during the past fifty years desertification has claimed an average 1,3 million hectares of land per year. Because of war, upheaval and economic pressures, at the end of 1994 almost six million of the region's people were refugees.

It is now widely recognized that HIV/AIDS is one of the world's leading problems and for many countries a major setback in human development. So far an estimated 20 million people are infected with HIV, and 2,5 million have already died from AIDS. Every day 6 000 new infections occur, that is to say, one every 15 seconds. No less than 90% of all new infections occur in developing countries, although in developed countries too, the situation is getting steadily worse: in North America and Europe AIDS is now the leading cause of death for adults under 45 years of age. As yet there is no cure and the cost of medicines, at least in our parts of the world, is so prohibitive as to prove a cause of an even earlier death for millions in the developing countries. International trade agreements have been designed to protect transnational pharmaceutical companies, and developing countries will face crippling punitive measures if they should dare to circumvent these international rules in order to secure affordable medicines for their people.

The landmark court case between the government of South Africa and international pharmaceutical companies will have far-reaching effects on all concerned, and its uneasy settlement has not brought any lasting solutions. My strong feeling is that the South African government, like others in the third world, shall not escape the bind into which globalization and unfair trade agreements have pushed us. The issue will not be resolved through a court judgment that has to balance international agreements and the needs of people, if the courts themselves are not courageous enough to challenge the fundamental injustices inherent in some international agreements as they now operate.

---

[30] Peter Vale & Sipho Maseko, "South Africa and the African Renaissance", *International Affairs*, 74.2, 1998, 271-287.

If the courts find themselves compelled to honour the rules of globalization as set by the rich nations of the world, the question of justice will still have to be placed on the agenda by the people themselves, and that is a confrontation the government, in the long run, cannot avoid.

The incessant, violent spats between political parties in South Africa on this matter have shown, to a frightening degree, I think, just how much the illness has become politicised. By "politicised" I do not mean giving the issue its proper place in the political debate, making of it a question of political responsibility of those entrusted with that responsibility, as opposed to keeping it a personal, privatised-religious, medical, or non-governmental issue. I mean rather that the reality of HIV/AIDS becomes filled with party-political interests, dragged down by political fly-catching rather than uplifted by mature debate; it suffers from public relations bombast rather than being humanised by genuine compassion. Instead of becoming a rallying point for a common, national effort toward a permanent solution, AIDS becomes the stage for political grandstanding, vain personality clashes and the vulgar display of juvenile one-upmanship. That fact has its own devastating impact, not only on the quality of public debate, but also, and much more tragically, on the real situation of people living with, and dying from, AIDS. Meanwhile, however, AIDS is monstrously rampant, seemingly unstoppable, and almost always fatal.

In Africa, the worst hit of all continents, the situation in Sub-Saharan Africa is, in turn, the worst. The latest reports on HIV/AIDS point to South Africa as the country with the greatest problem in this regard. The prevalence of HIV/AIDS has risen 20 times in seven years to about 4 million people and here more than 1,500 infections occur every day. More than 14 million children below the age of 15 have lost one or both parents due to HIV/AIDS, 11 million of them in sub-Saharan Africa.[31] By 2010 the number of orphans will have risen to 25 million, perhaps even more than 40 million. In South Africa alone the number may increase from 2.2 million (13% of all 2-14 years olds) in 2003 to 3.1million by 2010, i.e. 18% (!) of all children. "A 'Lord of the Flies' syndrome is emerging", writes Dutch theologian Frits de Lange, "children bringing up children. Stigmatized as an AIDS orphan, the impact of their destiny gets even more traumatizing. A vicious cycle begins, of depression, anger, guilt, and fear for their futures".[32] Poverty, social dislocation and a host of other social ills add to growing aggression, hopelessness and tendencies toward suicide. So while for some of us "2010" is the magic year which will bring the Soccer World Cup and all its marvellous opportunities to South Africa, for the growing millions of orphans, young people infected with HIV/AIDS and their families, the number is fast becoming a futuristic nightmare of apocalyptic proportions.

---

[31] Cf. Frits de Lange, *About Being a Church vis-à-vis HIV/AIDS*, paper read at the Barmen/Belhar Consultation, Stellenbosch 18-20 October 2004. The host of disturbing facts is to be found in Sonja Weinreich & Christoph Benn, *AIDS – Meeting the Challenge. Data, Facts, Background*. (Geneva: WCC Publications, 2004)

[32] De Lange, *op. cit.,* 2. Cf. also UNAIDS Report 2004, on the global AIDS epidemic, 62ff.

We now know that 1 in every 5 persons in South Africa is infected. Five years ago it was 1 out of 9. Truly frightening is the fact that the greatest increase per year now occurs among the age group 15 to 25. These are mostly youths in high school, where in some cases the percentage of infected children is as high as 50%. A doctor who works in the townships around Cape Town tells me of the hopelessness of these young people. This is the new generation, he says, who know nothing of the ravages of legal apartheid, who do not have to struggle for liberation as their parents did, who do not have to suffer the psychological effects of one of the most pernicious systems of racism the world has ever seen. These are the children of freedom and democracy. They have, he continues, no vision for this country, nor for themselves. They lack vision, they lack hope, they lack the spiritual values that might lift them out of their despair. Why? Because they are dying. As one colleague from the townships, who says that he buries several young people who die of AIDS every week, observes, "This, in contrast to the seventies, is now our *real* lost generation". The social and economic implications are incalculable, and the unpreparedness, and sometimes unwillingness, of the South African government to deal with this problem effectively is disturbing. One cannot help but wonder what it means when in the new parliamentary session of 2003, the Minister of Finance in his budget speech announces R3 billion more for the fight against AIDS, but the President, in his State of the Nation address, does not even deign to mention the disease, let alone discuss it.

And there's the rub. It is one thing to argue that the President's silence is a strategy to deal with a political problem, since the tensions between the government and the AIDS activists groups continue to run high, and this thus becomes easy fodder for the opposition. But how forgivable is it that persons, not persons as *voters* but as human beings, are dealt with as a strategy, not worth a mention because they have become a political problem that the government is finding increasingly difficult to handle? The question is not whether it is enough or not, or even better, that the problem is being handled by the Finance ministry which allocates money, instead of by the President, who makes pronouncements, since deeds are always better than words. That might be true.

But the issue that concerns us is not just the allocation of funds, the debate whether that allocation is enough completely aside. The issue surely is whether our politics, as reflected in the State of the Nation address, is seen to be a politics guided by cold realism or a politics infused with compassion. The politics of realism would weigh the political wisdom of a statement on AIDS to determine how much ammunition the opposition could get from it to blast the government. The politics of compassion would weigh that wisdom in terms of the comfort and hope it would give the victims of AIDS. The politics of realism would seek to limit any damage to government through attack on its policies or lack of them. The politics of compassion would seek to limit the despair of the victims and their families in their situation of hopelessness. The politics of realism has as its point of departure the belligerence of the opposition; the politics of compassion proceeds from the pain of the victims. It is, in the end, a question of caring.

For the church this is vitally important, for the politics of compassion is the politics of Jesus, whom the church confesses to follow.[33] The tradition into which Jesus was born spoke primarily of the holiness of God. Jesus spoke primarily of the compassion of God. In the Bible, we know, compassion is a feeling, localised in the abdomen. It is an empathetic stirring in the womb, a crying out of one's insides, as Jeremiah describes God's compassion for the plight of Israel[34] and in the Bible the association is decidedly feminine, revealing, with an almost casual naturalness, the fallacy of a male, patriarchal God. It means "being moved by", "feeling with" another and that person's situation. Just as God is moved by and "feels with" the least of these, writes Borg, "so the Jesus movement was to participate in the *pathos* of God".[35] This is the driving force in the political participation of the church: the pathos of God for the "least of these" infuses the politics of compassion. And that is the politics that should shape the soul of the nation.

But the guilt of the church in this matter precludes us from apportioning blame and pointing accusing fingers at the government. The ignorance, judgemental attitude and lack of compassion of Christians are just as appalling. In the Middle Ages the black death and the devastation of that pandemic were blamed on women who were accused of being witches. The church sought them out, hunted them down mercilessly, and every strong woman who had ever threatened or challenged a man's authority was judged and burned at the stake. Now with AIDS we experience that same misplaced zeal. There is an almost hysterical haste to blame homosexual persons, judge them and hang them. Today we know we are wrong, we ought to know better. AIDS is an illness that strikes everywhere and, in any case, in Africa it is a more heterosexual than homosexual occurrence.

But it is not just the ignorance. It is the more ingrained tendency to stand in judgement and the concomitant lack of compassion that should disturb us even more. When it comes to AIDS, Christians keep looking for somebody's *fault,* instead of looking at somebody's *need.* We act as if establishing the fault is somehow a prerequisite for Christian charity and action. When confronted with HIV/AIDS Christians ask: "Whose fault is it?" Is he gay? Is she promiscuous? While all the time the only question should be: what can we do?

When Jesus met the leper, he did not ask, "Whose fault is it?" He said, "Be made clean!" When he met the man with a withered hand, he did not ask whose fault it was. He said, "Stretch out your hand!" When Jesus met the woman who had been crippled for eighteen years, he did not look for somebody's fault. He healed her, even though it was the Sabbath, or even better, *because* it was the Sabbath. Jesus understood that the

---

[33] Marcus J Borg: *Jesus A New Vision. Spirit, Culture, and the Life of Discipleship* (San Francisco: Harper & Row, 1987), Chapter 7, writes insightfully about this.

[34] Jeremiah 4:19. The NRSV's rendering, "O my anguish, my anguish!" is a less successful translation of the expressive, passionate Hebrew. God's pain is God's compassion: "O my insides! My insides! O walls of my heart!"

[35] Borg, *op. cit.*131.

Sabbath was made for human beings, not the other way round. He understood that the Sabbath was meant to be a celebration of freedom, of liberation and the healing power of the realisation of our humanbeingness. Jesus understood that the many fruitless rules and regulations posing as Torah were binding the Sabbath, perverting God's liberatory intentions with God's own rest on that blessed day. Jesus' own spirituality freed him to celebrate God's rest in the work of liberation and healing he did in and for that woman, and the many who came to him on the Sabbath. On such a day, there is no room for finding fault or apportioning blame, there is only room for the celebration of freedom and life: "Woman, you are set free from your ailment!" (Luke 13:12). When Jesus met the man born blind, others argued about whose sins it was that caused the blindness. His response was different. "Neither this man nor his parents sinned, but the works of God must be revealed" (Jn. 9:3). We must have as much compassion for the victims of AIDS as Jesus had for the sick, the blind, the lepers, the poor. And for us. Our enemy is not the victim of AIDS. Our enemy is AIDS.

Our dilemma with the HIV/AIDS problem is, of course, not simply the fault of the new regime. The negligence shown by the apartheid regime toward people who were not white had been criminal, both in the responsible gathering of statistics and in terms of proper health care, education, housing, etc. Poverty, lack of education and inadequate health facilities now present formidable problems, aside from the fact that South Africa has to cope with an undetermined, and seemingly unstoppable, flow of illegal immigrants from areas where AIDS has been a major problem for the previous decade or more. Now, more than ever before, careful husbanding of our limited resources is called for.

Another problem that is increasingly exercising the leaders of Southern Africa, political as well as in civil society, is the question of international debt which is burdening Africa, as it does most countries of the Third World. Of the world's 42 low-income and highly indebted poor countries, 33 are in Sub-Saharan Africa. In 1962 Sub-Saharan Africa owed US$3 billion, by the early eighties the debt had multiplied to US$142 billion and today the burden stands at US$222 billion, representing about US$370 for every man, woman and child in the sub-continent.[36]

The impossible situation this presents to all these countries is summed up by the predicament faced by Mozambique, whose external debt totals US$5.5 billion. This translates to a whopping 327% of its annual GDP. Zambia's total debt of US$7 billion is 195% of its GDP and Tanzania pays up to 45% of its annual budget in servicing its staggering debt of US$8 billion.[37]

The *SADC Today* article on Sub-Saharan African debt asks the question we raised at the beginning of this section: "Who pays the price?" Again, it is an absolutely necessary

---

[36] *SADC Today*, a publication of the Southern African Development Community, Vol. 2, No. 2, June 1998, 9.
[37] *SADC Today*, August 1998, 8.

question. If the arrangement is that debt servicing takes priority in budgetary planning and resources, as the International Monetary Fund and the World Bank demand, the social sector cannot compete and the poor are the ones who continue to suffer. It concludes: "If the international financial community represented by the IMF and the World Bank does not use its power to cancel or reduce Africa's debt, the gulf between the rich and the poor is set to widen and economic reforms efforts on the continent are not likely to achieve any meaningful results".[38]

Of course there are factors, quite apart from the legacy of colonization in terms of poverty, lack of education and the ravages of war, that seriously impeded democratisation and sustainable development in Africa, and they are well known:

Φ The geo-political realities created by the tensions that resulted from the Cold War in which Africa had to perform a precarious balancing act, even while the lives of its peoples became zones of ideological clashes between East and West;

Φ The fundamental unfairness of the global economic system, where Africa was denied control over prices for its own commodities, denied access to world markets, and presented with loaded trade agreements as virtual *fait accompli*;

Φ The blackmail involved in international aid, which has become quite a common fixture of "aid". For example, in 1995 US subsidies for arms exports accounted for over 50% of US bilateral aid, and no less than 40% of total US aid. This emphasis on weapons exports comes at the expense of programmes designed to promote economic development and social welfare in recipient countries;

Φ The so-called "Cold War" was "cold" only as far as the superpowers were concerned. While only threatening each other with a nuclear war they knew was never likely to occur, they sponsored proxy wars in third world countries – Africa, Central America and Asia being only the most obvious examples. War-related deaths during the cold war have been estimated at more than 40 million;

Φ By the same token, war-related deaths for the superpowers occurred not at home, but on the battlefields of the Third World they have created for their own ideological reasons: the US in Viet Nam, for instance, or the Soviet Union in Afghanistan;

Φ The constant plague of ethnic strife, so easily manipulated by the political agendas of power elites, led to violent conflict and open civil war;

Φ The brutal but sobering fact is that wars not only cost money, they *make* money. War today is not just a struggle for power or land. It certainly also is about belief and renewed, narrow, nationalisms. But war is, above all, a highly profitable business, and we ignore that fact at our peril. The consequences of this are vast and remain truly frightening, and this is an area that needs to be addressed even more urgently. It helps explain the millions dead in wars since 1945, while the status quo of the Cold War remained untouched, and it offers meaningful insight into the heart of the problem, namely the common interests of the military-industrial complexes of the

---

[38] *SADC Today*, June 1998, 9.

West and East, and the power elites of the developing world. Those interests do not include democracy or the preservation of human rights;[39]

Φ The greed and rapaciousness of the new elites in independent and liberated countries, whose hunger for power and wealth completely gobbled up the people's hunger for freedom and justice and food.

This did not mean that the people themselves did not care. The very fact that authoritarian regimes reacted so harshly to their efforts to build sustainable democratic structures proves just the opposite. Organs of civil society in Africa do not have the financial resources of the sister organizations in Europe and the United States, and their infrastructure is often not as sophisticated. But this does not mean that their work for democracy and human rights does not flourish, and often they work with great success against incredible odds, as the recent developments in Nigeria have shown. They know that "independence" does not always mean true liberation, and "freedom" does not always mean political or economic justice. They know that for the vast majority of their people the struggle for true freedom is far from over, and will continue, until "every yoke is broken". And that decision will be made, not by the ruling elite, the all-powerful media or the political compatibles in the West, but by the people themselves.

People in Africa whose human rights are threatened on a daily basis know that it is not enough to invoke the term "democracy". It certainly will not do to define democracy in minimalist terms as is done so often by "African scholars" from the West, with the excuse that third world countries are "different". This is a definition that suits dictators and totalitarian rulers well, as does the endless debate over what actually constitutes human rights.

Certainly the last decade or two we in Africa have come to understand more and more that at the very least democracy should mean "government with the consent of the governed" and firm guarantees for the defence and protection of, and respect for, human rights, communal and individual. It must mean the full and meaningful participation of all people at all levels in building a culture of democracy in society, and accountability of government based on the availability of all information needed to make informed choices.

For those who have been fighting *this* battle, the debates between scholars, African and otherwise, about "minimalist" and "maximalist" theories of democracy are not nearly as compelling as the imbalances between progress and deprivation their people are subjected to.

As it is, the battle for democracy in Africa continues, and it is taking considerable effort to hold onto, and consolidate, the gains made so far. In Sub-Saharan Africa alone, democratic traditions had been reversed in four countries by the end of 1997, and those

---

[39] The 1997 edition of *The State of War ad Peace Atlas*, 3rd edition (London: Penguin), while an excellent and extremely useful publication, strangely makes no mention of this fact in its discussion of the causes of war, especially in the nineties.

countries remains dangerously volatile.[40] Bratton's outlook on the chances of second elections (and therefore the ultimate survival of democracy in Africa as a whole) is not wholly optimistic, and he concludes, "The fate of democracy in Africa continues to rest all too heavily in the hands of men with guns".[41] The pendulum-like fortunes of countries like Gambia, the Ivory Coast, Ghana, Sierra Leone and Liberia, to mention only some, seem to prove his point with depressing regularity.

This is the broader political and economic reality within which the new South African democracy emerged in 1994. Not only is the world expecting South Africa to play a significant leadership role in the continent, South Africa itself has claimed that leadership role, not just through the sheer charisma of Nelson Mandela, but also through the considerable claims staked out by his successor, Thabo Mbeki. Much will depend, therefore, not only on the quality of that leadership that South Africa *gives*, but on the quality of leadership that South Africa *has*. And that, in turn, depends on what South Africa itself understands under "quality of leadership" and what it perceives to be the soul of its politics, if anything at all.

The Iron Fist or the Hand of Peace

This leadership has already been tested in the region since 1994, and at times quite severely. In the Democratic Republic of the Congo, formerly Zaire, civil war has plagued that country since Laurent Kabila took over from Mobuto Sese Seko, an incredibly corrupt dictator. In yet another replay of events, rebels in turn accused Kabila of being a dictator, and even after his death with his son at the helm, the peace is not yet fully secured. As with the rebellion that toppled Mobutu, the interplay of regional forces is ever present and Uganda, Zimbabwe, Rwanda and Burundi are immediately involved, and there is a dangerous mix of the ethnic politics of the region, which caused such tragic events in the states of the Great Lakes. South Africa is playing a positive peacemaking role here, and is indeed giving leadership in an admirable as well as politically assertive fashion.

For the latter part of the last century, political responsibility rested primarily with the Organisation of African Unity. Recently, however, that responsibility has been taken over by the newly-formed African Union within which the countries of southern Africa playing an increasingly central role regarding peacemaking efforts in that part of the continent. This is not to be wondered at. The DRC is not a small country and shares a border with nine other countries, which will decidedly feel the effects of its ultimate destiny. Volatility or peace in the DRC will make a huge difference on the continent as a whole. One need only think of the potential that the DRC's enormous wealth and natural resources could unlock for its own people as well as for the continent, to realise how much is at stake here.

---

40 See Michael Bratton, "Lessons for South Africa's Second Elections", in: *Africa Insight,* Vol. 27, No. 4, 1997, 230-232. Bratton is speaking of Burundi, Congo-Brazzaville, Niger and Sierra-Leone.
41 Bratton, *Lessons,* 230.

The OAU has had a long-standing policy of non-interference in the internal affairs of another African country, a policy which sounds reasonable, but which in effect tended to leave Africa's despots firmly in place until internal pressures forced them out, more often than not entailing much bloodshed, upheaval and suffering. There are many who believed that, as in the case of ASEAN, (the Association of South East Asian Nations), it was no more than a self-protecting mechanism which serves to shield dictators from outside pressure and keep the restless population unsupported and therefore under control. With the establishment of the African Union and its mechanisms for what is called "peer review", its plans for economic development encapsulated in the New Plan for Africa's Development (NEPAD) and the commitment to good governance, the political scene in Africa is set to change irrevocably for the better. At least, such is the hope of all of us. South Africans take no small measure of pride in the leadership President Mbeki is giving in this whole endeavour.

The case of the DRC is important, because it brought strongly to the fore the issue of leadership which is the subject of our discussion in this section. Initially, South Africa, and later Southern Africa, became involved as a result of the stature of South Africa's then president, Nelson Mandela. It is, simultaneously, this fact which has caused the first serious tensions in the region about the way in which problems should be solved. Zimbabwe's Robert Mugabe, backed by Namibia's Sam Nujoma, opted for a military solution to the problems caused through the fighting between the DRC government and the rebels. Zimbabwe and Namibia chose military action, arguing that President Laurent Kabila was the legitimate ruler of the DRC and therefore has to be supported against the rebels. Mandela, on the other hand, was dead set against military intervention, believing that a peaceful solution, brought about by talks and a negotiated settlement, would better serve the country and the continent.

In this Mandela had the backing of his own country, since this was so evidently in line with his own political philosophy, a philosophy which had helped so much in South Africa's own peaceful transition. It also made eminent sense. This, however, led to serious problems with Mr Mugabe, who had lashed out quite openly at South Africa's insistence that peace talks could not be complete, or successful, without direct participation of the rebels. Mugabe accused South Africa of trying to undermine the talks and the authority of the SADC, thus ensuring peace and a solution for the DRC remained elusive.

This rift presented more than just personality clashes and Mugabe's attempt to challenge South Africa's (and by implication Mandela's) presumption of leadership, as some serious analysts have suggested. It was, I think, a question of fundamental belief: should, and can, problems always be solved through military intervention? Should Africa, under the flimsy guise of "non-intervention", forever back political leaders, even though their corruption is evident and their legitimacy tenuous, questioned and finally not recognised by their own people? Can Africa show the way to a more permanent, and by far superior, solution, thereby overcoming the persistent delusion that violence is the cure to every ill Africans may face? Such an example could impact not only Africa and other Third World countries, but indeed, with Nelson Mandela's extraordinary stature as a world leader, could present the whole world with this challenge.

If this was going to be the shape and content of South Africa's foreign policy, a new and brighter future was awaiting this country and a whole new set of rules was going to be presented to the world by Africa. In this Nelson Mandela had our wholehearted support. Clearly, Mandela was not going to be just another African leader. Braving the wrath of Robert Mugabe and Sam Nujoma, he has shown that he was not going to be intimidated by the very real debt we owe these leaders and their countries because of their unstinting support in the liberation struggle, nor by the unspoken demand for African solidarity, nor by the desire to be popular among his peers on the continent. Mandela was breaking the rules of the African old boys club and by doing that he was breaking up the club itself. No question: this action would have important ramifications for the politics of peace and intervention. This, we thought, was the kind of leadership Africa needed and which its peoples craved.

For South Africans like myself, there was yet another consideration of the utmost importance. The difference between this kind of thinking and the offensive, blood-thirsty aggressiveness of the apartheid regime was staggering and profoundly gratifying. This was the qualitative difference we had fought for and hoped to see. This was an object lesson in political morality which South Africans badly needed to see and experience. It was necessary, especially, not only for the apartheid remnants still prevalent all over the South African bureaucracy and armed forces, but also for those hardliners in the ANC itself who, in the name of "political realities", would just as easily want to continue the amoral thinking of the apartheid mentality without the hindrance of moral qualms.

It is with these reflections in mind that the South African invasion of Lesotho came as such a shock. In Lesotho, as so often before elsewhere, the clumsily worded constitution of that country led to serious disruptions over the outcome of a general election. The opposition took to the streets, challenging the government, occupying the palace grounds, calling for a recount of the votes, and, ultimately, for new elections and a change in the constitution.

For South Africans it was a familiar scene. The demonstrations were mostly non-violent. The opposition voices were, to my mind, eloquent and reasonable. It was as if we were witnessing ourselves in replay against the apartheid regime. Clearly it was something the government of Lesotho had to deal with in a democratic fashion, and the demands were not, most of us thought, outrageous. We were therefore shocked to see "SADC forces", which were really almost all South African, invading Lesotho to "restore law and order". The resultant mess was not unexpected, although both deeply disappointing and demoralising.

We watched in amazement as South African soldiers went in, got thrashed initially, then waded in again with a humiliated anger so depressingly familiar to those of us who experienced it in the streets of our townships a scant few years before. The damage to the capital city, Maseru, amounting as it did to more than R1 billion, caused only after the invasion, was great. But the damage done to South Africa's image was incalculable. We watched as government spokespersons explained that this was not an invasion, after all, because we were "invited" (according to Minister Buthelezi); and we did not do it "on our own", but "in concert" with the SADC (Minister Mufamadi). Invited by whom? The people who felt robbed or the politicians who rigged the elections? In concert with whom? With the politicians whose will bore no resemblance at all to the wishes of the people in South Africa and in Lesotho, whose hopes were so easily betrayed? Because that is what struck me most of all: the *ease* with which we did it. Since when do we wade into a country to thrash peaceful protestors who were simply claiming their constitutional rights? Since when do we go into a country, shoot down their people, loot their shops, disrupt their economy, create general havoc? Since always, it seems.

This was, to say the least, a stunning reversal of foreign policy. What had happened? Was it because Mandela had changed his mind, now believing in military intervention rather than peaceful settlement of disputes? Was this to be an object lesson to South Africans who might have in mind challenging their government in the streets, as they had done so often before? Had Mandela simply been overridden by the hawks in the ANC, sidelined by those who still believe in the power of the gun and for whom moral suasion in politics is just a waste of time, or a foolish concept not to be entertained at all?

Was the involvement of Sydney Mufamadi, South Africa's minister for internal security at the time, rather than the then foreign minister, Alfred Nzo, significant? It seems so. But that would mean that the whole exercise was merely a demonstration of political power play *within* the ANC, for which the people of Lesotho had to pay the price. Surely that would be a possibility too ghastly to contemplate? Was this a question of South Africa acting in the best traditions of superpower arrogance, reminiscent of the USSR's invasion of Hungary and Czechoslovakia; of imitating the US in its attacks on Grenada, Panama, and Iraq? Or was this the excuse the hawks in government had wanted and needed to prove to the people and the world just how necessary it still is to have a well-equipped defence force, a foundation well-laid in advance for the acquisition of those corvettes, tanks, fighter jets and submarines the government was so intent to buy and finally did, a scant few months later?

Are there answers to any of these questions? Perhaps it does not really matter. It may have been any one or all of these reasons. Every answer to every question is as depressing as the other, since all of them raise a central question: what is happening in South Africa's *politics?* What kind of country do we want to be? What is the spiritual quality of our politics? One thing is certain: the question of South Africa's perceived arrogance is now firmly on the agenda. When the invasion occurred, confusion about this country's intentions in foreign policy was rampant, both internally and externally. A question now hangs over South Africa's commitment to peaceful solutions and it may take some time to restore confidence in our integrity in this regard. The hawks in the ANC have flexed their muscles and the door to unwanted and unwarranted force has been opened. This episode has strengthened the "need" for programmes of armament in Africa, beginning with Zimbabwe, which, as always, has all sorts of unhappy consequences for social development.

And what are we to expect? Is South Africa's commitment to the iron fist of force and coercion as in the days of old, or is it to be the open hand of peace? Or worse still, are we seeing a new version of the Kissingerian "peace with honour" cynicism made infamous through Nixonian doublespeak?

The South African leadership had failed this particular test, and it is to the disadvantage of peace that Mr Mugabe's obstreperousness seems to have been vindicated. Maintaining the South African National Defence Force in Lesotho for more than a month cost the South African tax payer more than R1 million per day, while at home hospitals are being closed for lack of funds. Taken together with other issues, notably the government's policy on arms production, arms sales and arms procurement, the ANC's moral stance has suffered a telling blow and that, too, does not augur well.

Again, it is not so much the single political act that we question. It is, rather, the *spirit* that gives rise to such an act that is our concern. Behind and within all of these actions lies the question: what kind of country is South Africa to be? What inspires us? What makes us do what we do, for it reflects not what we purport to be, but what we are. As it is, we are in danger of seeking our identity as a nation in our admittedly catchy slogans, rather than in our political deeds of compassion and justice. The litmus test is not our obvious expertise at making ourselves feel good, but the thing we shall have to raise throughout this book: what is the spiritual quality of our politics? And the litmus test for *that* is the plight of the poor, the weak and the most vulnerable in our society.

Power and Authority: the Test of Leadership

South Africa is the region's strongest power. Its comparative power "simply dwarfs the region", in the opinion of political scientist Peter Vale.[42] While Vale is speaking of South Africa's military and economic power, I would suggest that these are not nearly enough to establish the kind of leadership Africa needs. The tensions with Robert Mugabe, over military intervention versus peaceful means, and over his increasingly anti-democratic stance in his country, prove that. And if Nigeria, with its more than 100 million inhabitants, should think along the same lines that will be a singularly fruitless basis on which leadership of the continent will be contested. It is, in my view, a futile and, in the light of Africa's deepest realities, rather pathetic understanding of our situation.

What is really needed is the moral leadership that South Africa enjoys, not because of the military power it has inherited from the apartheid regime, or its relative economic advantage since its colonisers never had a home to go back to; but because of the awesome resilience of its people, their strength in struggle, their persistence in faith and

---

[42]   Peter Vale, "Southern African Security, Some Old Issues, Many New Questions", in: *Confidence- and Security-building Measures in Southern Africa, Disarmament, Topical Papers 14* (New York: United Nations), 1993, 33.

hope of which the whole country is now heir, but which the people, with extraordinary magnanimity, have conferred upon Nelson Mandela and his successors. And although the Western world, with its obsessive inability to deal with more than just one black hero at a time, will not acknowledge this, that moral leadership is nonetheless the South African people's greatest gift to the world.

South Africa's leadership role cannot be taken for granted, and it was both a stroke of genius and God's providence that Thabo Mbeki, through his dream of an African Renaissance, created the space for that leadership to come to its full potential. It would be a great pity if that leadership and that opportunity were to be squandered. Here is a golden opportunity to turn Africa's fortunes, to reverse trends for the better, to set new examples and give new meaningful content to political concepts that have become worn with cynicism and meaninglessness. Here is a chance to inspire hope in Africa's peoples, to open up Africa not only to the world, but to the best that lies dormant within herself.

South Africa itself is facing formidable challenges and its battle against a legacy of destructive militarism, racist oppression, economic recklessness and the appalling waste of human potential is far from over. The ANC's generosity in dealing with its enemies has given it moral stature, but has also left it, and the democracy it espouses and is committed to defend, oddly vulnerable, and the world has not been as willing to help South Africa shore up that vulnerability as it was to applaud the spirit that gave rise to it. Its people's needs are great and they have, over many decades of struggle, been patient to a fault. Besides, in the final analysis leadership exacts a price, and the people will have to be the ones to pay it.

The judgement on Africa in general has been harsh – more so from those who have invested so much hope and expectation in the freedom of Africa's people, for whom *Uhuru* had become a rallying cry for the freedom of their own souls. President Thabo Mbeki, who is keenly sensitive to both the African realities and the African dream, has recognised this and pleads that Africa should "stop the laughter" emanating from a world that can no longer take African promises of a better life for all its people seriously, who "talk of a vision but do not have the will to translate that vision into reality".[43] From Thabo Mbeki, too, we learn of the bitter disappointment and disillusionment of many African Americans who, ashamed of their motherland, have turned their backs on her:

> I am an American, but a black man, a descendant of slave brought from Africa... If things had been different, I might have been one of them [the Africans] – or might have met some... anonymous fate in one of the countless ongoing civil wars or tribal clashes on this brutal continent. And so I thank God my ancestors survived that voyage [to slavery]...

---

[43] Mbeki, *Africa*, 289-295.

> Talk to me about Africa and my black roots and my kinship with my African brothers and I will throw it back into your face, and then I'll rub your nose in the images of the rotting flesh [of the victims of the genocide of the Tutsis of Rwanda]. Sorry, but I've been there. I've had an AK-47 rammed up my nose, I've talked to machete-wielding Hutu militiamen with the blood of their latest victims splattered across their T-shirts… I've seen cities bombed to near rubble, and other cities reduced to rubble, because their leaders let them rot and decay while they spirited away billions of dollars – yes billions – into overseas bank accounts… Thank God my ancestor got out, because, now, I am not one of them.[44]

Our indignation over a black man's gratitude for slavery because it spared him from being "one of them", meaning us, does not change the bitter reality that *what* he is upset about is undoubtedly true, however painful it might be to admit that. And he is not the only one. Stokely Carmichael, Black Power advocate of the sixties, and a consistent Pan-Africanist for the rest of his life, delivered judgement without apology and without mercy just before his death in late 1998. "Leaders in Africa are so corrupt" he said, "that we are certain if we put dogs in uniforms and put guns on their shoulders we'd be hard put to distinguish them".[45] This, coming from a man who has adopted the names of two of Africa's most revered leaders and has called himself Kwame (after Kwame Nkrumah of Ghana) Ture (after Sekou Toure of Gambia), and who lived in Africa till his death, calling it "home", is a harsh judgement indeed.

But this is far more than a condemnation of just Africa and African leaders. Ture's description will fit "leaders" the world over. What Kwame Ture was saying in effect was that as far as Africa is concerned, *Uhuru* has failed, Black Power has not fulfilled its potential, African people are still not free. Black Power has proved to be an empty slogan. It has not fulfilled its promises, but it has in fact shirked its obligations. It has not created genuine democracy, it has not allowed the people to govern. It has, instead, become a power that crushed all opposition, feared the voices of criticism and correction, stifled the cries of the lowly. Black Power, contrary to its own character, has not empowered the poor and powerless. It has, in the hands of black people, become a power to dread. African people, from north to south, have been betrayed.

South Africa still has an opportunity quite unique in recent history. It need not reach farther than its own people's lives for the inspiration it seeks. It need not contend for leadership in this continent. Just speaking with the voice of its people's faithfulness invests this country with an authority and an integrity whose natural child is leadership. Because it is to that faithfulness that the people of this continent, and of the world, have responded so deeply.

---

[44] Quoted in *Africa*, 240.
[45] *The Cape Argus*, 15 April 1998.

But it would need more than just *Realpolitik* driven by the interests of power for power's sake. It would need more than a mere continuation of the old apartheid mentality, albeit clothed in the transparent jargon of the new realists, who, for all their worldly verbosity, remain as naked as the emperors they once fought, but now seem doomed to emulate.

A step away from that is a step closer to the heart of its own people, and to the salvation of the continent. And that, ultimately, is what it is all about.

It is Thabo Mbeki who invites us to dream, see and create a new Africa, to recognise what Africa and Africans had been, have been able to become, have in many ways lost, but are able to be again. He says,

> When I survey all this and more besides, I find nothing to sustain the long-held dogma of African exceptionalism, according to which the colour black becomes s symbol of fear, evil and death.
>
> I speak of this long-held dogma, because it continues to still weigh down the African mind and spirit, like the ton of lead that the African slave carries on her shoulders, producing in her and the rest a condition which, in itself, contests any assertion that she is capable of initiative, creativity, individuality and entrepreneurship.
>
> Its weight dictates that she will never straighten her back and thus discover that she is as tall as the slave master who carries the whip. Neither will she have the opportunity to question why the master has legal title both to the commodity she transports on her back and the labour she must make available to ensure that the burden on her shoulders translates into dollars and yen.
>
> An essential and necessary element of the African renaissance is that we all must take it as our task to encourage her, who carries this leaden weight, to rebel, to assert the principality of her humanity – the fact that she, in the first instance, is not a beast of burden, but a human and African being
>
> And in the end, an entire epoch in human history, the epoch of colonialism and white foreign rule, progressed to its ultimate historical burial grounds because, from Morocco and Algeria to Guinea-Bissau and Senegal, from Ghana to Nigeria to Tanzania and Kenya, from the Congo and Angola to Zimbabawe and South Africa, the Africans dared to stand up to say the new must be born, whatever the sacrifice we have to make – Africa must be free![46]

---

[46] Cf. *Africa*, 242.

Such an invitation we cannot but accept. But we accept it in the spirit of Casely Hayford, who understood the needs of Africa, her vision and the kind of leadership she has always longed for, but did not always get; knowing the pain of her past and the hopes for her future, as he expressed it more than one hundred years ago in his powerful book *Ethiopia Unbound*:

> In the name of African nationality… whether in the east, south or west of the African continent, or yet among the teeming millions of Ethiopia's sons in America, the cry of the African, in its last analysis, is for scope and freedom in the struggle for existence. The African's way to proper recognition lies not as present so much in the exhibition of material force and power, as in the gentler art of persuasion by the logic of facts and of achievements before which all reasonable men must bow.[47]

It is this spirit, if made our own, that will redeem WEB Du Bois's words from the grave of unfulfilled emptiness. It is this generation that shall have to dream new dreams and make them Africa's new reality in this new century.

---

[47] As quoted in J Ayo Langley, *Ideologies of Liberation in Black Africa* (London: Rex Collins, 1979), 261. I found the quotation in Kwesi Kwaa Prah, "African Renaissance or Warlordlism", in Mkgoba (Ed.), *African Renaissance,* 45.

CHAPTER TWO

THE "AFRICAN RENAISSANCE"
In Search of the African Soul

The Discovery of our Soul

The man who took over from President Nelson Mandela after the 1999 elections is Thabo Mbeki, whose words took us toward the close of our previous chapter. Mbeki has been described as an able, intellectually strong politician, who understands the politics of power and compromise. He cannot, of course, hope to "fill the shoes" of Mandela, whose deification by the world makes that an impossibility anyway, apart from the question of the effects of that deification process on South Africa and South Africans. But like a good politician, Mbeki has understood the need to carve out his own niche, take his own stand as it were, create his own particular brand of politics, which must distinguish him from the overwhelming and sweeping presence of Nelson Mandela. Now, after the resounding victory of the ANC in the 2004 elections, his leadership affirmed by the vote, no one can say that Mbeki is not "his own man". President Mbeki is free to set his own political agenda, to shape his presidency in his own way. So besides continuing with the theme of "national reconciliation", which had become Mandela's trademark, Mbeki has introduced his own vision for the 21st century: the so-called "African Renaissance".

Much unnecessary debate has raged about this concept, mainly stirred by people who for some reason or another had misunderstood Mbeki. From the side of the Pan Africanist Congress Mbeki had been slated for daring to suggest that Africa needed a renaissance at all! As if Africans had no achievements to speak of, or as if African history had been completely swept away by European power and there had been no continuous, albeit largely ignored, history of which Africans could be proud. They thought Mbeki had swallowed completely the arrogant, imperialistic propaganda of the West, which had relegated Africa to the trash heap of history, politically, economically and culturally.

Others found the idea of an "African Renaissance" coming from a South African an exceptionally arrogant concept. Africa has had a proud history, they argue. It had known great civilisations which had given birth to great cities, unique cultures, courageous warriors and artists of infinite skill, philosophers, poets and story tellers of great renown. South Africa itself, we are reminded, has no recall of a "great state of Dahomey", say; cannot boast of an ancient city with the greatness of Carthage or Timbuktu; has known no ancestors who could have built the fortress which is now known as the "great Zimbabwe ruins". It is, they argued, somewhat presumptuous of South Africa, in truth a little upstart that got its independence a scant four years ago, to take upon itself the leadership of an "African Renaissance".[48]

Still others, falling back easily on their innate racism, scoffed that a renaissance meant that there must have been something to begin with! They could not see that. Africa was, after all, a dark continent, filled with "witchcraft, sorcery and ancestor-worship", plagued with internecine wars of the utmost barbarity, a continent steeped in ignorance and superstition, until white people came. Besides, they argued, there was only one Renaissance, and that was in Europe, and there was nothing at all to suggest that Africa is close to producing the scientific, cultural, artistic wonders that are associated with the European Renaissance. Their advice to president Mbeki was to abandon his grandiloquent pipe dream and stick to what is truly necessary: rid South Africa of crime.

These arguments express an almost deliberate wish to misunderstand Mbeki. They cloud the issues unnecessarily and make responsible debate well nigh impossible. In an important speech held early in 1998 and published widely, Mbeki has tried to flesh out further his vision of the African Renaissance and its implications for both South Africa and the continent.[49]

Renaissance: A Call to Rebellion

Africa, so Mbeki begins, is racked by war and destruction. Lesotho, the Democratic Republic of Congo, Sudan, Eritrea and Ethiopia, and Guinea Bissau are all areas of serious armed conflict. The language he uses is instructive in its honesty. He speaks of an "abyss of violent conflict", where the "silence of peace has died" and "war has usurped the place of reason". In Algeria he sees a war "without mercy, made more horrifying by a savagery which seeks to anoint itself with the sanctity of religious faith".

"Thus we can say", he says, "that the children of Africa, from north to south, from the east and the west and at the very center of our continent, continue to be consumed by death, dealt out by those who proclaimed a sentence of death on dialogue and reason and on the children of Africa whose limbs are too weak to run away from the rage of the adults…"

On top of that there is the random violence within states, employed with blatant cynicism for political gain and self-interest. As examples, he mentions Sudan and KwaZulu-Natal. Here Mbeki does not resort to the euphemisms of polite and politically correct

---

[48] The question of "leadership" seems to be considered permanently attendant on the issue of an "African Renaissance", as well it should. We cannot discuss that subject fully here, but reference will be made to it. A full discussion can be found in Peter Vale and Sipho Maseko, "South Africa and the African Renaissance", *International Affairs*, 74.2, 1998, 271-287.

[49] This speech was published in full in *The Cape Times*, 18 August 1998 and is now published in an anthology of Mbeki's speeches, which gives us the most recent and most detailed exposition of Mbeki's ideas. See Thabo Mbeki, *Africa – the time has come* (Cape Town: Tafelberg and Mafube, 1998).

speech, and his judgement is swift and without adornment: "Africa has no need for the criminals who would acquire political power by slaughtering the innocents…"

Third, he tackles corruption. Mbeki is adamant that Africa has no need "for the petty gangsters who would be our governors by theft of elective positions, as a result of holding fraudulent elections, or by purchasing positions of authority through bribery and corruption". He slates the African elites who forget the plight of the people in their desire for wealth: "Their measure of success is the amount of wealth they can accumulate and the ostentation they can achieve…They seek access to power…so that they can corrupt the political order for personal gain at all costs". In this way, the poverty of the masses "becomes a necessary condition for the enrichment of the few and the corruption of political power…"

Logically, Mbeki believes that poverty is not just the accidental flip side of wealth and power. It is, above all, an enemy which has to be fought with "sustainable economic development". The "upper echelons" have become a "mere parasite on the rest of society, enjoying a self-endowed mandate to use their political power and define the uses of such power that its exercise ensures our continent reproduces itself as the periphery of the world economy, poor, underdeveloped and incapable of development". So Mbeki wants Africa to "conduct war against poverty, ignorance and the backwardness of the children of Africa".

Next, Mbeki turns to Africa's intellectual heritage and in doing so he seeks to respond to those Africans in the north who think that he is usurping a role he cannot fully claim historically. But here Mbeki speaks as an *African*. Not for him the narrow confines of the Sub-Sahara. His sweep is wide as he recalls "with pride" Sadi of Timbuktu, a scholar from the Middle Ages who had mastered Law, Logic, Dialectics, Grammar and Rhetoric. Clearly he thinks that Africa can regain the glory days of these giants: "We must ask the question – where are Africa's intellectuals today?"

They are, in their hundreds of thousands, not in Africa, he laments, but in their "places of emigration in Western Europe and North America", whence they need to be recalled to rejoin Africa. We need them, working together with all Africans, "to open the African door to the world of knowledge, to elevate Africa's place within the world of research, the formation of new knowledge, education and information". In truth, Mbeki knows that Africa has been there before. In words strongly reminiscent of the language of the philosophers of *Negritude* and *Black Consciousness*, he urges intellectuals to recreate the mastery of those Africans in Egypt who were "two thousand years" ahead of Europeans.[50]

---

[50] See the works of Basil Davidson cited above. Davidson disdains the notion, so popular in the West, that it was Europe that gave rise to "organised" kingdoms and stimulated commerce in Africa. In fact, the situation was the "reverse". "The kingdoms of the Congo preceded the Portuguese; and the Portuguese, far from creating them, had in truth destroyed them". *Black Mother*, 103-104.

Then, still in this Black Consciousness mode, Mbeki takes up his final point, the psychological damage done to Africans by the European colonisers, who made of Africans "beasts of burden, slaves and sub-humans". They sought, in essence, to enslave the African mind and destroy the African soul. "In the end, they wanted us to despise ourselves". So this becomes Mbeki's quest: "The beginning of our rebirth as a continent must be our own rediscovery of our soul, captured and made permanently available in the great works of creativity represented by the pyramids and sphinxes of Egypt, the stone buildings of Axum...the rock paintings of the San..."

So, Mbeki concludes, the call for Africa's renewal, its renaissance, "is a call to rebellion". We must rebel against "the tyrants and the dictators...those...who steal the wealth of our people...against the ordinary criminals who murder, rape and rob...". We must "conduct war against poverty..." – this is the call Mbeki continues to make.

Participation in this renaissance, in this rebellion, is to be truly African. Therein lies, in fact, the true African identity: "Without equivocation", Mbeki believes "that to be a true African is to be a rebel in the cause of the African Renaissance, whose success in the new century and millennium is one of the great historic challenges of our time".

It is these lofty ideals Thabo Mbeki has in mind when he speaks of the African Renaissance. They form, in a very real sense, the visionary framework of his politics, both domestic and international. They speak to the heart of many Africans, at a time when prospects for Africa in the world are decidedly dim. They are meant to elevate him above the petty party politics that hamper him at home, and lift him up as an African of deep insight, capable of leading the continent to the great heights where it once stood. It should, for all sorts of reasons – not least Mr Mbeki's fervour against war and poverty – stir the hearts of Christians. His is a dream with an alluring evangelical ring to it.

A secular newspaper responded with words calculated to link Mbeki to one of the 20th-centuries' greatest personalities and prophets of the church, Martin Luther King Jr. "Mbeki's dream" it declared, "can and should be our dream. It is a dream of a continent where poverty, ignorance and disease are eradicated, allowing her people to take their rightful places among the family of nations in order to help build a planetary civilisation".[51]

For these reasons it is important not to dismiss this ideal out of hand, but rather to engage Mr Mbeki in earnest and critical dialogue. In a groundbreaking and insightful essay, scholars Peter Vale and Sipho Maseko started that dialogue.[52]

---

[51] *The Cape Times*, Editorial, 18 August 1998.
[52] Peter Vale and Sipho Maseko, "South Africa and the African Renaissance", *op. cit.*

"A Workable Dream"

This is what the President's office, as well as Mbeki himself, calls his ideas.[53] This dream was to be realised through engagement in five crucial areas: "The encouragement of cultural exchange; the emancipation of African women from patriarchy; the mobilisation of youth; the broadening, deepening and sustenance of democracy, and the initiation of sustainable economic development".[54] With this deliberate choice of words Mbeki himself infuses his politics with an element of idealism that is admirable. He thereby invites a discussion that rises above the cold-blooded "realism" he and his followers are so wont to employ.

This looks like a programme to fulfill this dream and at the same time establish firmly South Africa's leadership in the region and, indeed, the continent. At least, such is the thinking of scholars such as Vale and Maseko, who speak of South Africa now standing "on the threshold of fulfillment of its destiny – its time finally at hand".[55] They speak of "the country's capacity to offer leadership…enhanced by the role model which its successful transition offers to the continent…(and) the international standing of Nelson Mandela…"[56] All of this made for a fortuitous mix, but it was nonetheless "the lyrical appeal of Mbeki's imagery which turned the obvious, the commonsensical, into the tryst with history".[57]

Yet for all their appreciation of the historical moment, Vale and Maseko confess to some unease, for "when analysts and commentators searched the idea of the African Renaissance for policy content, there appeared very little to anchor what was obviously a fine idea…more promise than policy…high on sentiment, low on substance".[58]

What Kind of Awakening?

Apart from the expectations read into the President's dream by *The Cape Times,* which may or may not reflect the expectations of the masses, other responses may give us a clue as to where all this might lead. Vale and Maseko speak of the "globalist" and the "Africanist" interpretations and seek to discover where Mbeki himself stands.[59]

The globalist interpretation understands the African Renaissance to be essentially economic progression linking South Africa's economic interests and leadership through the logic of globalisation. This process will end history as we know it. Embracing the

---

[53] Cf. Vale and Maseko, 274, footnote 16. Mbeki himself introduced the term in an address in Montreux, Switzerland, June 1995, referring to a "non-racial, non-sexist and prosperous South Africa". *Africa,* 51.

[54] Vale and Maseko, *op. cit.*

[55] *Op. cit.,* 276.

[56] *Op. cit.,* 276.

[57] *Op. cit.,* 276.

[58] *Op. cit.,* 276, 277.

[59] *Op. cit.,* 278-283.

"free market", privatisation, exchange control relaxation and cuts in public expenditure, it will, as it did elsewhere in the world, erode the power of national governments, lessen the hold of ideologies on the economy and, by the same token, the potential for conflict. South Africa, committed to these ideals, might set in motion a chain of events which might lead Africa to the same economic success the Asian Tigers enjoyed.

In this rendition, the African Renaissance posits Africa as an expanding and prosperous market alongside Asia, Europe and North America in which South African capital is destined to play a special role through the development of trade and strategic partnerships. Mbeki's aides have welcomed this interpretation, since they see the Asian economic model as "a miracle…one of the most important socio-economic developments of the twentieth century … (offering) hope to all the people of Africa…" No wonder that the idea of an African Renaissance understood thus has been "enthusiastically embraced by moneyed elites from across the racial spectrum".[60]

It was not totally unexpected that this enthusiasm caused disquiet on the continent, not only in light of the continent's experience with South African arrogance in the past, but also in light of Africa's experience with "market solutions". Of course, recent economic developments and the virtual collapse of the Asian economies have punched more than just a few holes in this bubble and the subsequent scramble for new economic role models has not yet produced anything that Africa can safely emulate.

One continues to wonder, however, if it did not dawn on those who were so impressed with the Asian "miracle" that that miracle was achieved at a price South Africans might not be willing to pay, namely the lack of democratic freedoms, personal and collective, and the stringent restraint of trade union activities in those countries.

But there is an even deeper question: are the desire for an Asian-type of economic miracle and the social contract inherent in the idea of an African Renaissance, the "emancipation of Africa women from patriarchy" and the "broadening, deepening and sustenance of democracy" not fundamentally in conflict with each other? Not a single one of those Asian countries even pretended that "the deepening and broadening" of democracy was a goal for them, certainly not to be set above economic achievement. How are President Mbeki's social goals to be achieved along with the economic growth he seeks?

One of the central tenets of globalisation is the "internationalisation of labour", meaning that companies close their plants in countries where trade union activity is considered too vigorous and too "uncontrolled", wages deemed too high, and government regulations regarding health and the environment considered too stringent and inhibiting. There are reasons why companies have closed their plants in the United States, for instance, and have moved to Indonesia, Vietnam and Guatemala. Already South Africa has experienced that phenomenon, with plants being closed and moved to China, for instance. It seems to me to be short-sighted in the extreme to simply embrace

---

[60]   *Op. cit.,* 279.

the broad concept of "globalization" without taking cognisance of these very hard realities and taking pre-emptive action.

The Africanist response to these ideas has been decidedly critical. They see an African Renaissance driven by globalist politics as an "externally driven consumerist movement" in which Africans are valued simply for their ability to "absorb and popularise foreign ideas, trinkets and junk".[61] For them, the essence of such a Renaissance can only be cultural and psychological, centring on "the African identity in the making". So Mbeki's search for the "African soul" resonates with them, but cannot live alongside the more materialist interpretation favoured by Mbeki himself and applauded so happily by the financial Establishment. Mbeki reveals a strong commitment to the central tenets of globalization and his engineering of South Africa's neo-liberal macro-economic policy shows him to be a "moderniser among the South African business community",[62] which observation prompts Vale and Maseko to ask the pertinent question: "Who will benefit from the African Renaissance?"[63] This question is not rhetorical, but critical.

Some of the most stringent critique has come from "within", with the South African Communist Party's Jeremy Cronin unceremoniously writing off the idea of an "African Renaissance" and the president's New Economic Plan for African Development (NEPAD) as "a kind of fluffy, feel-good third-wayism for the African continent".[64] It is a "voluntaristic" (which in this context means "opportunistic" and therefore meaningless) promise of the "African century", no more than an "escape from the contradictions and difficulties of the present…" With these plans, Cronin asserts, Mbeki is proving himself to be no more than a lackey of the West, "a shop steward and conduit" of Western, neo-liberal capitalist ideas, and as such "playing with a death wish on the global stage". This is very harsh criticism indeed, and nor is it all.

Mbeki, says Cronin, fancies himself a "bridge between North and South", going about it with a "kind of swollen-headedness about South Africa, that bad old South African habit of exceptionalism", thinking that we are better than the rest of Africa. What Mbeki does not understand, Cronin contends, is that the issue is not a continental one, but rather a *structural* one. In other words, it is a battle between ideologies that is being fought on a global scale, not merely a question of the development of Africa as a continent. Clearly it irks Cronin that Mbeki does not understand this, or if he does, chooses simply to ignore it. Mbeki's idea of an African Renaissance he dismisses as "the sort of sound of white colonials in Africa, of Anglo-Indian or whatever…" Whatever it might purport to be, Cronin's opinion is that the African Renaissance is "a threadbare notion".

---

[61] *Op. cit.*, 280.
[62] *Op. cit.,* 285.
[63] *Op. cit.*
[64] These remarks are made in the interview with Cronin by Irish intellectual Helena Sheehan which caused such upheaval in the ranks of the alliance. See the transcript of the Cronin interview with Helena Sheehan, available from the ANC, which I used for our purposes here.

Moreover, Cronin believes that Mbeki is using these grand ideas as an escape route, because he is unwilling, or unable, to deal with "the hard issues" facing South Africa itself. Cronin insists that "there are more pressing points of focus like job creation and development. The African Renaissance, because it is vague and general and continental, can too easily become short on detail and rather fuzzy on content and can become an escape mechanism from dealing with the hard issues…"

This criticism goes to the heart of what the President sees as the defining elements of his presidency, this vision for Africa and his own country. But it is a vision that the "left" within the ANC does not share, for it is not built on the principles for a "democratic socialist revolution" not just for South Africa, but for the continent as a whole. Hence Jeremy Cronin's scathing reference to the structural issues involved here. Jeremy Cronin himself has to concede that "the paradigms have failed". The dream of a world-wide socialist revolution is no longer attainable, if it ever was. The South African government under Thabo Mbeki has chosen a different path, not just for South Africa but for the continent as well. This is a path that does not correspond with the "socialist agenda". That is clearly traumatic for the Communists, but it is not all politics at play here. One does not have to agree with them on the issue of the "socialist democratic revolution" and its attainability or benefits for this country and the continent to realise that what they are saying about the "pressing issues", the "South African realities" and the danger of political escapism into the vagueness of continental grandiosity, is as close to the mark as one can get. Jeremy Cronin does not speak for me, but clearly, even though the African Parliament is now a reality, the idea of an African renaissance is still very much under discussion, as it should be.

Equally important is the point that Vale and Maseko raise almost at the end of their critique. "The majority of Africans", they say, "consider themselves marginalised from the affairs of their countries, the continent and the world. Unless this is changed, there will be no renewal". And further, "To carry the day, in policy terms, the African Renaissance will have to evince both a capacity to deliver the stuff of politics and a consciousness of the pain and humiliation of African people in a continent, and a world, which remains entirely dominated by the cultural values of people who are not black".[65]

This last is a profound insight, touching as it does on the interesting link between the African Renaissance and Black Consciousness, which Mbeki himself makes (the search for the African soul) but does not explicitly recognise (as do Vale and Maseko[66]); neither does he acknowledge the role that that phenomenon has played in the recent political history of South Africa. As we have seen in chapter one, it raises the question whether this omission is simply an oversight or a *political* decision, since it brings into play the political philosophical activism of the seventies and the eighties, a period which the ANC seems either to want to appropriate for purposes of domestication, or ignore,

[65] Vale and Maseko, *op. cit.*, 281, 282.
[66] *Op. Cit.*, 281

for purposes of control. It may, of course, be a question of Mbeki's simply not being acquainted with, in the sense of having personally experienced, the impact of Black Consciousness, Black Power and Black Theology on the thinking and actions of two generations of black South Africans during the struggle years. It may also explain to a certain extent the observable distance between the ANC leadership and so many of the activists of those years, and the estrangement of the youth who, according to news reports, were not eager to register for the 1999 elections, out of lack of interest or disillusionment.[67]

But Vale and Maseko wind up their discussion by returning to the question of South Africa's leadership, which they feel, the country cannot, indeed dare not, give. Making the same point as Cronin in a different way, they argue that this cannot be, since South Africa is too much condemned by its own past; the country's residual power skews, rather than balances the prospects for sustainable and equitable development, and without equity, "followership can only be reluctant and enforced".[68]

Be that as it may, the question of South Africa's leadership of the region or the continent is not, we feel, the most important question here. We are intrigued by what Mr Mbeki has himself said about the African Renaissance, issues which Vale, Maseko and Moletsi Mbeki, the President's brother, in his address to the South African Institute of International Affairs,[69] did not touch upon, but issues which Christians, precisely because these matters echo so much the heart of the gospel, cannot afford to ignore. Those are the issues we will now seek to engage.

African Renaissance and the Miracle of the Rainbow Nation

Quite correctly, Vale, Maseko and others link the idea of an African Renaissance to South Africa's peaceful transition and the "miracle" of 1994. This must not be romanticised. The "miracle" is as much due to the grace of God as it is the result of the sacrificial efforts of so many over such a long time. Yet one must not belittle this achievement. South Africa did, after all, manage to effectuate the transition from apartheid state without the bloodshed many had feared and fully expected for years. That in itself was a major triumph and those of us who had fought so hard for space for non-violence as a legitimate method of struggle and reconciliation as the end-goal of our struggle cannot thank God enough for this.[70]

On the other hand, those who thought purely in political terms, trumpeted the negotiated settlement as a triumph and vindication of the kind *Realpolitik* which would become the

---

[67] Only 0,9% of youths between 16 and 18 years old registered for the 1999 elections; 1,5% of those between 18 and 20 years old, and of those between 20 and 30 only 28,3%.

[68] Vale and Maseko, *op. cit.*, 284.

[69] *The African Renaissance, Myth or Reality?*, Address to the SAIIA, Jan Smuts House, Johannesburg, 21 October 1997, quoted in Vale and Maseko, 279, note 38.

[70] See Allan Aubrey Boesak, "The Task of the UDF in South Africa Today", key-note address at the formation of the UDF, in: *Black and Reformed*, Johannesburg: Skotaville, 1984, 174.

hallmark of politics for the African National Congress. Indeed, for them South Africa has become an object lesson in "politics as the art of the possible". The ANC and the National Party were both praised for their ability to "restrain" their supporters, and make them understand the (long-term) benefits of political compromise.

This included what was called "incremental democracy", a strategy which meant that "majority rule", which would have been the logical outcome of the first one-person-one-vote elections, would in fact not materialise. Instead, the opposition, the white political parties and the Inkatha Freedom Party were promised participation in government, at Cabinet level, *beforehand*. Together they would form a government of national unity. It was an arrangement to pacify those whites who could not conceive of government by a black majority alone right away: majority rule had to be tempered by the presence of whites. Over time that arrangement would be revisited and new deals would be made.

This was not a coalition government of the kind one is used to see in Europe, where power-sharing arrangements are made *after* elections and no clear outright winner has emerged, and deals are then made with other political parties who more or less share the same political programme and who could be (more or less) trusted when voting time comes around. In South Africa, however, the deal was made *before* the election: Mr F W de Klerk would, by prior arrangement, become a Deputy President (along with Mr Mbeki) and Chief Buthelezi would, again *by prior arrangement*, be a member of the Cabinet, *no matter what the real outcome of the elections.*

Thus the outcome of the struggle was not based on the people's struggle and their sacrifices, but on an accommodation of power elites:

> The older, more moderate ANC leadership was encouraged by De Klerk to believe that an *accommodation among elites, resulting in majoritarian rule with various checks*, was possible.[71]

Hence no one was really surprised when the ANC *just* fell short of the magical two-thirds majority it needed to govern alone and hence also the fortuitous election outcome of the provinces. So the goal was achieved: the ANC does have its majority, and the election results justified *a postiori* the compromise that had been made.

Of course, it has been argued that all this was necessary under the circumstances, that the ANC, considering the geo-political situation and pressure from both the US and the USSR, had virtually run out of options; that power-sharing arrangements are made

---

[71]   Marx, *Lessons of Struggle, South African Internal opposition, 1960-1990*, (Cape Town: Oxford University Press, 1992) 262. Emphasis mine. The degree of anger over this fact is both remarkable and sobering, as is the anger over the perception that the ANC as an exile organisation is undeservedly claiming all the credit for the democratic victory, a victory which really was that of the oppressed masses in South Africa itself. Cf. e.g. Martin Legassick, "Armed Struggle in South Africa", in: *Journal of Contemporary African Studies*, Vol. 21, Number 2, May 2003, 285-302. Legassick remarks, "The price that will be paid for aborting a worker-led democratic revolution in favour of a negotiated compromise will be high".

all the time and that the electoral system of proportional representation was perfectly legitimate. Also, Namibia's experience underscored the critical importance of political reconciliation and of ensuring that more than one party is able to secure a role in the ongoing political process.

I have no problem whatsoever with multi-party, proportional representation. Except that during that decisive phase the ANC strenuously denied any power-sharing arrangements with the National Party or anybody else, that the system of proportional representation was not ever explained to the followers of the ANC, even though it is, in my view, a very acceptable way of doing things and would suit South Africa very well indeed, and that the term "incremental democracy" was used only in intellectual circles. The real reason, we were left to surmise, and sometimes told, was the fear of violence. Violence from Inkatha, which had turned Natal into killing fields second to none, and a "counter-revolution" from the far right-wing whites, whom de Klerk had to control.

The point I want to make is this: if South Africa's "democratic miracle" has been achieved by being less than honest with South Africa's people, how much of a miracle was it? If violence could drive the outcome of negotiations to the extent that it apparently did, then how would we ever escape the threat of violence in the future if ever some or other group wants to have their way? Is this the reason why in KwaZulu-Natal the ANC was so ready to make a pact with the Inkatha Freedom Party and whoever else might be a handy partner, not taking into account any "principles"? And all this in the name of a "peace deal"? The ever-present threat of violence as a not so subtle form of political blackmail in that province has been given more political credence than is healthy in our democracy and we should carefully consider our response to these matters as a matter of principle, rather than expedience.

In the Western Cape during the nineties, an extremist Muslim group called *Pagad* was terrorising the Cape Flats, planting bombs, calling for violence openly, threatening the lives of intellectuals and civic and religious leaders in their communities who dare speak out against them. In the name of a *Jihad* (a holy war) they aimed to make the country "ungovernable" through violence if they did not get their way.[72] There are many reasons for the existence of *Pagad*, but certainly one of the most important is the extraordinary success of violence as political blackmail in South Africa's recent history, which *Pagad* could not have failed to note. That door, once opened, might prove extremely difficult to close.

Also at issue is another matter. Obviously, the compromises struck here were compromises between power blocks. In the case of the ANC it was numbers; for the old apartheid establishment it was the financial power of the Afrikaners, the ability of the right wing to create havoc through armed rebellion and the possibility of disruption

---

[72] *The Cape Times*, 12 January 1999. Although the state has tackled Pagad quite vigorously, with key leadership in prison, the organization's support base is still very much alive, since their ostensible *raison d'être*, crime, drugs, etc. remains a growing concern for the communities of the Cape Flats.

of the bureaucracy. With the English-speaking elite it was their financial power and their strong international links, and for whites in general it was, as well, the solidarity of the Western world. But in such a case, what happens to the hopes and the needs of the masses who, of necessity, have to be left out of the equation, since in the scheme of things (the "balance of power" the ANC used to say) their contribution was not the greatness of their needs, the weight of their sacrifices or the justice of their cause, but the strength of their numbers? They, the ordinary people, were almost certain to fall between the cracks. And mostly they did.

Over and above that, and inextricably linked to this issue, is the question of trust, without which no democracy can survive. It is my contention that South Africa's people could have been entrusted with the truth about necessary political compromises. I do not accept the argument that the people of this country were not politically sophisticated enough to understand the reasoning behind necessary but honest compromise. If South Africa's people were sophisticated enough to understand the appeal of Black Consciousness, could rise above the indoctrination of ethnic thinking imbued into them for decades and launch political action that would ultimately lead to the formation of the United Democratic Front, they would understand. If they were sophisticated enough to know that the suffering caused by sanctions was necessary to overcome ultimately the greater suffering of apartheid, in spite of South Africa's draconian laws and the extraordinary propaganda of the white controlled media, then they would have the sophistication to understand. It is all a question of trust.

In time, many black South Africans will come to think again about these arrangements and wonder why their leadership did not take them into their confidence. And hence, what *truly* was behind these compromises. In a situation where government needs to explain why delivery of essential services is so excruciatingly slow, why there is no money for education or health; where corruption is so rampant and so little is done about it; or why the inviolability of (white) property rights had to be enshrined in the new constitution; or, why the situations of the poor masses and the rich have changed so disturbingly little, one cannot afford to squander trust.

Second, while political power is being shared in South Africa, real economic power remains virtually intact, and untouched, in white hands. Experience around the world, from the United States to the Caribbean and Africa itself, has shown that political power without economic power is like owning a rowboat without an oar. To make matters worse, South Africa's economy is controlled by tight monopolies which in turn are controlled by just a few families. We can be sure that "economic empowerment" will be just as rigidly controlled, and already it is clear that the way forward has been chosen: create a few black millionaires overnight and use them as buffer to keep the poor hungry masses both poor and at bay.

Third, control of the information industry remains largely in white hands. That is true for all newspapers and almost all magazines, and by far the majority of radio stations that are now allowed to operate since the "liberation of the air waves". The first private television station allowed to operate besides the national broadcaster, the SABC, has plenty of black faces but the money and control are firmly in white hands, with the considerable financial backing of American media giant Time Warner in the background.

What this means for *information* as opposed to *infotainment* is all too clear, if one only looks at what passes for "objective news" on US television networks. This also means that we can forget about news that will truly inform South Africa's people and allow them to make intelligent choices based on truthful reporting, reflecting the realities of South Africa not acceptable to the moguls who profit from ignorance.

Fourth, and very disturbing indeed, is that South Africa's new democracy in its first ten years has had to function largely within the structures and strictures of the old apartheid era. The ANC has committed itself to no sweeping changes in the civil service, the police, the army and the judicial system. It is difficult to understand how we thought democracy would be served by leaving in positions of considerable power persons who had spent their whole lives fighting democracy. We are hoping to build democracy while we have left every weapon to destroy democracy in the hands of those who always were the sworn enemies of democracy. The long-lasting inability of the police to effectively fight gangsterism in the Western Cape, the open and constant failures of the justice system, the strains in the National Defence Force, now openly blamed by ANC politicians on the "slowness of the transition" and "anti-democratic" elements,[73] are all signs of some serious short-sightedness in this regard. The present row about racist white judges on the Cape bench is not surprising, but nonetheless disturbing.[74]

Now, slightly more than ten years into our democratisation project, the realities of the "new South Africa" often belie the miracle everyone is expected to believe in. The Government of National Unity collapsed with the walk-out of the National Party in 1995, but new deals are always in the making and we are not sure that the essence of these deals is aimed at strengthening our democracy. The Truth and Reconciliation Commission, hailed by the white English liberal press as an instrument of healing, has faced acrimonious court actions and has lost much credibility in the black communities, while many Afrikaans-speaking whites, bitter at being forced even to acknowledge some of the atrocities of apartheid done in their name, don't think reconciliation was served or effected at all. On television, many white South Africans sarcastically referred to the Truth Commission as "the Kleenex Club". In many ways, English-speaking whites are even worse, and the dismal failure of the reconciliation campaign spearheaded by Mary Burton and Carl Niehaus is a sad, but tellingly true, reflection of the state of affairs.

---

[73] See, for instance, the speech of Thabo Mbeki at the 87th anniversary rally of the ANC held in the Western Cape, 8 January 1999, reported on SABC's *One 'o Clock Live*, 8 January 1999, and the ANC initiated debate in early 2005 regarding transformation of the judiciary as just the most recent examples of the ANC's acknowledgement of this problem.

[74] Cf. Sunday paper *Rapport,* October 3, 2004. The debates raged on through the weeks that followed. These issues are not recurring, they are also symptomatic.

Racism is rampant, to a degree this writer finds shocking, in all communities in South Africa and the persistent denial of its existence even more so.

The new black elites are doing well, while the situation of the vast majority has scarcely changed. New-found wealth has shifted the issues fundamentally. "Solidarity" is now the solidarity of the rich. The interests of the new black wealthy class are the same as the interests of the old rich white establishment. The trade unions, in the struggle for the workers, now find themselves increasingly at odds with the government, while in theory it is still an "alliance partner". Increasingly also, the issues of fundamental difference do not end with internal economic policies such as GEAR – it now includes foreign policy as well as the growing dispute over Zimbabwe shows. When will this paradox become too much to bear, or too painful to ignore? And what will the consequences be?

But there is a still deeper question. As we move into the 21st century, will South Africa, exactly because of its struggle against injustice and apartheid, be the example of justice and tolerance that so many had hoped it would be, or would the price to be paid for an appropriated revolution prove too much for the poor, already taxed beyond endurance? This is not just a question of political and economic realities. This is, at its deepest level, a question that raises moral issues for South Africa, and in a wider sense, for the Southern African region where South Africa plays such a key role. When the President makes the "African Renaissance" the main theme of his politics for the 21st century and the wider framework within which he sees this country's role under his leadership, it has not just economic and political implications. Its moral ramifications are vast.

The Long Walk to Freedom

This is the title of President Mandela's acclaimed autobiography. In that book, the "long walk to freedom" is essentially the South African oppressed people's struggle for freedom under the leadership of the ANC, and, of course, Mr Mandela's own role in it. For our purposes I would like to suggest that that title more aptly describes the road that lies ahead, rather than the road we have come. I am suggesting that the long walk to freedom has just begun and that South Africa's description of itself as a "miracle" and a "rainbow nation" might prove to be a dangerous exercise in the politics of delusion.

I am very much afraid that starry-eyed, uncritical enthusiasm over the continent's newest democracy is simply proof that we are looking at South Africa through the eyes of the powerful and the privileged. Countless people in South Africa feel that they are still "on the other side of the Red Sea", that Jordan "still has to be crossed". One cannot blame them.

This is not to say that South Africa has not come a very long way from where we have been and that there are no reasons to celebrate. There is the new constitution, the removal from the statute books of all those obnoxious laws that have made this country such a hard one to live in. There are new laws which seek better conditions for workers and children and the empowerment of women. There are permanent Commissions on gender equality and human rights. Government is certain to point out progress made in the provision of water, electricity and housing. But the poor South Africans who point out their continued plight are concerned with the realities of their everyday lives, and what they experience to be the government's *priorities,* as well as the *quality* of what is being delivered.

One of the startling realities of the "new South Africa" is not only that the rich are growing richer and the poor poorer; but that the gap between the rich, including the new black elite, and the poor is wider than ever. The first four years of black majority rule produced a surprising number of new, black "empowerment achievers" who are worth millions. By 1999 33 black-controlled organisations have been listed on the Johannesburg Stock Exchange and by late 1998 the value of black-controlled corporations was around R48 billion.[75] All this new wealth is concentrated among the aristocracy of the new political ruling class. Meanwhile, the misery of the vast masses of poor people is growing. There is no doubt that the greatest enemy South Africa is facing is poverty. Recently, two[76] major reports have focused on the plight of the poor and the danger of poverty in South Africa.

Φ The richest 10% of people in South Africa control 50,1% and the poorest people have access to less than 1% of the wealth of the country.

Φ By the same token, 6% of the population earn more than 40% of the income, while 53% live below the poverty datum line of US$60 per month.

Φ This 53% of the population, the poorest of the poor, receive only 40% of the educational resources.

Φ The economic and human development status of South Africa has been declining over the last years and is now at the same level as it was during the 1960s, before the sharp economic growth of the late 1960s and 70s.

Φ Currently over 9 million people are living in informal shacks and more than 2 million black South Africans are nutritionally compromised.

Φ During 1996, in the Western Cape alone, 6 000 teachers were fired, while only one black in 2 000 is at university, compared to one white in just 30.

Φ In 1997 an estimated 563 501 children between the ages of six and fourteen were not attending school, while over-enrolment at schools (because a lack of teachers and facilities) results in a wastage of some R1 billion per year.

Φ There was, in 1996, a country-wide shortage of more than 64 000 class rooms and the overall pupil/class room ratio varied from 31:1 (Western Cape) to 55:1 (Eastern Cape).

---

[75] "New Directors Are Making Up For Lost Time", *The Cape Times*, 26 February 1999.
[76] The HRSC Report on poverty, Pretoria: Human Sciences Research Council, 1995; and Julian May, *Experience and Perceptions of Poverty in South Africa*, Durban: Praxis, 1998.

Φ About 38% of poor children suffer from stunted growth and 23% of those under the age of six suffer chronic malnutrition or stunting.

Φ Tuberculosis has overwhelmed health care in South Africa and 3,5 million new cases were to be expected by 2005 if current trends continue.

The very latest research results from the Human Sciences Research Council confirm this disturbing trend.[77] "South Africa's poor are getting steadily poorer" it says, "and it has become so bad that 85% of the country's people in some municipal districts live under the poverty datum line". Taken together says the HSRC, no less than 57% of the country's population live beneath the poverty line, "and the gap between the rich and the poor is widening". The government has failed in creating the jobs required, and with the slow trend in this process "it does not look as if things will be changing anytime soon". The study used what the HSRC calls the "poverty gap" [the average income of the wealthy classes versus the income of the poor masses]. In 1996 it was about R58 billion. In 1998 it rose to about R81 billion. In other words, the government is not reaching its goals, and all the talk about the growing economy in line with globalization expectations is just that: talk. It is probably worse: the most recent up-beat reports about our economy mean that the prosperity of the already wealthy is not "trickling down" to the poor, something we have already discovered in Reagan's America to be a delusion. The government's goal of bringing down unemployment to half the present number is not realistic, says Dr Miriam Altman, executive director of the HSRC, even if the labour force is reduced. The job-creating prognosis is not good: apart from the 100 000 to 300 000 jobs that are being created, a further 200 000 to 300 000 need to be created every year, if the government wants to reach its goals. In other words, GEAR is not working, and our reliance on neo-liberal capitalism as the foundation for our faith in globalization is not meeting our expectations, to put it mildly. And as always, the real losers are the poor.

These are bleak and utterly grim statistics. But poverty is more than just statistics. It means unemployment, lack of access, education and skills, poor health, deprivation of knowledge and communication and an inability to exercise one's basic political and human rights. It means the absence of dignity, confidence and self-respect. These are the South Africans who remain excluded, and their exclusion ranges from basic needs to justice in the courts. For them, the difference between apartheid South Africa and post-apartheid South Africa is non-existent. That is a time bomb that has to be defused. Quickly.

Behind these realities, the 1997 UNDP *Report on Human Development* reminds us, "lies the grim reality of desperate lives without choices". That is, I think, the final humiliation of the poor: to be without choices or options, which in effect, make of poverty a state of effective slavery, in a democracy that came into being on the blood, sweat and tears of the poor. An African Renaissance which does not take this into account is no awakening at all. Or rather, it might be an awakening for those in the privileged classes,

---

[77] Cf. *Die Burger,* 11 October, 2004.

but certainly not for those to whom it should really matter in order to be real. When Thabo Mbeki therefore calls upon us "to make war on poverty", the poor have a right to know what he means and how serious he is in doing just that.

We must again point to the threat posed by HIV/Aids. South Africa still has to come to grips with the shock of now being the worst-hit country on the continent with its one HIV infection every 15 seconds. More than 80% of HIV/Aids deaths occur among 20- to 45-year-olds. In other words, Aids claims people in the prime of their lives. In South Africa, as is the case in the inner cities of the United States for example, poverty is a major factor underlying the spread of the disease. Poor women, men and children are often forced into prostitution in order to survive. The children generally have to leave school early, which means they remain illiterate and subsequently have no or little access to accurate information regarding the disease. Add to this equation inadequate nutrition and sub-standard living conditions as well as an unemployment rate of over 40% and the vicious downward spiral is complete. If the Aids epidemic is not checked, the economic and human disaster that will surely follow will put paid to any idea of an African Renaissance.

Governments, including that of South Africa, are not doing nearly enough. If governments the world over would have policies that were people-driven, rather than motivated by greed or the hunger for power, or have the courage of Uganda, things would be different. But that in itself would not be enough. The tragedy of Aids is not just the neglect or the lack of political will, but the lack of understanding, and therefore compassion, and therefore justice. The stigma attached to Aids is like a polluted cloud hanging above a fog of misunderstanding and judgement. It makes of the Aids patient and their families double victims: first of the virus, then of discrimination.

This means that education about Aids is far more than just about the regular use of condoms, or even, as Thabo Mbeki has suggested, abstention. It has a spiritual dimension to it government cannot hope, and cannot be expected, to give, and about which, frankly, our politicians know precious little. It has to do with our reading and understanding of the Scriptures, our judgement of our own prejudices, our capacity to love our neighbours as ourselves. All this has to do not just with ignorance but with a sinfulness no government campaign can adequately address.

Poverty, and all its attendant miseries is, as Thabo Mbeki has correctly seen, an enemy. But it is no longer an unbeatable enemy. The 1997 UNDP report is unequivocal. "Poverty is no longer inevitable. The world has the material and natural resources, the know-how and the people to make a poverty-free world a reality in less than a generation".[78] In fact the whole report is devoted to a methodology for the eradication of poverty and it makes fascinating reading. The Report makes the point that the progress in reducing poverty over the 20th century is remarkable and unprecedented and that those advances are found in all regions of the world, even though, because of political unwillingness,

---

[78] *UNDP Report* (iii).

those advances have been uneven and marred by setbacks, and so poverty remains pervasive.[79]

In order for such strategies to succeed, policies must become "people-centred", not just remaining the well-worn slogan we are currently hearing, but by deliberately building assets for the poor, fostering a creative commitment to gender equality, encouraging investment in human development so that countries "are ready to face the challenge of globalisation".[80] Eradicating poverty is no longer a point for leisurely debate. "Eradicating absolute poverty in the first decades of the 21st century is feasible, affordable and a moral imperative ... It is a practical possibility".[81] This is clear language. In other words, it is possible, if we have the political will and if governments were to get their priorities straight. There are no more excuses. In this respect too, the church must change both its language and its mindset. We should be done with talk of charity and "poverty alleviation" as if this were our highest calling. We should speak of and demand, and work for the total eradication of poverty. It is possible.

But lacking political will is exactly what the new government is being accused of by black theologian and activist Dr Molefe Tsele, General Secretary of the South African Council of Churches and one time South African Chairperson of Jubilee 2000, an international group working for the cancellation of foreign debt of Third World countries.[82] Social benefits remain woefully inadequate in spite of budgetary efforts. One reason, experts agree, is the paralysing drain on South Africa's limited resources by the legacy of apartheid, and the debilitating effects of South Africa's foreign debt, again part of that fatal legacy. But that legacy should not be seen as having simply been dumped on us by the apartheid regime. Some of that legacy has been willingly accepted by the ANC as part of the negotiated settlement, part of the "sunset clauses" granted the previous government, for which the poor must continue to pay.

One particularly blatant, if scarcely known, example of this is the Government Employees Pension Fund (GEPF). This fund, Dr Tsele has pointed out in an informative article,[83] is the largest single component of apartheid's internal debt. This fund came into being as a result of an effectively secret deal between "a dying apartheid regime and its most senior officials in 1989". However, because of the ANC's negotiated deal with the National Party, it continues to be vigorously defended by the new government's ministry of Finance, who argue that "meddling with the Fund would both create financial havoc and destroy the life savings of ordinary South Africans after a lifetime of hard, honest work". But it is not the poor, hard working masses who struggled against apartheid who benefit from this Fund. The senior officials of the apartheid regime, the police and army generals who were "criminally responsible for the terror and murder of the apartheid

---

[79] *Op. cit.*, 2, 3.
[80] *Op. cit.*, 6, 7, 9.
[81] *Op. cit.*, 12.
[82] *The Cape Times*, 25 February 1999.
[83] "Truth About South Africa's Apartheid Debt", *The Cape Times*, 25 February 1999.

death squads" and who "took early retirement on full pension", says Tsele, "are the direct, intended beneficiaries of the unusually generous scheme created in 1989".

And that is not all. Contrary to the claims by the government, the fund does not consist entirely of pensioners' contributions. "The reality is that the vast majority of the fund is public money put there by the government since 1989". The impact on the poor is devastating. "Therefore", Tsele concludes, "while the recipients of child benefits - officially defined as being among the poorest of the poor - have had their meagre benefits slashed in order to spread the benefit more widely, the GEPF, reflecting all the inequities of the apartheid wage structure, is said to be untouchable". This ensures that those discriminated against by the apartheid regime continue to be discriminated against through the fiscal preferences of the new regime.

"Making budget allocations from limited resources is like distributing the proverbial five loaves and two fishes" the Finance Minister is reported to have said in his budget speech on 17 February 1999, when he defended his allocations relating to social responsibilities and foreign debt servicing, illustrating the ever-present danger when politicians seek to use biblical texts for their own dubious ends.[84] Of course (this just in passing), the church knows that the Minister's biblical reference is slightly out of joint. In the gospels the poor are not being sent away hungry and empty-handed, because Jesus has other priorities. There, his first priority, *above* his desire to feed their souls, was to feed their bodies, to still their hunger. There no one was sent away as were the poor in the cartoon accompanying this newspaper report. In the gospel story there was, in fact, more than enough for everyone. "*And all ate, and were filled*" exclaim all three gospels, jubilantly. No, the meaning of the gospel passage illustrating the concern of the Man who taught us to pray "Give us today our daily bread", and whose mother's revolutionary song about filling the hungry "with good things" and sending "the rich away empty", still fills our ears as it must have filled his, is quite contrary to the concerns of the new government. The meaning of the gospel is not to show the *shortage* of food; it is to show the *abundance* of food; reflecting the wideness of God's mercy, the limitless care of God's grace, the unending depths of God's justice, the all-inclusive sweep of God's faithfulness.

But even if the foreign debt *were* "only" 5% of the total debt, Dr Tsele argues - bringing to bear the realism of faith on the facts, over against the "realism" of politics - this 5% translates into R15 billion. For the government, Trevor Manuel says, this is "trivial".

Φ Yet, a mere 0,17% of R15 billion would restore the rail service to what it was before the recent cuts (thereby bringing public transportation back within reasonable reach of the poor);

Φ R4 billion would provide housing for the 200 000 families on Cape Town's housing waiting list;

---

84 *The Cape Times*, 18 February 1999.

Φ R400 million would provide all our schools with textbooks (thereby alleviating one of the most acute crises in education for the poor. The more wealthy, historically white schools do not suffer from this problem).

It is within this context that Molefe Tsele is justifiably upset about the government's unwillingness to support the call for cancelling South Africa's foreign debt. In spite of huge popular support at home and abroad, and the undeniable need for doing so, the government will not join the call because it fears "upsetting foreign investors". So once again, as before, the voice of capital, of power, of the "Washington Consensus", is louder than the voice of the poor who, for all practical purposes, remain voiceless. This raises the spectre that the government, despite its oft-expressed concern for the poor, is in reality drifting farther and farther away from the poor, whose plight matters little when power talks to power.

For these reasons, among many others, the church should be far more vigorous in participating in the debate about the African Renaissance, and not just as it relates to the question of Aids or poverty, but as it relates to the spirituality of struggle. The poor deserve it; the God of the poor demands it.

Prophetic Faithfulness and the African Renaissance

In South Africa the role of the church in the struggle for liberation has brought to that struggle a spiritual dimension without which we would have been much the poorer. The fact that politicians are now using that spiritual tradition as an ideological tool in a process of "national reconciliation" that serves a political agenda rather than genuine concern for God's will cannot take away that fact and should not discourage us.

Besides, people of faith have always known that the struggle needs more than just political slogans. We do not just know those slogans, we *invented* them. We have experienced that, when such enormous sacrifices are called for, when standing up for justice almost inevitably means laying down one's life, when dealing not only with the progressive brutality of the system one is fighting, but also, inevitably with one's own brutalisation, and when one has to face the temptations that come with fighting for a just cause, one cannot live by bread alone, but indeed by "every word that comes from the mouth of God".

No matter how much the ideologues of the new secular religiosity have hated it, are still chagrined by it, or are now stubbornly trying to act as if it were never the case, in the process not only trying to *rewrite* history but also *writing out* the driving force behind that history, the truth remains and deep down South Africa's oppressed people know it. We were, in the final analysis, not inspired by Lenin, or Stalin, or the lofty ideals of "democracy" or "freedom", but by our faith.

If it were not for that faith, the struggle in South Africa would not have had the resilience or the persistence or the hope, and it would have taken another turn completely, and Mandela, ironically, would have had nothing to appeal to in his call for reconciliation in the face of a most horrendous history of oppression. That this is now being denied by those in power is one of the greatest tragedies of current South African history making, and one that will surely come to haunt us in years to come. The irony is the greater, since this spirituality is essentially what Mbeki's African Renaissance is calling for.

Of course there is political work to be done. The African Renaissance is nothing if not political, and the call for political action to fulfil the promises of the lofty language is very much the business of the church. We must work hard to ensure that people understand that democracy is meaningless unless it also means the genuine empowerment of people. The church, more than others, must ensure that the question, "Who will benefit from the African Renaissance?" is answered correctly. It must be a people-driven, people-centred process, in which all our people can take pride and participate with joy.

There are those who insist that what is needed is simply simple common sense. In the US, for example, with a view to "better military protection for the 21st century" the United States has current procurement plans for the following: 30 Centurion nuclear submarines, total cost, US$40 billion; 442 F22 advance tactical fighters, total cost, US$72 billion; 120 C-17 "Globemaster" transport planes, cost, US$340 million each; 20 B-2 Stealth bombers, at the cost of US$2,2 billion per plane.[85] The cost of just one Stealth bomber would be an amazing advance for research to combat diseases such as Aids, and to scrap the nuclear submarines would free $40 billion for education. The UNDP Report is right: we really could wipe out poverty and disease, if we wanted to. If we would only make the right choices.

But clearly, more is called for than just "common sense". Experience shows that greed (for both power and money) speaks louder than common sense. Yet the arms trade is not profitable for governments; it is profitable for the arms manufacturers, who in turn share these profits with politicians. The armaments industry is heavily subsidised, slurping up monies that could have been used for domestic projects such as housing, transport, education and health care.

William Hartung[86] has shown that in the US the hidden costs of the arms trade boils down to "welfare for weapons dealers", which is the title of his 1996 study of the arms trade. Export subsidies in 1995 amounted to $7,6 billion on exports of US$12 billion, a subsidy of 63%. Were the $7,6 billion in export subsidies used instead for domestic projects, they could support construction of 100 000 low-income houses plus preschool education for 130 000 children. On top of this, there would be a net increase of over 88 000 jobs. There are, Hartung points out, almost twice as many workers employed building F-16 fighter aircraft in Turkey than there are at Lockheed Martin's principal plant in Fort Worth, Texas. So the argument for job creation is weak.

---

[85] We can safely assume that under George W Bush and his "wars on terror" and advocacy of "regime change" these numbers will be significantly higher.

[86] William Hartung, *Welfare for Weapons Dealers: The Hidden Costs of the Arms Trade*, quoted by Terry Crawford-Browne, *Submission to the Joint Standing Committee on Defence*, Cape Town, 19 May 1997.

Yet knowing all this, South Africa continues to buy, manufacture and export arms. To continue such a heavily subsidised industry is detrimental to South Africa's economy and its ability to fight the real enemy: the dismal poverty of 70% of our people. With our people desperately needing education, good health care, housing, clean water, decent police protection, jobs - why is it necessary to spend R30 billion (now, with "unexpected" escalation already over R60 billion) on arms from Britain, Sweden and Germany as the South African government has stubbornly decided to do?

The same is true for Britain which, under Tony Blair even more than under Margaret Thatcher, is doing its best to entice South Africa even further into the arms trade. Professor Michael Cooley, who was a leading aircraft design engineer at Lucas Aerospace, has spent much time pioneering strategies to convert the arms industry to peacetime production. He speaks bluntly on the issue of how defence contracts sustained jobs.

> In many ways that's a downright lie. If they want to have a defence industry for military reasons, that's their political issue, but it must not be confused with jobs. In some areas of the defence industry, it costs 600 000 pounds Sterling to create just one job. Now if the government put a fraction of that money into alternatives, almost anything would be possible. I can list 5 000 new products beginning with systems for renewable energy to monitoring and control devices, used in aircraft design, that could combat our biggest killer, cardiovascular disease. At the end of the Second World War in Britain, 3, 5 million people were demobbed and 2, 5 million were taken out of the defence industry. How? *There was a national plan and government support ... it can be done, it needs only the political will.*[87]

In South Africa, too, the economic benefits of the armaments industry are not what the government purports. During the 1970s and 80s, the years of apartheid South Africa's strongest onslaught on the democratic forces, the arms industry became a significant provider of jobs, as more than 150 000 persons were employed. But these were "highly capital- and skill-intensive and reserved for whites, given the strategic concerns of the industry. Thus the employment benefits of domestic arms production perpetuated the racist structure of the labour market ..."[88] It remains capital- and skill-intensive and the legacy of apartheid education policies will continue to ensure the racist and therefore insignificant (in terms of the vast uneducated black masses) basis for the provision of jobs.

Economists and peace activists are agreed on this. Sue Willet of the University of London's Centre for Defence Studies has pointed out that the economic benefits in terms of foreign exchange earnings, balance of payments considerations and job

---

[87] Quoted in John Pilger, *Hidden Agendas* (Vintage, London: 1998), 151, 152. Emphasis mine.
[88] Peter Batchelor, "South Africa's Arms Industry, Prospects for Conversion, in: *From Defence to Development*, Jacklyn Cock and Penny McKenzie, Eds. (Cape Town: David Philip, 1998), 102.

creation appear to be "relatively marginal". She shows that the industry has absorbed a disproportionate number of South Africa's scarce scientific and technological graduates, "with little obvious benefits to the civilian economy".[89] Peter Batchelor makes the same point and speaks of a "misinvestment".[90]

Armscor's *Rooivalk* attack helicopter project is a case in point. It has soaked up some R1,17 billion in research and development money and has failed to create more than just a few hundred jobs, although the industry promised "thousands".[91] The conclusion is quite clear: "Arms production is inefficient and expensive. It may encourage growth in the short term, but it distorts the structure of the national economy in the long run and has only limited export potential, particularly at present when international demand for weapons systems is declining and the arms market is saturated".[92]

With these considerations in mind, and with the unfulfilled promises of the past, one should not place much hope in the promise that South Africa's initial R30 billion will result in "at least R60 billion" investment in job creation, especially since most of it seems to be destined for the arms industry anyway. Church groups and non-governmental organisations, including the South African chapter of *Economists Allied For Arms Reduction*, have called this promise "economic nonsense", holding that a straight investment of R30 billion would have made much more sense.[93] We have heard much of the Coega project, but the fulfilment of promises is at best partial. The economics is not working.

The point is clear. South Africa, with the new government supposedly representing the interests of the poor masses who had voted it into power, fighting the frightening legacy of apartheid, having decided to push for an African Renaissance, cannot afford an armaments industry, heavily subsidised at that, or squander money on so-called "defence" when there is no discernable military threat to the country. Moreover, the South African arms industry, despite the massive subsidies injected into it for the sake of its survival, has reported a loss of more than R390 million for this year, proving Hartung's point.

South Africa's first democratic Minister for Defence, the now deceased Joe Modise, and Aziz Pahad, current Deputy Minister for Foreign Affairs, both strong exponents of the new "political realism" of the government, have declared that the arms industry is "integral to the right of self-defence and the maintenance of sovereignty of territory of the state". But South Africa is not facing any military threat and the notion that a militarily strong country is an important country is fallacious. The sovereignty of Third World countries is being undermined rather than enhanced by maintenance of armaments industries, because of the strongly negative impact on socio-economic

---

[89] See Terry Crawford-Browne, 1997, 16.
[90] Cf. Batchelor, 102.
[91] Cf. Jacklyn Cock in Cock and McKenzie, 9.
[92] Cf. Willet and Batchelor, quoted by Cock, *op. cit.* 22.
[93] Cf. *The Cape Times*, 28 November 1998.

development. Long-time peace activist and economist Terry Crawford-Browne states that the greatest threat to South Africa's security is not a military one, but poverty, and the acquisition of arms which diverts public resources away from socio-economic investment is nothing less than "a betrayal of the struggle against apartheid".[94]

Still, the ANC government, like the apartheid government, has become a major supporter of the defence industry and its export drive. In 1982 South Africa's arms exports amounted to about US$20 million. By the early nineties the figure had climbed to more than US$270 million. Mr Mbeki announced that since April 1994 South Africa had sold arms worth more than US$600 million.[95] These arms are sold to "whoever can pay", without regard to the human rights records of the countries to which they are sold. So countries like Saudi Arabia, Indonesia under Suharto, Iraq and China featured high on South Africa's customer list.

This is done in spite of all the political and economic arguments we have seen above, and in spite also of the pleas of at least one church leader. "The arms industry," said Bishop Peter Storey of the Methodist Church, "was born in secrecy and its purpose was to facilitate the wars of destabilisation ... (it is) associated with bribery, corruption and murder. R130 billion was squandered in defence of apartheid and it is shocking that this industry is not being phased out in the new South Africa".[96]

And it is not just a matter of questionable economics, and not only an issue of concern for South Africa internally: "The conclusion is that, in both local and global terms, South Africa's arms industry is a source of moral contamination".[97] Yet these sensible arguments are not finding a ready audience in the new South African government.

No, as we have seen with the GEPF and the cancellation of foreign debt, it is not just "common sense" that is needed. What is needed is *moral courage* to set the right priorities and make the right choices. Let me take this a bit further. South Africa has an obligation to the poor who marched and sacrificed, who gave their blood and saw their children die for "liberation" and whose needs are now being made subservient to the dictates of the arms industry. We cannot feed the poor, or build roads or schools or clinics, or pay doctors or teachers or nurses. We close hospitals for lack of funds, and the "impact of staff losses (in hospitals and clinics) bordered on devastation".[98] We are way behind the schedule for housing needs and the houses that are being built are shameful, glorified shacks; but we want to buy corvettes and fighter jets and submarines, spend precious resources on developing new weapons. The consolidation of South Africa's democracy

94 Terry Crawford-Browne: *Poverty, not War, is South Africa's Sword of Damocles*, in: *The Cape Times*, 21 November 1998.
95 Peter Batchelor, "Arms and the ANC, in: *The Bulletin of the Atomic Scientists*, September/October 1998.
96 Cf. Batchelor, *South African Arms Industry*, in Cock and McKenzie, 99.
97 Cock and McKenzie, 22.
98 According to Peter Marais, Health MEC for the Western Cape, *The Cape Times*, 10 March 1999.

and the quality of our own renaissance depends, to a very large degree, on the capacity of the new democratic government to meet human needs and to defend human rights.

The arms industry, driven by state-owned and -funded Armscor and Denel, is the most jarring remnant of South Africa's apartheid past. It was the flagship of white South Africa's defiance of world opinion, its most effective sanctions-busting tool. Its products destabilised the whole region, supported civil war and proxy colonialism in Mozambique, Namibia and Angola for years and ravaged neighbouring countries. They were used in our townships, devastated our communities and killed our children.

Armaments and military expenditure to do just that during 1977 to 1994 has cost South Africa about US$28 billion. The implications for social and economic progress were horrific. And remain so. The very existence of Armscor and Denel is an affront to those who stood in our streets and faced their weapons. To support them with the taxes of the poor and to export their deadly products to secure the death of the poor and the innocent on the rest of the continent, is to spit on the graves of the martyrs of our struggle. This is not just nonsensical: it is symptomatic of the gap in experience, understanding and values between an exile-led government and the masses who stayed and fought at home.

Moreover these arms are sold, not to Europe or the US, but to poor Third World countries, including Rwanda, Burundi and Sudan, which in turn cannot feed their own children. A common argument in government circles is that if we don't sell these countries arms, someone else, the US for example, will do so. For me there is no question: let the US try and live with its own conscience. Since when do we take the behaviour of the US government as the moral measure of our conduct?

For us the issue is far more fundamental. How can South Africa set an example of, and take credit for, a "transitional miracle", speak of "reconciliation", boast of our "rainbow nation", while our weapons fuel wars in other poor countries, bolster ruthless dictatorships, and blow other people's chances of reconciliation to smithereens? How can a country with no less than four Peace Laureates make peace impossible in the same continent we want to lead in its "renaissance"? How can our struggle for human rights be reconciled with massacres in Burundi and Rwanda? South Africa's successful peace efforts in the Democratic Republic of the Congo and Angola, and the efforts toward peace in the Great Lakes districts contrast sharply, and painfully, with our convoluted commitment to the arms industry.

Do we really believe the utterly fallacious argument advanced by the armaments lobby that "engagement is the most constructive way of doing business - that influence can be more effectively brought to bear on governments through dialogue rather than by strident public criticism", so that selling arms to countries with bad human rights records is more likely to restrain them than confronting them with the diplomacy of advocacy? Have we so soon forgotten what we thought of that argument when it was used by Ronald Reagan and Margaret Thatcher in their support of white, apartheid South Africa?

As for the argument that selling arms brings in foreign exchange, how can we help to kill the poor elsewhere with the intention to feed our poor – and then we only feed the already well-fed? For certainly the money we earn from selling arms has not alleviated in any appreciable measure the plight of the poor or the desperation of the sick in South Africa.

All this raises a fundamental question. Not: why don't we do the common-sense thing? But: what kind of country does South Africa want to be, especially in light of the kind of country we have been up to now? What is the content, ultimately, of this Renaissance we hope to be the leader of? It is not a question of political common sense only; it is a question of morality. And that brings us back to the question of the church. Can the church once again infuse our politics with the spiritual power that kept us strong in the face of one of the most oppressive ideologies of the 20th century?

Can the church, with prophetic clarity, hold the government not only to its promises, but to its obligations to the poor? The danger with Mbeki's African Renaissance is that it so closely resembles the dream of the church and the demands of the gospel that we may be lulled into thinking that we need not be concerned. Can the church remind the new government not only of our political dreams, but of our spiritual roots? Can the church tell the government unequivocally that we cannot be both agents of reconciliation *and* merchants of death? Can we, with prophetic courage, expose those empty arguments that are designed once again to victimise the victims and satisfy the rich? Can we be what we have been, and, in so doing, be more than we have been?

Can we tell the government that embracing globalization so uncritically, producing and selling arms and thereby encouraging war, enlarging the gap between the rich and the poor, making the needs of the poor and needy subservient to the greed of the powerful, is not just contrary to their idea of a renaissance, but a denial of the gospel? Dare we tell the government and Mr Mbeki that the call of the gospel therefore might very well be a call to rebellion against the government's appropriation of the language of the church, which is designed to domesticate the church? Against an awakening that speaks of *poverty* but not of the *poor*, of the *soul* of Africa but not of its salvation; of *politics* but not of its spirituality?

These are questions we cannot avoid, and we have no desire to. They are vital for South Africa's democracy, and for our future.

"A Regeneration Moral and Eternal ..."

Just over ninety years ago a brilliant African intellectual and one of South Africa's most famous sons, Pixley ka Isaka Seme, became the first to introduce the theme of the *African Renaissance*. Writing in *The African Abroad* on 5 April 1906, he called it "The Regeneration of Africa".[99] It is a vivid and moving piece of writing. In a time more stiflingly racist

---

[99] Documented in: Karis and Carter. *From Protest to Challenge* (Stanford: Stanford University Press, 1973), Vol. I, 69ff. Even though the president makes no reference to Pixley, he was the first to make this call and use this language.

than we can imagine and unbearably Eurocentric, his voice rings with pride: "I am an African!" he declares, and in those four words threw down the gauntlet to the European mixture of lies, half-truths and myths about Africa and her children that ruled the day. Even though for some reason Mbeki does not mention it, Pixley was the first to raise this cry, and it is his understanding of it that should give us primary guidance. Thus long before Marcus Garvey rediscovered Africa, and long before Leopold Senghor, that modern day prophet of *Negritude*, long before the children of Black Consciousness learned to take pride in their Africanness, Pixley raised the standard which Thabo Mbeki now seems to have picked up once more.

"Come with me" Pixley invites his readers, "to the ancient capital of Egypt, Thebes, the city of one hundred gates". He speaks glowingly of the "grandeur" of Thebes, of the gigantic proportions of its architecture which "reduce to insignificance the boasted monuments of other nations". The pyramids, he says, "seem to look down with disdain on every other work of human art and to vie with nature itself". Foreseeing European efforts to somehow divorce Egypt from Africa because such a barbarous and uncivilised continent could not possibly have given birth to such wonders, Pixley exclaims, "All the glory of Egypt belongs to Africa and its people!" He praises Africans' "great and original genius" as he speaks of the pyramids of Ethiopia. "In such ruins Africa is like the golden sun, that, having sunk beneath the Western horizon, still plays upon the world which he sustained and enlightened in his career". He mourns the denial of his continent, and the historical circumstances that brought it low:

> "Whither is fled the visionary gleam, Where is it now, the glory and the dream?"

But now, he insists, "a great century has come upon us". The twentieth century will yet see "a new Africa arising". His expectations are high. "Cast your eyes south of the Desert of Sahara ... you too would be convinced that the elevation of the African race is evidently part of the new order of things ... The brighter day is rising upon Africa". Pixley knows that Africa is complex, that slavery and colonialism have had a devastating impact on its people, their culture, their psyche. So he asks the question: "Who is an African?", to which he answers: "The African people, although not a strictly homogeneous race, possess a common fundamental sentiment which is everywhere manifest ... a people *with a common destiny*" (emphasis mine). Not being able, or willing, to find commonality in the past, Pixley Seme takes the only sensible route: binding Africa and Africans together in a common destiny, which is the regeneration of Africa and its peoples, its reawakening, "The entrance into a new life, embracing the diverse phases of a higher, complex existence".

Then Pixley identifies what he calls "the most essential departure" of his "regeneration", which is a "new civilisation": "It shall be thoroughly spiritual and humanistic - indeed regeneration moral and eternal!" It should be needless to point out that Pixley's use of the term "humanistic" should not be understood as it sometimes is by Western theologians, meaning thoroughly secular, depending solely on human effort. What he means is that this regeneration should be humane, thoroughly rooted in community, in that rich African concept *ubuntu*, reflecting the spirituality he calls "the great triumph of Christianity, which teaches men (*sic*) everywhere that in this world they have a common duty to perform both towards God and towards one another".[100] It is in that new spirituality that Pixley finds a common destiny, a renaissance, for Africa and its people. Which is exactly the point we are trying to make. It is Pixley's vision which sets the standard.

The Root of the Evil

We must wander a little farther along this historical excursion and go back a few more years before Pixley wrote his immortal sentences. There was a reason why Pixley did not simply fall back onto a romanticised African past in order to draw inspiration for his regeneration. It is not, we have seen, that he does not have appreciation for Africa's greatness and the achievements of its people. But he knew that Africa's history is chequered, at best, like the history of other continents and peoples, filled with ambivalence, fraught with contradictions and the failures of human frailty and our stubborn unwillingness to do what is right.

One of Africa's great failures, the truly devastating consequences of which last to this day, is Africa's complicity in the slave trade of the 18th and 19th centuries. Historian Basil Davidson has devoted several chapters to this in his *Black Mother*, a work already cited above. "European traders sold their fellow-countrymen to the oversea states of Egypt and North Africa. Pressured by the need for European goods, the lords of Africa would sell their own folk to the mariners who came from Europe".[101] Even though the slaves naturally resisted, fighting for their lives, escaping when they could, rising up in bloody rebellion when presented with the chance; the trade, as joint venture between Europe and Africa, could not be stopped and vast numbers were forced to leave the continent. There was too much money in it for the courts of Europe, and "The Black Mother had already shown how fertile she could be, and how blind to the consequences".[102] This was so because those who profited from the slave trade thought those consequences were only impacting upon those who were their victims and the source of their profit, the powerless and the defenceless, those they considered lesser than themselves: "The trade of slaves is the business of kings, rich men, and prime merchants" said John Barbot in 1683. Quite so.

This is the key to understanding the system, its successes and its consequences, throughout Africa. Slavery meant the acquisition of wealth and power with astonishing speed, and African kings and chiefs, like their European counterparts, could not resist the temptation. There grew, in time, a greater dependence and solidarity between the

---

[100] In; "Native Union", article by Pixley ka Isaka Seme in *Imvo Zabantsundu*, 24 October 1911, in: Karis and Carter, Vol. I, 72.

[101] *Black Mother*, 43.

[102] *Op. cit.*, 63.

African and European slave traders than ever there were between African chiefs, kings and their subjects.

> Whether in the accumulation of wealth by custom-dues, gifts or trading profits; or in the political authority which salving lent to those who organised it; or in the military superiority which derived from the buying of fire-arms, slaving built chiefly power where it did not exist before, or else transformed that power, where it was already present, from a broadly representative character into an autocratic one.[103]

The slave trade did not just destroy Africa's social structures, civilisations and communal and family life. It was, more so through African participation, the destruction of the African soul. Davidson calls it something "even more binding and pervasive in its consequences":

> Men (*sic*) became mere trade goods. Not only that. Men (*sic*) became the only trade goods that really mattered. African chiefs found that the sale of their fellow men (*sic*) was indispensable to any contact with Europe: unless they were willing - and not only willing, but active in delivery - the ships went elsewhere.[104]

So the destruction went both ways: it destroyed the souls of both the captured slaves and of the ruling classes who sold them for money and power. So the African ruling classes and the aristocracy became rich beyond their wildest dreams, and their power waxed exponentially, but the price paid was a heavy one, and they too would not escape the consequences of these policies, as we shall see.

There is irony upon painful irony in our reflection upon this piece of African history. Africans' desire to become rich and powerful was inextricably linked to the slave trade, and in this desire they grew more and more dependent on the goods the Europeans brought in trade. What were these goods Africans craved so much that they sold their brothers and sisters for them? Davidson supplies us with one such a list: two guns, two barrels of gun powder, musket balls, two swords, two dozen common sheath knives; five pots of Dutch ware, four barrels of brandy, ten strings of glass beads.[105] Almost invariably slaves were sold for consumer luxuries or the means of war, with the result that "the enrichment of the ruling groups could not, in the circumstances, lead to any compensating gain for their peoples as a whole".[106] The African purchaser had bought nothing that could help to uplift his people in any way whatsoever.

---

[103] *Op. cit.*, 92.
[104] *Op. cit.*, 91. Already we can see the power of that old adage, and the economic blackmail which would continue to wreak havoc in North/South relations, "Capital goes where it is well-treated".
[105] *Op. cit.*, 146.
[106] *Ibid.*

The African dependence on consumer goods, and especially on arms, grew steadily and it became a chain of cause and deadly effect. Consider the case of Dahomey. This country at first resisted the slave trade. But the new state of Dahomey could defend itself effectively only if it could lay its hands on adequate supplies of firearms and ammunition. And these it could obtain only in exchange for slaves. This situation spells out clearly the dilemma that African states were confronted with, and one cannot mete out blame as if they had had very many options left open to them under the circumstances.

But it is clear that the system of slavery lay at the heart of Africa's dehumanisation and the enslavement of its soul, and at the heart of *that* problem lay the arms trade. And the Europeans knew it:

> Hence Dahomey's power to resist ... depended on delivering slaves to the coast: the drastic but inescapable alternative was to enslave others - in order to buy firearms - or to risk enslavement oneself. This indeed was the inner dynamic of the slaving connexion with Europe, and it pushed Dahomey, as it pushed other states, into wholesale participation in slaving.[107]

Once Africa yielded to the temptation, a downward spiral was set in motion from which Africa could no longer extract itself. Once it tasted the wealth that the slave trade brought, it wanted more. But wanting more meant wanting more power, which in turn translated into the need to purchase the firearms which secured the slaves. Huge quantities of firearms were poured into West Africa during the major period of the slave trade. Like the Africans, the Europeans were themselves caught in the bind: "They had to have slaves, and to get slaves they had to pay with guns".[108] Needless to say, the Africans bought those guns not to fight the Europeans and chase them off their shores, but to fight each other, to attack weaker nations and capture them to be sold.

As a result, African states, despite the "trade" with Europe, proved incapable of recovery and progress. Davidson poses the question: how was it that chiefs who were forceful and intelligent and well aware of the nature of their adversaries, failed repeatedly to learn the lesson of their losses and defeats? Where, he asks – and that question becomes also ours – was the root of the evil?[109]

> The answers to these questions lay largely in the character of the trade: a demand for slaves on the one side, and, on the other, a monopolist interest among African chiefs in obtaining European consumer goods, especially firearms.[110]

---

[107] *Op. cit.,* 211-212.
[108] *Op. cit.,* 212.
[109] *Op. cit.,* 142.
[110] *Op. cit.,* 143.

So while Africa was buying arms to "strengthen" itself, it was in reality weakening itself, breaking down its spiritual defences, undermining the foundations of its own societies, enriching a few, but impoverishing its masses, making itself vulnerable to the worst Europe had confronted it with. The common people were constantly threatened by enslavement and many fell victim to it, while the chiefs and their henchmen made a good thing out of it. In the end, for the Africans as for the Europeans, it boiled down to profits, and their failure to resist the temptation, which led to their failure to foresee the disastrous consequences for the future.

African kings were alarmed only when the Europeans, in their insatiable greed, began to forget the deals made and captured not only common folk, but the sons and daughters of the royalty and the aristocracy. But by then it was too late, and the fervent plea by King Mani-Congo to his Portuguese "Royal Brother" King John III, was to no avail:

> We cannot reckon how great the damage is, since the afore-mentioned merchants daily seize our subjects, sons of the land and sons of our noblemen and vassals and our relatives ... Thieves and men of evil conscience take them because they wish to possess the things and wares of this kingdom ... They grab them and cause them to be sold: and so great, Sir, is their corruption and licentiousness that our country is being utterly depopulated ... That is why we beg of Your Highness to help and assist us in this matter, commanding your factors that they should send here neither merchants nor wares, because *it is our will that in these kingdoms (of Congo) there should not be any trade in slaves nor market for slaves.*[111]

Like David, who could not find succour for his grief nor comfort for his soul when Absalom died (II Sam 19), because he could find no tears for Tamar when she was ravaged by Amnon (II Sam 13), King Mani-Congo's cries went unheard, his tears unseen, his pleas unheeded. His "royal brother" was, after all, not his brother, but a slave trader and gun seller, a merchant of death. "Every Christian intention of the Portuguese", is Davidson's sober and sobering judgement, "went forfeit to that inexhaustible commercial appetite, and, on the African side, every reasonable hope of direct and fruitful contact with the world of the far north".[112] This is an African tragedy of immense proportions.

These historical lessons highlight, as we have intimated, the supreme irony of our own situation. The most salient features of our situation and consequently of the renaissance we are speaking of, are the unbridled optimism with which we abandon ourselves to the neo-liberal capitalism of globalization and the concomitant inequities that exacerbate the already existing inequalities we have inherited from apartheid, and the grim determination with which we pursue our share of the arms market resulting

---

[111] *Op. cit.*, 138-139.
[112] *Op. cit.,* 139.

in the careless abandonment of our human rights values in foreign affairs. If the slave trade had as its constant and inseparable companion the arms trade with which Europe first tempted Africa, then ensnared her, and finally deserted her once caught in the trap, and left her with the tragic consequences, what in the world are we doing, falling for the same trick all over again?

The same factors we have seen at the beginning of this tragic relationship remain in play. Davidson's question plagues us still. Why do we still fail to learn the lessons of our losses and defeats? How else, for example, do we explain the fact that South Africa is buying these new weapon systems from Britain and Sweden at twice and thrice the prices being paid for the same items by Chile and Argentina? We deprive our own poor of basic necessities in order to enrich yet further the arms dealers of Britain and Sweden. The price of one British Aerospace Hawk is roughly the amount needed to provide 1,5 million people in the Third World with fresh water for life. On top of that, existing navy vessels, army armoured vehicles and air force aircraft have been decommissioned and mothballed because of the financial crisis the country is facing. The air force reportedly has no less than 85 aircraft out of commission. So why is South Africa spending billions on weapons, when the country cannot afford even to operate its existing equipment?

If our renaissance is made to be dependent on the sale of arms, which in turn depends on the creation and encouragement of fear, enmity, greed, distrust and death, and on the inhumane opportunism of global commerce which leaves no room for genuine concern centred on people, but rejoices in get-rich-quick policies for the few, we are planting our tree by the side of a poisoned brook.

Pixley ka Isaka Seme was right. There will be no renaissance in Africa unless there is a moral re-awakening. South Africa's role in Africa lies not in its "strength" as a military power. We will never be able to compete with the likes of the United States, Britain, France, Germany or even Sweden, which has moral qualms about selling toy guns to its children but no such qualms in selling Saab-Gripen fighter aircraft to poor Third World nations for use in real wars in which real people are killed. And we must not even try to compete.

South Africa gave so much hope to the world, not because we fought a successful revolution. The armed struggle waged by the liberation movements never really made a dent in white South Africa's military supremacy, and it is high time we stop pretending that it did. We did so because we brought apartheid to its knees through our persistent struggle, our willingness to sacrifice, and the extraordinary moral courage of our people. What captivated the world during all those years was not our military successes, but our spiritual strength.

I submit that it is the spiritual quality of our politics, more than anything else, that will help Africa, if indeed such help is needed, to face the 21st century, face the challenges, make the right choices, and find the courage to set the right agenda. And before an African Renaissance can begin, South Africa itself would need to find the courage to admit that to itself, and the church would be well advised to remember and proclaim, in season and out of season, that essential truth from the gospel: "What does it gain a person to win the whole world but to lose their soul?"

CHAPTER THREE

CALLED BY A HIGHER POWER
Christian Faith, the African Renaissance and the New World Order

---

World Orders, Old and New

We are living in a changed and constantly changing world. This is, to be sure, a trite observation, but nothing is more true as we stand at the dawn of the new century, having to take stock of, and deal with the results of what, scarcely more than one hundred years ago, we had thought of as impossible. Certainly these changes are not as obvious as in earlier times, for example, the time of the industrial revolution, or the advent of weapons of mass destruction in the middle of the last century. The changes in the last quarter of the twentieth century have been more subtle, even hidden, but nonetheless just as fundamental, and their impact on the lives of ordinary people is far greater than we sometimes realise. The context of the call for an African Renaissance this time around could not be more different, or more challenging.

Christian faith is called to witness to this changing world today, as it was from the beginning. We cannot do that unless we first seek to better understand the world in which we now live. That means we should attempt to understand the ways in which our world has changed. It is not the world in which Isaiah or Jesus, John Calvin or Pope John XXIll lived. The world in which South Africa's call for a new renaissance is heard is not the world of Pixley ka Isaka Seme.

It is an increasingly complex world, with a complexion that mirrors the ambiguity of human progress, as it mirrors also the human paradox: the more we know, the less we learn; the more we gain, the less we have; the more we discover, the less we understand. To paraphrase Dr Martin Luther King Jr, our knowledge of the universe has grown by leaps and bounds, but we remain pitifully ignorant of simple human justice and compassion.

The end of the twentieth century has made abundantly clear the failure of the great systems human beings have tried to build, and consequently it was a time of great disillusionment, of less and less faith in human ability to do what is right and good. It seems as if the dream of a caring, beloved community has remained just that: an unattainable, impossible dream. In South Africa itself our painful paradoxes in our new situation have compounded the old weariness and have given birth to a new wariness, both of which stand in tension with the high expectations and joyful hopes with which our people entered through the doors of a new democracy.

Talk about a "new world order" is not entirely new, of course. Right through history potentates of all sorts have tried to create "new world orders" to reflect their victories and control of the world in which they lived and of the peoples they have conquered. This was as true of Alexander the Great as it was of the Caesars of Rome; as true for Bismarck as it was of the Spanish conquistadores. As true as it was for Hitler, it was also true of the rulers of the Soviet Empire and the regimes of the Pax Americana.

The true foundation for the "new world order which still exists today", argues the father of the *Theology of Hope,* Jürgen Moltmann, "was laid in 1492", with its claims of the "discovery" of "new" territories, which always in reality was an act of appropriation in which both the land and its peoples were moulded to the will of the "discoverers".[113] The islanders and the peoples of the main lands had long before given names to the land, the rivers, the mountains. But Columbus "baptized" them, claimed them by giving them names that were Spanish and Christian, thereby taking possession of them. These were not political acts in isolation.

> With the conquest of America, European Christianity also came forward with a claim to world-wide domination. It won souls, not for the gospel, but for the Christian imperium. The decisive question was not belief or unbelief; it was baptism or death.[114]

The other foundation stone of that new world order Moltmann identifies as the seizure of power over nature. In the century between Copernicus and Sir Isaac Newton the new sciences stripped nature of her magic and her defences, and took from her the divine mystery which up to then had been called "the world soul". The dictum of Francis Bacon became the driving force of human endeavour: The *novum organon scientiarum* is the *ars inveniendi:* the new scientific instrument is the art of discovery. What it meant was this: scientific reason is instrumentalizing reason, a reason whose epistemological drive is utilization and domination.[115]

All this gave rise to what Moltmann calls "the messianism of modern times", the confidence that flowed from the unquestioning belief that what was done was done in the name of God, who blessed the Western world with "progress". European history's "fine messianic top coat" however, has its ugly apocalyptic underside; the success story of the "First World" has never gone "unaccompanied by the story of the Third World's suffering".[116] So the progress of the modern world and the foundations of the modern world order have been acquired only at the expense of other nations, at the expense of nature, and at the expense of coming generations. "If the real costs had to be met," says

---

[113] Jürgen Moltmann, *God for a Secular Society, The Public Relevance of Theology* (Minneapolis: Fortress press, 1999), 6
[114] *Op. cit.,* 7.
[115] *Ibid.*
[116] Op. cit., 12

Moltmann, "the actual progress would have been negligible".[117] Relating this history for our modern contexts remains immensely important since:

> the memories of the perpetrators are always short, while the memories of the victims are long. For the repressed people in the countries of the Third World, and for the exploited and silenced earth, the messianism of modern times has never been anything but the apocalypse of their annihilation. [118]

This is the context we must keep in mind in our subsequent discussion.

In 1971 US President Richard Nixon arranged and announced a new economic world order which opened the door for the most dramatic changes since the Second World War. That was an arrangement that responded to the need to have an economic order more suited to the demands of the world created after World War II. In other words, it reflected the response of the rich, Western world, and particularly the United States, to the new political and economic challenges of the new, post-colonialist era. Nixon's plans were an attempt to further solidify the position of the United States as the "other" great power over against the Soviet Union in a world order which had thrown the world at the mercy of the ideological battle between "East" and "West".

That world order has effectively come to an end. The most recent discussions around a "new world order" were given currency by former President George W Bush as he spoke of the new geo-political realities in a post Cold War world.

Historically, talk of new world orders always emerged in the wake of military conquest and expressed the desire of the conquerors that the world should reflect the new political arrangement of the world as a result of their military victory. It is therefore not altogether surprising that Mr Bush spoke of the new world order in direct relation to the Gulf War. For him, the fact that the United States could wage that war without fear of interference either from international bodies or another "superpower", was the true reflection of the fundamental changes that had brought about a new world. More than the United States' invasions of Grenada and Panama, or the proxy wars fought in Southern Africa and Central America, the first war against Iraq spelt out the terms and scope of the new world order.

The subsequent, heated debate in intellectual and political circles gave both the event of the Gulf War and its international consequences the significance of a genuine turning point in international politics. But whether George Bush Sr knew it or not, casting the "new world order" in terms of the US military adventure in the Middle East was as antiquated as the stated goals of the war were ambivalent. As a result, much of the discussion around the issue tends to be misleading.

---

[117] *Ibid.*
[118] *Op. cit.,* 12, 13.

The "new world order" is mostly seen as a result of the end of the Cold War in which the West (read: the United States) was the victor. But then, there was no military conquest of the Soviet Union, unless one wants to accept the dubious argument that the sheer economic costs of the ideology of the "balance of terror" was an indirect military onslaught which the Soviet Union could not hope to withstand. This view would also credit the Cold War warriors in the United States with a foresight which would be difficult to sustain. But that is an argument we cannot pursue here.

At the very least that means that our understanding of the term "new world order" must now be different from what was historically meant by it. It still emerges out of conquest, but not necessarily military conquest. And if there were a conquest, it was not a conquest by the United States, and the need of many in that country to believe otherwise still does not make it so.

For many the "new world order" simply means the total re-arrangement of the balance of power in the aftermath of the Cold War. That, I think, is an essentially optimistic reading of history. The sheer weight of the moral superiority of "Western style democracy", they argue, had caused the collapse of Communism as a political system in Eastern Europe, marking the end of the Cold War, while at the same time affirming the destiny of the United States as the true leader of the world - a world that could indeed now truly be free. As expected, these events opened the world to liberal democracy. In many countries multi-party systems have now displaced one-party, military, or authoritarian regimes and a veritable wave of freedom has swept the globe. In 1993 alone there were elections in 45 countries, often for the first time ever. And the spectacular sight in 1994 of long lines of people waiting patiently to cast their vote in South Africa seemed to capture the essence of it all.

Others, while acknowledging the above, were more concerned about the implications for international politics. The bi-polar superpower structure - the US and its allies on the one hand and the USSR and its allies on the other - no longer existed. We now live in a "uni-polar" world. The US, the only remaining superpower, would from now on have the field to itself. Hence the much-used, and much debated term "US Leadership", whatever it may mean for both sides of the political divide in the US itself, let alone in the rest of the world.

In separate articles in the Spring 1995 issue of *Foreign Policy* magazine, Secretary of State Warren Christopher and Senate Majority Leader Robert Dole both wrote about American foreign policy. Between them, they used the word "leadership" (of the US) 36 times. The fact that this leadership is highly contentious, not always accepted, as in the case of US policy decisions on Iran, Bosnia or Cuba, or when US trade sanctions on Japan created tensions with Europe, does not change this. In fact, the very dispute over US leadership among its allies proves the point.[119]

---

[119] *Foreign Policy Magazine*, Spring 1995.

It also distracts from the real problem, namely that at the United Nations the US is now able to drive through its will, bend the will of the UN to its own, force the UN into essentially US-conceived and US-driven interventionist actions (Sudan and Haiti, for example); veto with impunity resolutions it dislikes, and stage military interventions at will, while flouting and even breaking international law, as in the case of Panama under George Bush Sr, and recently the case of Iraq under his son. Moreover, the fact that the US succeeded in drawing the UN into supporting its actions in the Gulf through resolutions and Security Council actions, while simultaneously sublimely ignoring resolutions of this same body regarding Israel, must be regarded as one of the most serious and disturbing issues challenging the integrity of this world body.

And the US does all this without feeling the obligation, morally or otherwise, to pay its dues. In the eyes of two thirds of the world, the US is deliberately weakening the UN politically and financially, constantly trying to reduce it from being "the servant of the world" to becoming a mere instrument of US foreign policy. In this way the UN ends up legitimizing uni-polar action, rather than being a forum for seeking consensus on global governance, hardly what the drafters of the UN Charter had in mind more than fifty years ago.

For those Americans who find this not troublesome at all, this attitude is justified by US superpower status based on economic and military power, and the assumption that the end of the Cold War and the collapse of Communism is solely an American victory. Columnist Charles Krauthammer speaks for many when he states in the same issue of *Foreign Policy Magazine*, that "(President) Clinton leads the sole remaining super-power, fresh from victory in the Cold War ... in command of the world's dominant military force ..."[120]

Almost as a matter of course, but sobering in its consequences, it also means that the US is able to force its political will on smaller countries more than ever before, on a wider scale and with very little prospect of having to face criticism. Haiti is a case in point. And there are some who say (though I think this is a bit far-fetched) that South Africa under an ANC government is another. In the light of all this, it is not correct to speak of the new world order as "the end of the super-power age" as does Jonathan Clarke.[121] On the contrary, the US constantly refers to itself as "the one remaining super-power" or the "only super-power" and its unilateral arrogance as seen under Mr George Bush Jr has irrevocably changed the face of international politics, as it has challenged, and undermined, international law.

More Than Military Conquest

All of the above is true, but as important as it is, it is not, in my view, the real essence of the new world order. The most basic difference between the traditional understanding

---

[120] *Op. cit.*
[121] *Foreign Policy Magazine*, Spring, 1995.

of "world order" and that of our day can be seen in two fundamental shifts: first, the fact that the "new world order" is no longer determined by military conquest or even political ideology, and second, the shift in power in the last fifteen years away from national governments to trans-national corporations (TNCs) and international financial institutions.

Critical observers have noticed this and have expressed concern over this shift and, even more pertinent, over the fact that TNCs – despite the sweeping nature of their power, or perhaps *because* of it – do not have to concern themselves with public accountability. Christians have pointed this out[122] and in the circles of the World Council of Churches there has long been a very constructive debate on these issues. Franz Hinkelammert makes the telling observation that "the 'invisible hand' of Adam Smith, has now grown powerful enough to prevail throughout the entire world and in every area of human life: it can now judge over life and death but cannot itself be judged in terms of the effect it has on the life of every individual".[123]

But also someone like Admiral Hyman B Rickover, certainly "no enemy of the capitalist system", as Miguez Bonino describes him, sounds an alarming, if sobering, word of warning:

> Political and economic power is increasingly being concentrated among a few large corporations and their officers - power they can apply against society, Government, and individuals. Through their control of vast resources these large corporations have become, in effect, another branch of government, but without the checks and balances inherent in our democratic system. With their ability to dispense money, officials of large corporations may often exercise greater power to influence society than elected or appointed government officials - but without assuming any of the responsibilities and without being subject to public scrutiny ... (They) are hidden behind the remote corporate screen and are rarely, if ever, held accountable for the results ...[124]

As we consider the effects of globalization in this century, we are only beginning to understand how true those words are. Warnings concerning the nature of big business are not new, however. Early in the 20th century American educator and philosopher, John Dewey, recognised that institutions of private power were absolutist institutions, unaccountable and basically totalitarian in their internal structure. In the seventies it was the World Council of Churches who again (as in so many other instances) sounded a prophetic warning against the nature and role of trans-national companies and called

---

[122] Cf. Franz Hinkelammert, "The Mystique of Transnational Business and the Vision of a Just Society", quoted in Jose Miguez Bonino, *Toward a Christian Political Ethics* (Philadelphia: Fortress Press, 1983), 15
[123] *Op.cit.*
[124] Cf. Bonino, 14

upon the churches to begin to realise the ways in which our world was changing and the central role of trans-national corporations in those changes.[125]

Somehow the words were never heard, or if heard, not heeded. Today the power of TNCs is far greater than most of us begin to comprehend, according to an in-depth study by Richard Barnett and John Cavanaugh.[126] They point out that under current US law, corporations have more rights than individuals and these are better protected.

The top 200 corporations in the world control over one quarter of the world's total assets and total sales by the largest multinational companies exceed the gross national product of many medium-sized economies. In 1992, for example, General Motors and Exxon were two companies whose sales exceeded the GNP of countries such as Norway, Indonesia and even Saudi Arabia, in spite of all that oil!

TNCs, private financial institutions, international banks, together with multi-lateral institutions like the World Bank and the International Monetary Fund have virtually created a new "imperial image". They wield enormous power, control huge amounts of money, and enforce their conditions for "development" and societal (re)structuring all over the world. The G-7 (the seven richest nations, namely the US, Canada, Germany, the UK, Japan, Italy and France),[127] the European Community and its Council of Ministers have effectively more power than the UN to effect change in the world, since it has the direct involvement of the leaders of these nations on a far more dedicated scale that the UN has ever had or could ever hope to have.

At the UN itself the only meaningful change the powerful nations are willing to contemplate, in spite of dozens of proposals to make the UN more effective, is two additions to the permanent membership of the Security Council: Germany and Japan, and that only because of their economic status and the fact that the economic interests of these countries coincide with the interests of the G-8 of which they in any case form a part. Even if the powerful nations concede the membership of one member from the developing world, the influence of that country can be expected to be minimal, unless the rules on veto powers are changed. The placement of either Japan or Germany or both on the Security Council as has been advocated will in no way endanger the political and economic agenda of the rich nations. In fact, it will simply solidify and legitimise the combined power of those already in the G-8.

---

[125] Ulrich Dunchrow, *Global Economy: A Confessional Issue for the Churches?* (Geneva: WCC Publications, 1987), 77-83.

[126] Cf. Richard Barnett and John Cavanaugh, *Global Dreams, Imperial Corporations and the New World Order* (New York: Simon and Schuster, 1994).

[127] The G-7 has now become the G-8, with Russia as the newest member. Russia is not counted as a "rich" nation, but it was considered politically wise to include this former superpower because of its important political role in the part of the world where it held sway for so long. Russia's position on the Security Council, with veto powers, was also a consideration. All in all, it was safer to allow Russia to count itself "in" rather than "out". Whichever way one considers it, the inclusion of Russia in this exclusive club is symbolic of the paradigm shift that has taken place since 1989, illustrating the point we made above.

Political leaders who do not pay obeisance to global economic power do so at their peril. The presence of political leaders at the annual meetings of the World Economic Forum in Davos Switzerland is now a matter of course and in itself eloquent testimony of the hold of international economic power on governments. We can safely assume that what is being discussed in all those "private conversations" is not in the interests of the poor and needy. The question of whether non-governmental organisations and groups of concerned citizens should allow themselves to be drawn into discussions at these forums should be discussed much more seriously. It is a question whether representatives of the ordinary people should be seen to endorse this process, if their contributions are not making a difference in the way these corporations behave in the world.

It has always been thus, though: structures of government tend to coalesce around formations of power. First it was the monarchy, then the military. In our day, it is economic power that forms that centre of cohesion. In my view, this is by far the most fundamental characteristic of the new world order we are facing. In this regard, the question really is how to make that worn-out phrase "people's power" work again, so that governments are forced to acknowledge *that* power from which their legitimacy derives, rather than the power from which they derive their comfort.

The Politics of Globalization

Following the leadership of the US after the Wall Street crash of 1929, the proliferation of post-war international agencies was part of a movement to develop strong and effective systems of international economic co-ordination. This applied particularly to money and finance.

At the Bretton Woods conference, thinkers sought to devise a system in which global finance would serve "productive purposes", that is, finance, trade and productive investment. They saw speculative capital flows as inimical to the health of a modern industrial economy. What emerged was a system of management for the world economy, premised on the regulation of financial markets.

This era has now come to an end, contends an authoritative report entitled *States of Disarray*, compiled by the UN Research Institute for Social Development in Geneva for the World Summit on Social Development held in Denmark in March 1995.[128]

In 1981, the writers of the report state, the Reagan administration cut taxes in order to attract capital investment. Other countries followed this example, reducing their direct taxes on income, interest and profit, and shifting the burden more to indirect taxes. The cost of social services accumulated and governments reacted by cutting social provisions and expenditures, privatising public enterprises, trying to make governments more "businesslike", market-oriented and efficient.

---

[128] *States of Disarray*, United Nations (New York: 1994).

This gave rise to the development of off-shore "Euro-markets", the first relatively free international capital and money markets to be created after the Second World War. These markets grew rapidly and more money was more freely available than ever before. This enabled more and more governments to increase their debt, especially developing countries, who took heavy loans to fund their balance of payment deficits.

Between 1972 and 1981 the debts of developing countries rose from less than $100 billion to more than $600 billion. At the time interest rates were between 5 and 10 per cent. It did not seem so risky then. But in the 1980s the US raised interest rates to unprecedented levels to prevent catastrophic depreciation of the dollar. By the mid-1980s rates were above 15 per cent. This triggered an international debt crisis the developing nations still have not overcome, and are not likely to any time soon. Poor countries are now transferring more than $21 billion a year into the coffers of the rich, according to the report.[129] The necessity for seriously calling for the cancellation of debt for Third World countries was never more urgent than now.

Governments that borrow on the international markets have to maintain favourable risk and credit ratings, so they become increasingly accountable to the discipline of market forces. Increasingly also, these market forces, rather than domestic realities and the needs of their people, dictate the policies of these governments.

Market operators constantly scrutinise government policies and they can respond rapidly by moving vast amounts of liquid capital around the globe. These flows have steadily eroded national autonomy. National borders no longer correspond with political authority and economic activity. This has not only reshaped global capitalism, but it has also restructured the state as we have come to know it. Nation states have become attuned to, and in many cases subordinated to, international economic forces.

Rich industrial nations who benefit from these arrangements keep a close watch to see that these arrangements remain in place. World forums are designed to continue the global political climate that make these arrangements possible. The G-8, G-10, the General Agreement to Borrow, the Working Party Ill of the OECD, "all these forums continue today" confirms the UN report, "ensuring that international money is managed by a privileged and powerful inner circle".[130]

Structural Adjustment

The recession that followed the first oil shock in 1973 brought a reversal of fortunes for industrial countries. Inflation doubled, unemployment rose, output fell from 4,9 to 2,7 per cent. Economists and financial experts, perhaps predictably, blamed high taxes, government intervention and too generous social benefits. Governments, the US and the UK foremost among them, consequently embarked on a series of radical reforms,

---

[129] *Op. cit.*
[130] *Op. cit.*, 34

instituting a global drive in favour of private enterprise, reducing state intervention in the economy, privatising public enterprises, deregulating utilities and cutting benefits for the needy.

All this signalled a fairly radical swing in world politics. But at the heart of it all was a fundamental shift in power relationships. The rise of market forces has greatly enhanced the power of international investors and creditor countries as well as of the major multi-lateral financial institutions. By the same token it weakened the position of countries heavily dependent on foreign capital or aid. At the same time, within countries, owners of capital benefited greatly while the working classes lost out significantly.

This global drive in favour of private enterprise has helped to significantly widen the gap between rich and poor countries, and between the rich and the poor within countries. And it has had dire consequences for the poor in rich as well as poor countries. Nearly one third of the population in developing countries live in absolute poverty, but by the same token the gap between rich and poor in the US, for example, has grown wider than ever, and wider than in any industrial country today, even Britain. One half of one per cent in the US own 33 per cent of the total wealth of the country, 9 and one half per cent own 36 per cent, and the rest (30 per cent) is shared by the rest of the population (90 per cent).[131]

In order to address the economic ills of developing countries, and as a condition for financial aid, the International Monetary Fund and the World Bank have imposed conditions on these countries in a process called "structural adjustment". This process has brought more efficiency to governments in a limited number of cases. But on the whole it has caused serious long-term damage, enhanced existing distortions even while creating new ones, and heightened tensions within societies already under historical political, social and economic strain.

Countries like South Africa that, in a real sense, are just emerging on the world markets need to seriously assess the workings of globalization before they embrace it, as South Africa has so enthusiastically done. We need only look at Mexico, for example, which since the mid-1980s has been a world pace-setter in pursuing policies conducive to globalization.[132] It has deregulated financial markets, exposed agriculture and manufacturing through the reduction of trade barriers and privatised public assets on a large scale. All these things have been done or are being planned for South Africa.

For owners of capital in Mexico, the privatisation of state industries and the 1992 land reform, allowing investors to purchase smallholder land, have created new sources of wealth. In the midst of one of the worst economic crises the country has ever faced, the number of billionaires increased from 10 to 15. In 1996 their combined wealth was equal to 9 per cent of Mexico's GDP. In contrast, the share of the population living in absolute poverty increased from 19 per cent in 1984 to 24 per cent in 1989, and in rural

---

[131] *Ibid.*
[132] See the 1997 UNDP Report, United Nations (New York: 1997), Box 5.3, 88.

areas, where more than 80 per cent of those in absolute poverty live, the number of poor people increased throughout the period, rising from 6,7 million to 8,8 million.

This sort of inequality, coming on top of the iniquitous inequities inherited from apartheid, will be devastating for South Africa's social fabric and the country will not be able to bear the strain. Already the creation of sudden wealth for a very chosen few and the growing gap between the rich and the poor, coupled with the government's chronic inability to deliver satisfactorily on basic goods and services, should be cause for grave concern.

The neo-liberal doctrine of globalization, writes academic Noam Chomksky, was a bad idea for the subjects, but not for the designers and local elites associated with them, and the key is the pattern that continues to the present: "placing profits over people".[133] Explaining the fundamental dishonesty of rich nations in international economic relations, Chomsky refers to the fact that the United States and Japan have recently announced major new programmes for government funding of advanced technology (aircraft and semiconductors, respectively) to sustain the private industrial sector by public subsidy. This is, of course, nothing new, but merely the continuation of a long existing trend. Virtually all of the world's larger core firms have experienced a decisive influence from government policies and/or trade barriers on their strategy and competitive position, "and at least twenty companies in the 1993 Fortune 100 would not have survived at all as independent companies if they had not been saved by their respective governments, by socializing losses or by simple state take-over when they were in trouble".[134] These state interventions in the "subject states" are of course forbidden by the rules set down by the powerful nations. This boils down to a form of "socialism for the rich",

> within a system of global corporate mercantilism in which 'trade' consists in substantial measure of centrally managed transactions within single firms, huge institutions linked to their competitors by strategic alliances, all of them tyrannical in structure, designed to undermine democratic decision making and safeguard the masters from market discipline. It is the poor and defence- less who are to be instructed in these stern doctrines.[135]

"One conclusion seems fairly clear" says Chomsky, "the approved doctrines are crafted and employed for reasons of power and profit".[136]

---

[133] Noam Chomsky, *Profit over People, Neo-liberalism and Global Order* (New York: Seven Stories Press, 1999), 26.
[134] *Op. cit.,* 38.
[135] *Op. cit.,* 39.
[136] *Ibid.*

"Market Democracy"

Nothing spells out the new relationship between politics and money better than the term "market democracy". The extension of liberal democracy has come to mean also an increasing reliance on market forces to the extent that the one (democracy) is now deemed inadequate without the other (the market).

That means that democracy as the full and meaningful participation of all people at all levels of government, acting on the basis of freedom and full information, has been made subservient to an understanding of democracy protective of, and dictated to by, the interests of the market. But, as Noam Chomsky and others have consistently argued, the term "market" is itself misleading. The question whether the market is indeed "free" as is claimed, or whether those free marketeers are indeed subjected to the rigours and dictates of the market, is an entirely legitimate one, although this is not the proper place for that particular debate. We should here merely note the tensions caused in international discussions, the dishonesty around agricultural subsidies and price fixing in rich countries, which are deemed anathema in developing countries by these same rich nations. For "market" we should read: those forces which shape and determine the economic order of the world.[137]

This new "market democracy" has a few salient features which might help to illuminate our understanding of the "new world order".

Φ The predominant actors in this new world order are the trans-national corporations. 37 000 parent TNCs and their 200 affiliates control 75 per cent of all world trade commodities, manufactured goods and services. They, together with the owners of capital, plus certain sections of the professional and managerial classes, have been by far the biggest beneficiaries of the changes in the world economy. The gap between these groups and the poor has grown out of all proportion.

Let us take but one example: Guatemala. After the US had helped overthrow the only democratically elected government in Guatemala in the 1950s, that country, through US investments, has become Central America's largest economy, with a diversified cosmopolitan elite and a thriving group of TNCs consisting of over 200 US firms. In their eyes, Guatemala is a "sound and profitable" place to invest. But for the vast majority the realities are these: 87 per cent of the population live in poverty, and over two thirds in "extreme poverty". With high infant mortality and low literacy and life expectancy rates, says one study, Guatemala has the "lowest physical quality of life" in Central America, and the third lowest in all of Latin America.[138]

Φ The most striking aspect of these changes is the mobility of global capital. Computerised dealing systems dispatch huge sums across national borders. A single

[137] See, for example, Noam Chomsky, *Year 501, The Conquest Continues* (Boston: South End Press, 1993), 99ff.
[138] Cf. Mark Lewis Taylor, *TNCs and Violence*, unpublished paper, 1995. Cf. also Chomsky, *op. cit.*, 173.

building in New York houses a computer that moves $1 trillion around the world each business day. But contrary to the hopes of the Bretton Woods conference, to which I referred earlier, the bulk of this money is not for investment or trade, but for speculation. In 1970 90 per cent of international capital was used for trade and long-term investment, and 10 per cent for speculation. By 1990 those figures were reversed. Furthermore, this is unregulated capital of which governments have very little knowledge, and over which they have no control. When even governments as powerful as that of the US have problems with this state of affairs, what are governments in the developing world to do?

Φ Actual banking operations can take place in off-shore regions where there is no supervision. So there is no way of knowing whether a bank is transferring legitimate profits or, say, laundering drug money.

Φ There have also been substantial changes in world trade. There were expectations that the liberalisation of trade should get a considerable boost from the last round of GATT (The General Agreement on Trade and Tariffs) and NAFTA (The North American Trade Agreement), but many have had their doubts. I tend to agree with the doubters. First of all, these agreements are heavily biased in favour of the rich nations in general and private capital in particular, so that the disproportions are actually built in. Second of all, one third of this trade is intra-firm, making it very difficult for governments and international trade organisations to exert any control.[139]

Φ Furthermore, any attempt by governments to exercise such control might give, and has indeed given, rise to flights of capital, skills and enterprise. Weaker countries that are dependent and vulnerable, and even stronger economies, cannot really withstand such pressure. Moreover, monies that governments don't know of and cannot control cannot be taxed. This has serious consequences for any government anywhere. Given also the power of the main stream media, which are owned by big capital and from whom therefore no serious critical analysis can be expected, it is not too fanciful to speak of a hostage situation. It does not take too much to see that the South African government already finds itself in this unenviable situation. The question is what really stands to happen when the masses from which this government draws its support begin to understand this as well.

Φ Integration of the world economy is also closely linked with what is called the "internationalisation of production", in other words, the shifting of production to regions and countries where cheaper labour is available. Exporting jobs to high-repression, low-wage, low-risk areas is extremely profitable. Unionising is essentially impossible, since unions cannot organise internationally, while corporations can and do, and repression is usually immense. Since the International Labour Organisation's recommendations and decisions are subject to the ratification of the governments who support its work, this organisation's international clout is severely curtailed and the ILO can often offer no more than moral support to the workers of the world.

---

[139] Cf. Chomsky, *op. cit.*, 60.

Companies are constantly closing down factories in countries where they have to pay decent wages and deal with strong, organised unions, and moving these factories to countries where there is no minimum wage and the workers have no choice, because of conditions of extreme poverty, but to work for as little as 30 US cents an hour.

Φ Trade agreements such as NAFTA and GATT are not designed to help the poor. Through NAFTA, it is estimated, Mexico would lose 25 per cent of its manufacturing capacity. US agricultural exports, produced with public subsidies there, will drive several million people off the land. That would mean a substantial increase in the unemployed work force, which will drive down wages, and increase urbanisation and levels of poverty. It also means more distress, more systematised injustice, more powerlessness and a deeper sense of despair and hopelessness.

Φ "This new global financial system operates outside the control of any single government, and increasingly sets its own agenda - working systematically in the interests of financial operators", the UN Research Institute summarises. "Despite their massive influence and reach, TNCs remain largely untouched by any form of international regulation".[140] TNCs represent the greatest concentration of power and freedom without responsibility and accountability, except to owners and stockholders.

The trans-national corporations which control global capital are the same companies that control the information flow in the world. They control the technological revolution which governs and guides it all. Whether through technological advancement, entertainment or war, they are the real beneficiaries in the end. When we endeavour to speak of a new world order, that, surely, is the heart of the matter.

The Third World is Everywhere

The bitter truth that people in the rich countries have to come to terms with is that what happened between rich and poor nations globally is also happening between rich and poor within nations: the third world is everywhere.

It is seen, as we have shown, in the widening gap between rich and poor in the US, and the situation in the UK and in many parts of Europe is no different. Dutch theologian Coen Boerma has provided us with a fascinating study on Europe's poor.[141] In example after example, he unmasks the face of the poor of that rich continent. In the land of the *Wirtschaftswunder,* charitable organisations distribute daily soup and bread coupons to needy Germans. Two-thirds of all German families shoulder debilitating debt, and 60% of them are no longer capable of paying because of unemployment. During the freezing winter of 1984 the *clochards* in France froze to death on the streets. The Metro stations were kept open at night so that the homeless could survive. In Britain "it is even worse", Boerma says. "The country which has been called 'the paradise of home-

---

[140] *States of Disarray*, 123.
[141] Coen Boerma, *The Poor Side of Europe, The church and the (new) poor of Western Europe* (Geneva: WCC Publications, 1989).

owners and shareholders' and where a small elite is steadily becoming richer, has some 4 million unemployed people. The poor are getting poorer…"[142] But it is also seen, and not by accident, in the US and the UK especially, in the systematic destruction of the trade unions. This destruction has been a long process, but it was perfected under President Ronald Reagan and Prime Minister Margaret Thatcher.

Since the destruction by Reagan of the Air Traffic Controller's Union in 1981, replacement workers, scab labour, growing unemployment, the closing of factories and mines, and the internationalisation of production, the right to strike in the US and Britain has been under siege and is now, in the view of many, not much more than a paper tiger. The economic consequences for workers have been considerable, but the political impact has been just as great. No effective unions means no organising force, no mobilisation of workers, no collective bargaining power and diminishing political influence. The disempowerment of the workers as workers is also the disempowerment of the workers as voters. In Britain the Thatcherisation of British society is continuing apace under Tony Blair, and trade unions in South Africa are worried whether this is not perhaps the goal of the South African government under President Thabo Mbeki.

Almost every recent study has to take note of what is called the "paradox of American society": the economy is weak, but profits are strong. What it means is this: most Americans are working longer hours for lower pay and considerably less security. Real wages continue to fall. Now that is a typical "third world" phenomenon. One ILO study shows that in 28 countries in Africa the real minimum wage fell by 20 per cent in the 1980s. Since 1987 real wages, also for the college-educated, have declined steadily in the US. Poverty is now becoming endemic; the poor of 1989 were significantly poorer than the poor in 1979. Hunger as a social phenomenon has grown by 50 per cent since the mid-eighties to engulf some 30 million people in the richest country in the world. One in eight children under twelve years old suffers from "real hunger" and a black man in Los Angeles or Harlem has the same life span as a man living in Bangladesh. In inner cities malnutrition is pervasive.

In all of this we would do well to remember that the "Third World" is a designation of class, no longer of geography; it describes economic realities rather than political boundaries. It is no longer the mainly powerless, underdeveloped and dependent cluster of nations outside the influential circle of the Northern rich; it is now also the points of explosion inside the circles of wealth, the simmering conscience under the surface of prosperity.

In the US all of this is exacerbated by the growth and newly acquired respectability of racism, from the quite blatant attempts to roll back the gains made through the civil rights struggle to the reintroduction of the so-called "bell curve". But in my view, racism in America finds its most deadly form in the relentless attack on education at all levels, the disparity in employment and the criminal justice system, and the long-term

---

[142] The whole first chapter makes for very instructive reading on this subject.

effects of these on what America calls its "minority communities". By the same token it is only a matter of time before this systemic racism will once again find overt, public, perhaps shocking expression, as it did not so very long ago. American racism's cloak of respectability will not be able to hide the barbarous nature that lurks within all forms of racism.

Another aspect of this is the resurgence of sexism and a self-destructive patriarchalism under the guise of "family values". It is a calculated, nation-wide *political* phenomenon, a rekindled anger at what Adolf Hitler, according to Naom Chomsky, called "the denial of the ancient truth that a woman's world is her husband, her family, her children, her home".[143] It calls upon men of all races to reaffirm their traditional roles as "promise-keepers", even as it appeals to the most base inculcation of macho manhood to feed a truly frightening homophobia. It does not question in any way whether the "tradition" is wrong, or how the tradition has changed, and therefore how the relationships between women and men have subsequently changed. It claims to be non-racial, but it is only ostensibly so. The outrage is directed, not at the resurgence of racism or the many forms of existing systemic injustice, but at the rise of feminism. Moreover, racism, homophobia and sexism are the children of the same prejudice, the same bigotry, the same intolerance, the same misguided appropriation of the Scriptures for evil ends. It is what Dr H Beecher Hicks of the Metropolitan Baptist Church in Washington DC calls "baptised bigotry".[144]

It is no wonder that the same Adolf Hitler, who knew so well the place of women as he knew the place of Jews, knew also the place of black people, as he claimed to know the will of God: "It is a sin against the will of the Almighty" he wrote, "that hundreds upon thousands of his most gifted creatures should be made to sink in the proletarian swamp while Kaffirs and Hottentots are trained for the liberal professions".[145]

Within this broader context the races are pitted against each other, men and women who should be allies, fighting side by side for fundamental change and equality in society, exposing the real enemies to the fulfilment of their human potential and the humanisation of their society. They are engaged in a bitter "gender" battle, divided by the quasi-religious fascism of an American neo-conservatism which, like so much of that land's dubious culture, is spreading globally.

"A Systematic Destructive Force ..."

In May 1993 the World Bank's Vice-President for Africa, Edward Jaycox, made the startling public submission that World Bank experts have been a "systematic destructive force in Africa".[146] Like the Stalinist regimes' "catastrophic attempts" to

---

[143] Chomsky, *Year 501*, 277.
[144] H Beecher Hicks, in a sermon I listened to in his church in Washington D.C.
[145] According to Chomsky, *op. cit.*, 277.
[146] Cf. Dot Keet, "Systematic Destruction: IMF/World Bank Social Engineering in Africa", in: *Track Two Magazine*, Cape Town: February, 1994, 10-11.

create communism in Russia and China, economist Dot Keet writes, the IMF/World Bank mission to restructure dozens of countries around the world according to a preconceived free-market blueprint has had "disastrous effects". Thus, "the IMF/WB prescriptions are among the fundamental causes of economic crisis in Africa, since they do not take on board, and in fact exacerbate, the deeper structural weaknesses within African economies and the damaging role of the international factors in Africa".[147]

The "solutions" offered by the IMF/WB were sweeping, uniform, ignoring the complex and diverse political, demographic, environmental and cultural factors within and between African countries. Instead of genuine economic empowerment, these "solutions" have led to "disproportionate economic power and profit accruing in the hands of insufficient and inefficient middlemen", widening the existing gap between rich and poor and aggravating social problems.[148]

After a decade of "development" in Africa, the World Bank's own figures show that the number of people living below the minimum poverty line (i.e. $US1 per day) increased in Africa from 68 million in 1982 to 216 million in 1990. And it will not stop there. The World Bank predicted that under its ongoing tutelage this figure would continue to rise - to more than 300 million, *half* the population of Africa, by the year 2003. And that is another deadline Africa has seen come and go without any real hope of change.

Meanwhile the demands of the IMF/WB themselves prevent African governments from responding to this critical situation with appropriate health, educational and other essential services, and the role of government, not only in the broader economy, but even in the provision of these services, continues to be reduced. The results continue to be dismal and the conclusion is inescapable: "In every direction the IMF/WB are reviving and reinforcing Africa's traditional subordinate role: dependent insertion into the world economy".[149]

This then is the new world order. A uni-polar power arrangement with undue influence of one nation on the institutions of governance globally; a greater propensity for war and violent conflict in spite of the end of the Cold war; and a fundamental shift of power from national governments to private capital, which necessitates a new power alliance between rich nations and global capital. This world order depends not primarily on military conquest but on control of the global economy to reach its goals and it employs the old methods of domination: ignorance, racism, classism, sexism and the politics of divide-and-rule.

In light of all this it is puzzling that South Africa has so enthusiastically, and with the minimum of critical thought, embraced globalization and made it the centre-piece of the African Renaissance. I am not saying that South Africa can, and should, ignore the reality of the processes of globalization. But I am saying that it is a fatal mistake

---

[147] *Op. cit.*
[148] Keet, *op.cit.*
[149] Keet, *op. cit.*

to embrace it without a thorough critical awareness of the realities either way. The highly selective nature and skewed priorities of globalization are not being questioned - or not nearly enough. It seems that we have swallowed whole the updated, but still flawed, logic of Reagonomics: the unreal optimism of the trickle-down theory – the rising tide of wealth that is supposed to lift, automatically, all boats. But, as the 1997 Human Development Report observes, "The yachts and ocean liners are indeed rising in response to new opportunities, but the rafts and rowboats are taking on water - and some are sinking fast".[150]

Of course globalization has huge benefits, and it is expected that those benefits should exceed the costs. The problem is that the losses will be carried by those countries that can least afford them. While the new trade agreements will increase global income by an estimated US$212 - 510 billion, the least developed countries will lose up to $600 million a year, and sub-Saharan Africa US$1,2 billion.[151] Globalization also means increased foreign direct investment. Once again, however, most direct investments go to North America, Europe and Japan which, together with the eight Chinese provinces and Beijing, receive more than 90 per cent of global FDI. The rest of the world, with more than 70 per cent of the global population, gets less than 10 per cent.[152] And in spite of a much admired "national reconciliation" and huge concessions to established white economic interests in South Africa to appease Western opinion, the promised foreign investment in South Africa has not yet materialised.

The reasons for these skewed realities are obvious and range from bad policy to bad terms to bad rules. The playing field has remained hopelessly uneven because the rules are still being made by the rich nations. The problems are acute in the field of textiles and agriculture, to name but two of the most glaring examples. The major exporters, notably the European Union and the United States, have continued to subsidise their production and exports, making a cruel joke of the much-vaunted "competition of the open market". The UNDP calls such unequal competition a recipe for the destruction of livelihoods on a massive scale: "Whatever sway the concept of a level playing field in world agriculture may exercise over the imagination of free traders, it is conspicuous by its absence in the real world".[153]

The same is true for the new vigour with which rich nations are now enforcing intellectual property rights. Earlier on, industrial countries, even Japan after the Second World War, exploited a free flow of ideas and technology without which their industrialisation would not have been so rapid. Now those same countries are enforcing policies that will impose steep licensing charges for developing nations for using foreign technology, thereby virtually ensuring that those countries remain forever behind.

---

[150] *UNDP Report 1997*, United Nations, New York, 82.
[151] *Ibid.*
[152] *Op. cit.*, 84.
[153] *Op. cit.*, 86.

"Globalisation is thus proceeding apace, but largely for the benefit of the more dynamic countries in the North and South", is the conclusion of the 1997 UNDP Report.[154] The report of the UN Research Institute is far more blunt: "The new law is the law of the jungle: only the fittest can survive.[155]

If globalization's "survival of the fittest" is the conclusion of a secular body working only with the statistics and the facts, what then should be the response of Christian faith? To that response we shall now turn.

The New Order Versus the Inverted Order

Over against the "new world order" with its "law of the jungle" stands the church with the proclamation of the kingdom of God with its justice and its law of love. The church has nothing else to proclaim but the power of the inverted order of the kingdom of God with its saving grace, its radical demands for justice, peace and the liberation of God's people; with its good news for the poor that God has indeed heard their cry, taken their side in their struggle for life and the fulfilment of their human potential.

Now, more than ever, the church cannot compromise on this. It needs to proclaim God's passion for justice and God's anger against injustice; God's choice for the poor, the weak, the stranger, the despised and the dispossessed. The kingdom of God is in fact God's new order against which all orders of this world shall be measured. It is an inverted order in which the last shall be first and those despised by the world shall be the chosen ones of God. It is the inverted order of which Hannah sings, for which Mary glorifies the Lord and which comes to light in the life and work, death and resurrection of Jesus the Messiah.

It is the continued proclamation of the faith of Israel in the God of the covenant, who has made a slave people his own, and led them out of that iron smelter which was Egypt with a strong right hand (Deut. 4). It is the unflinching truth of the prophets that to do justice is to know the Lord (Jer. 22), and that the poor, the hungry and the naked are our own flesh (Is. 58). It is God's injunction to break every yoke and to let the oppressed go free. It is a radical call to conversion, for confrontation with evil and the powers and principalities which dehumanise God's children and God's world.

It is, in short, the biblical message of liberation so forcefully proclaimed by liberation theology. We are discovering that liberation theology, far from becoming irrelevant as has been claimed by some, has acquired a new urgency and must be proclaimed with greater insistence than ever before. The triumph of evil in the continuation of injustice and oppression and the prosperity of the wicked is not a triumph over the Kingdom of God. It is a triumph over an unfaithful church that has found the quiet comforts of compromise easier to live with than the painful pathos of prophecy; a church that has

---

[154] *Op. cit.*, 87.
[155] *States of Disarray*, 33.

lost its passion for the poor in the desire to placate the rich; a church whose amazing failure to resist religious complacency can only be explained in light of its amazing ability to resist the radical power of the gospel.

One of the most persistent strains in the popular propaganda of the "serious press" in the last few years has been the dissemination of the deliberate fallacy that Communism collapsed because capitalism is "right". The church, for its part, would do well to remind itself that in God's scheme of things it may well be that the collapse of one system of injustice and oppression had simply preceded the collapse of another system of injustice and oppression. The so-called triumph of capitalism may yet prove to be an empty victory and the price for that victory will once again have to be paid by the poor and the powerless. It is utter foolishness to rush to bow down before the idol of capitalism just because, like Dagon, it survived one more morning. In the book of Revelation, the fall of Babylon is announced, not by the mighty voice of the angel, but in the sober reflection of the seer:

> *"For God has put it in their hearts to carry out his purpose by agreeing to give their kingdoms to the beast, until the words of God will be fulfilled". (Rev 17:17)*

God waits, not for the angel to announce, but for the church to speak.

But this misconception has also had theological consequences. In South Africa, for instance, we are now told in so many words that it is "anachronistic" to speak of the theology of liberation. It is the theology of "reconstruction" that is all the rage now. Just as it is not considered acceptable to speak of oppression and liberation from oppression, since liberation has now been "achieved", so all talk of liberation theology has become out of place. Likewise the theologians of the "new South Africa" have shifted their concern from liberation to "culture".

This is based on two assumptions. The first is from the court theologians of the new, ruling elite. The struggle is over, the age of reconstruction has begun. The call for "continued struggle" and "liberation" does not speak well of a situation in which democracy is now a reality and the achievements of the people ought to be celebrated. What is needed now is for the church to help create "a better life for all", precisely what the election campaign slogans called for. Worldwide, the unprecedented spread of democracy and the new opportunities for prosperity of a new middle class have rendered "confrontational" theological models obsolete. This is true in all places where liberation theology had found a voice, but in South Africa there is the added dimension that the official ideology of "national reconciliation" demands a theological agenda that excludes genuine confrontation with both the past and the present.

This is a reasoning which suits those who now have a stake in the status quo, and also white theologians from the old liberal school, whose ascendancy in the last few years has been remarkable. Their language is the language of "realism" and "pragmatism" reflecting the new realities of the compromise of power blocks which is the hallmark of politics in South Africa today. Its main concern is to support the programme of "nation building" as that concept is understood and spelt out by those in power. It reflects also the "understanding" of such compromise politics, which is peculiar to the privileged classes. The theological model is not liberation and justice, but their interpretation of the "Christian realism" of Reinhold Niebuhr. The context of their theology is the "new democracy" as if that is already an accomplished project within which "nation building", "national reconciliation" and "reconstruction" are the finishing touches. Here again, as was the case within the apartheid context, all depends on where one stands, whose viewpoint forms one's point of departure, and with whose eyes one looks at our new situation.

The new theological emphasis on culture has a similar agenda. Their attention is wholly taken up by the Africanisation of religion and theology as well as the church. There is a legitimate place for the discussion of theology and culture, and the long battle to free the African church from its colonial bondage is far from over. But I am one of those who have never seen a tension between what we used to call "African theology" in the mode of that doyen of Africa's teachers, John Mbiti, and "liberation theology". In fact the true Africanisation of the church cannot but be the liberation of the church. But there is much more to the task of the church in Africa today than ridding ourselves of European ecclesiastical colonialism, whichever way we perceive it. The question of culture is important, but it is in my view not nearly as pressing as the issues we have been discussing. It is cold comfort for the poor in South Africa to be told that their churches have been "Africanised", while that same "Africanised" church moves not one finger to secure justice, peace and human dignity for those still deprived of them. Besides, in South Africa we run the distinct risk of using the issues of culture as an escape from the real issues of justice and equality. What is the meaning of an "Africanised" church where the AIDS-stricken person cannot find a home, consolation, healing of the soul? Or where the gay Christian is condemned to hell? Or where women cannot find dignity of place?

Moreover, it is a field in which the dangers of being co-opted by the dominant culture, pandering to it rather than critically engaging it, are real. What we have seen of the government's expectations of the church's support for the "national agenda" should make us aware of how often the church and theology have been used as tools *for* the dominant culture, instead of being the vanguard of a *counter-culture* inspired not by overt or disguised nationalist notions, but by the demands of the Kingdom of God.

The second assumption is made by those who believed all along that liberation theology was not a biblical theology at all, but merely an expression of the ideology of communism. Repressive governments, conservative theological interest groups and some church establishments treated it as such. With the collapse of communism they expected liberation theology to have lost its "power base", so to speak. But the inspiration for and source of liberation theology never was any ideology, but rather the gospel of the poor and God's unequivocal choice for the weak and downtrodden. There is now more need than ever for that voice to be heard.

In Europe those who are sensitive both to the ongoing situation there and the unchanged demands of the gospel look towards the radical edge of liberation theology to give new life to the political theology that was once the prophetic spur to true engagement in the churches of Europe. Once again we listen to Jürgen Moltmann, who speaks of "a shortfall of solidarity" in European countries "as a result of globalization", the "serious danger" to the disabled, the old and the "useless", and the slow but sure decline into their own apartheid:

> The more we in the countries of the industrialized West are clear about this development, and the more we discover the oppressed, impoverished and abandoned world in our own backyard, the more relevant we shall find (the...) theology of liberation. It is better to heed its insights now, rather than to wait for the tragic end of capitalism, which has not foundered on its socialist alternative but is surely condemned to failure because it is increasingly at variance with human dignity, the life of this earth, and it own future.[156]

Moltmann speaks as a man after my own heart. These are the theological insights South African theologians and the South African church should rush to claim, rather than run away from, as most of us are currently trying to do.

The former Dutch Reformed Mission Church, when it wrote and adopted the Confession of Belhar in 1986 as participant in that great theological movement which also produced the *Kairos Document* and *The Call to Pray for the End of Unjust Rule*, did not know just how relevant that confession would remain in the new situation in which we find ourselves. So it is fitting that the voice of protest and caution that is raised in regard to the South African government's economic policies is that of liberation theologian, Molefe Tsele, one of the theologians who drafted the *Kairos Document* in 1985 and whose insights have served us well.[157] The period of the seventies and eighties now seems to have been a time that produced a theological tradition still extraordinarily relevant to the new times in which we live. Tsele, drawing from that tradition, speaks of the "neo-liberal free market system" as the dominant feature of our time, the only "'rational' alternative" for whose "attractiveness" a case could be made.[158] He means, of course, the much vaunted system of globalization which so enchants South Africa's new rulers. He, like me, is worried though that this system requires sacrifices for its success and those sacrifices are the poor and weak members of the community.[159] He confesses to a "sense of betrayal by a liberation project that is incapable of engaging this system".[160] The liberation movement, perhaps out of necessity, has made a deal with this system,

---

[156] Moltmann, *God for a Secular Society*, 67.
[157] Molefe Tsele, "Kairos and Jubilee", in: H Russell Botman and Robin Petersen, *To Remember and to Heal* (Cape Town: Human and Rosseau, 1998), 70 – 78.
[158] *Op. cit.*, 70.
[159] *Op. cit.*, 71.
[160] Op. cit., 72.

but has now been left with "an illusion at best, and a sham sense of power at worst" - the liberation movement having become just another "servant of power", which has taken the place of the old apartheid regime.[161]

The real power, Tsele says, "does not lie with our elected officials, but is located somewhere else ... Our cherished dream of democracy turns out to be a fraud. We believed in the ballot but nobody told us that we should rather invest our power in the stock market ... Real power is negotiated at the stock exchange, not in parliament".[162] This presents us "with a fundamental crisis", which can be confronted only with the message of liberation theology. "The greatest challenge is to be able to proclaim God's continuing liberatory work even in the midst of this despair".[163] It presents us, Tsele believes, with a new kairos,

> And it implies a confession that something better is demanded of us and is possible in our history. Our affirmation of the kairos is therefore simultaneously a call for the Jubilee of God. It is the refusal of our human spirit to succumb to the finality of history and to the absoluteness of any one particular system, however popular and successful it may have proved. The path from kairos should lead to jubilee.[164]

Among South African theologians Tsele's voice is rare, but I have no doubt that this is one of the crucial issues that should now engage us.

Against Powers and Principalities

No image catches the realities of the "new world order" better than the New Testament image of "powers and principalities". We must learn to listen anew to the words of Scripture:

> *"For our struggle is not against flesh and blood, but against principalities and powers, against the world rulers of this present dark age, against the evil spirits in heavenly places" (Eph 6:12)*

And again:

> *"God put this power to work in Christ when he raised him from the dead and seated him at his right hand in the heavenly places, far above all rule and authority and power and dominion, and above every name that is named, not only in this age, but also in the age to come. And he has put all things under his feet". (Eph 1:20-22)*

---

[161] *Ibid.*
[162] *Ibid.*
[163] *Op. cit.,* 73.
[164] *Ibid.*

And yet again:

> *And you, who were dead in trespasses and the circumcision of your flesh, God made alive together with Christ, having forgiven us all our trespasses, having cancelled the bond which stood against us with its legal demands- this he set aside, nailing it to the cross. He disarmed the principalities and powers and made a public spectacle out of them, triumphing over them in him". (Col 2:13-15)*

The Bible not only acknowledges the existence of powers and principalities, it knows that they are the enemy. They are powerful, their claims are all-encompassing, their presence frightening. Their totalitarian nature is an attack on our life in its totality. Our relationship with them is not one of peaceful co-existence or humble submission; it is one of struggle. They are the rulers of the world who are responsible for the present darkness in which we live, and in their powerful reach and boundless arrogance they seek to occupy even the "heavenly places". This means that they elevate themselves to the place of God, act as gods in place of God, challenging God not only on earth where God's will is to be done, but in the very heavenly places where God's will originates. We must not underestimate them, for their spirit is evil. The dangerous illusion here is not that they are "evil spirits", but that our struggle is actually against mere "flesh and blood".

Those who experienced Hitler's Nazi Germany, South Africa's apartheid, or the plight of the poor in Latin America, whose virtual destruction was, and in many ways still is, engineered by the most powerful nation on earth; those who have seen the forces of destruction at work in Africa's killing fields, or the US-sponsored death squads in Central America, know that this language is not simply psycho-religious babble. For millions these are realities that are as merciless as they are inescapable.

For that reason it is crucial to know that over against the powers and principalities God has put His power "to work" in Christ, and raising Christ from the dead, put him at His right hand "in the heavenly places". Evil shall not be allowed to occupy the space of God. In Christ God reclaims the heavenly places, and in Christ's resurrection God's power challenges the powers and principalities in their own domain: death. And God conquers. And if they are conquered in their own terrain, how can they continue to challenge God in "the heavenly places"? Or on earth, where God's will is to be done, and where God's tent is to be pitched among God's people?

The writer of Ephesians is emphatic: not only is Christ raised from the dead and put at God's right hand, Christ is now "far above all rule and authority and power and dominion". Not "above" as in "removed" or "aloof", but "above" as in having gained the victory, as now having subjugated all pretence of power, both for this age and for the age to come. "And he has put all things under his feet " is not just poetic repetition, but the joyful affirmation of a certainty, the constant echo of God's new reality, in the same way that the church repeats the liturgical affirmation each Sunday morning: "Our help is in the name of the Lord, who made heaven and earth".

We know the powers in their over-powering, oppressive presence. But the church knows something else. Real power is not to subjugate and to oppress but to create and liberate. God's power is a power that makes and keeps human life human as American theologian Paul Lehmann has taught us, and it is to the exercise of that power that human beings are called. That is the kind of power that rules in the "heavenly places" and should likewise prevail "on earth". *That* is the perfect will of God.

We know the powers not in their capacity to serve or to liberate or to create community and humanity or to preserve justice, but in their insistent hatred of God and God's creation, in their desire to "lord it over us" in their dominion over us. But because we know God, we know that their claim of ultimate meaning and truth, and their demands for ultimate loyalty and submission are idolatry and as such ultimately meaningless.

We have heard it all before. In the derision of the question of the Pharaoh: "Who is the LORD, that I should heed him?" (Ex 5:2). But we have also heard him say: "Rise up, go away from my people ..." (Ex 12:31).

We have also heard the voice of the people: "I will sing to the LORD, for he has triumphed gloriously; horse and rider he has thrown in the sea ... Who is like you, o LORD, among the gods?" (Ex 15).

We have heard, too, the voice of the prophet: "Their idols are like scarecrows in a cucumber field, and they cannot speak; they have to be carried, for they cannot walk. Do not be afraid of them..." (Jer. 10:5).

But we know even more. We know Jesus the Messiah who has come to set the captives free, give sight to the blind, to let the poor hear the good news and to proclaim the year of the Lord's favour. His presence shattered the pretensions of the powers of the world and broke our enslavement to them. By living freely and challenging them Christ shatters the myths and illusions of their absolute authority over us and of our own perceived powerlessness to resist them. Through his life and resurrection we know that the powers not only exist, but they exist in rebellion to God, and therefore have no legitimate claim on us.

By his self-giving life and death on the cross, he demonstrated his own freedom from them, disarmed them and exposed them for what they are, and not what they claimed to be in their idolatrous self-glorification. By freeing us from the paralysing stranglehold of sin, Christ makes us share in his freedom, freeing us also from the slavery to the powers and making a public spectacle of them. Their true impotence is there for all to see. Their claims of omnipotence and invincibility, their arrogant presentation of themselves as the ultimate arbiters of our lives and well-being, their sinful presumption that they are the determiners of our hopes and fears, our dreams and joys, our prayers and responses - all this Jesus exposed as pure deception. Christ has triumphed over them.

More than forty years ago Dutch theologian Hendrikus Berkhof spoke to this issue in a wonderful and still relevant little book, called *Christ and the Powers*.[165] He takes us to the heart of the matter:

> The scribes, representatives of Jewish law, far from receiving gratefully him who came in the name of the God of the law, crucified him in the name of the law. The priests, servants of his temple, crucified him in the name of the temple. The Pharisees, personifying piety, crucified him in the name of piety. Pilate, representing Roman justice and law, shows what these are worth when called upon to do justice to the Truth himself. Obviously, none of these rulers of the age, who let themselves be worshipped as divinities, understood God's wisdom ... Now they are unmasked as false gods by their encounter with Very God; they are made a spectacle.[166]

This Jesus is raised from the dead by the power of God, who seated him at God's right hand in the heavenly places – those same places that the powers and principalities thought they had occupied. The risen Christ reclaims God's space and so makes room for true humanity, free from the fear of and enslavement to the idols and false gods.

The evil spirit of these powers is challenged and conquered by the liberating, life-giving, re-creating, empowering Spirit of God who shatters the weapon, says Berkhof, from which they heretofore have derived their strength.

> This weapon was the power of illusion, their ability to convince that they were the divine regents of the world, ultimate certainty and ultimate direction, ultimate happiness and ultimate duty for small, dependent humanity.[167]

This is the message the church is called to proclaim still. In doing this we must not be afraid to call the demons by their names. The brutal disparities between rich and poor, the continued victimisation of the weak and defenceless, the growing concentration of power in the hands of a few persons and institutions, the contrived consensus forced upon us by media subservient to the interests of the powerful only and who feed us with the watered-down milk of ignorance about the issues that really matter; the hardness of conscience that seems to have become the hallmark of political leadership the world over - these must be spoken to and acted against.

Our faith in the kingdom of God means, I think, as I have said often before, that we are called to challenge the structures of the world, to fight them, to subvert them,

---

[165] Hendrikus Berkhof, *Christ and the Powers* (Scotdale, Pennsylvania: Herald Press, and Ontario: Kitchener, 1977) a translation of the Dutch *Christus en de machten* (Callenbach: Nijkerk, 1973).
[166] *Op. cit.*, 30.
[167] *Op. cit.*, 31.

until they conform to the norms of the kingdom of God. Until the choices they make reflect the choices of God. And here I am not speaking of the *fata morgana* of vague Utopian ideals, of opportunistic slogans designed to hoodwink the masses, but rather of prophetic faithfulness and civic responsibility. That means that we shall not vacate our places of responsibility in the world for them to be taken over by unaccountable powers, powerful politicians, or a conservative theology emanating from the shadow of government or a right-wing religiosity that so vainly, if loudly, claims the name of Christ. The church knows the might of the powers that rule this world, but the church is called by a Higher Power.

Sharing the Mind of Christ

Dutch theologian G ter Schegget,[168] in his brilliant exegesis of the Christ Hymn in Philippians 2:5-11, says of the injunction, "Let the same mind be in you that was in Christ Jesus" (no selfish ambition, no conceit, but humility, regarding others as better than yourselves): "How dare Paul admonish them thus, encourage them thus, call upon them in this way, these people who already live under the reign of terror which Rome was, who live 'without God and without hope in the world'?" (Eph 2:12). How dare he deny them the very understandable "flight toward inwardness" in order to escape the miseries of life? Is it not inhumane to ask so much of these little people? "The ground of Paul's own courage and of his encouragement is one thing only, and on that one thing he calls, to that he appeals: that which in Christ is true and real".

Their victory is won. They have only to accept it, make it true, realise it by living it as the church. They have to learn to see that the power of the Messiah is realised in a different way than the power of Rome. Christ's *doxa* is a totally different glory than that of the Caesar. The way to that glory is a different one. The manner in which it is achieved is different. The quality thereof is different. "But it is nonetheless a concrete, political alternative". For God reveals that it is in this Jesus, the One who has "emptied Himself", taking the form of a slave, identifying with the humiliation and the pain of slaves; in this love to the very end, that God has entered into the human story, demonstrating true majesty. For "precisely as slave is He very God".[169] "If God is the God of *this* Jesus, the hidden victory shall come to light".[170]

Ter Schegget goes on: the servant, the emptied One, is Lord; the slave reigns. His is the power and authority in heaven *and on earth*. His serving love, his solidarity in our suffering and humiliation has conquered all counter-powers. This is the truth that questions and conquers the lies by which the world lives. And this truth is not simply an idea, a philosophy, but reality, as surely as this Messiah is seated at the right hand of God.

---

[168] *De Andere Mogelijkheid* (Ten Have: Baarn, 1973) 44-45.
[169] *Op. cit.*, 48.
[170] *Op. cit.*, 49.

What this means in practice has never been unclear to the church. At least, we have always known what was expected of us.

> To be faithful to Jesus demands a constant affirmation of our belief in the One Living God, and at the same time a permanent confrontation with those human realities which tend to become the objects of idolatry. In other words, the proclamation of Jesus as the Lord excludes the acceptance of idols such as mammon and false security, dominance and unlimited growth, irresponsible accumulation and profit backed by injustice and the violation of other people's rights.[171]

That means that we should not surrender our right to protest, to act for justice and peace just because the goal posts have been so dramatically shifted in the past few years and the entities we fight are so deeply hidden and seemingly so completely divorced from the painful realities they create. Even though the powers that seek to rule the world in our day are mostly hidden, they still need the legitimisation of the structures of democracy, at least in those places where democracy is claimed. And even though governments may do their utmost to keep people ignorant and to limit their meaningful participation, they in turn need legitimisation by the people. It is in this chain of need and legitimacy that our opportunity lies. As long as this is so, it means that we can mobilise people by telling them the truth, by speaking truth to power and thereby holding power accountable, and by living that truth that God is a God of liberation and justice, hope and life.

The challenges posed to the powers by ordinary people who claim the right to know what is negotiated and agreed to in their name, as we have seen in Seattle, Prague, Quebec City and Johannesburg in the last year or two, are the hopeful signs of people who refuse to be intimidated into silence and acquiescence. The church should support all non-violent actions that seek to hold these powers accountable and as human as possible.

We really cannot allow the "power of the people", for which we fought such long and hard battles, to be usurped by the power of elitist cliques, national or global, political or economic. We cannot allow politicians, even our elected representatives, to assume our political responsibility. That would inevitably lead to political estrangement, to our capitulation before government, which in turn leads to apathy which in turn leads to tyranny. Political passivity is the doorway to misuse of power. "And that", says Moltmann, "is not just political estrangement, it is the beginning of every political idolatry".[172] Quite so.

The crown sits on the constitution, said John Milton, not on the head of a man.

---

[171] Duchrow, *op. cit.*, 77, quoting the WCC TNC working group report, "The Churches and the Transnational Corporations", 26.

[172] *Op. cit.,* 45.

John Quincy Adams, the sixth president of the United States, long ago spoke a profound truth which sorely needs repetition not only in the present dark age of American politics driven by neo-fascist Christian fundamentalism, but in every democracy, including our own, deeply tested as we are by the merciless powers from without and the ravaging temptations from within:

> *"Democracy has no monuments. It strikes no medals. Its coins do not bear the likeness of any person. Its true essence is iconoclasm"*. [173]

The church is called to live the kingdom of God as a fundamental, and constant, interruption in the reign of evil and as a persistent reversal of the ways of the world. If the church takes this seriously, the rulers of the darkness of this age, the creators of orders old and new, cannot, and will not, sit easily upon their thrones.

---

[173] Cited by Moltmann, *op. cit.* 45.

CHAPTER FOUR

"MY POWER AND THE STRENGTH OF MY HANDS"
Unremembering as Ideological Tool

Unremembering and forgetfulness

The role of religious faith, and consequently of the church, in the struggle for liberation in South Africa can hardly be in dispute.[174] Or so one should think. It can be legitimately said that if the church had not played that role, earlier already, but especially in the 1970s and 80s, the challenge to apartheid would have suffered immensely and the end of apartheid would have been significantly retarded. Throughout the struggle for freedom and human dignity, religion – even more, religious faith – was seen as central by the oppressed themselves. During the 1980s, the time of our darkest oppression, faith, as the deepest source of inspiration for struggle and sacrifice, was the most salient feature of the struggle against apartheid and the resultant conflict between the church and the apartheid state had reached a level never experienced before.

Yet, apart from the blandest of acknowledgements, there is no attempt at all to take seriously the impact of their religious faith on those who participated in this struggle. The church, not as a single monolithic body, nor as the institutional hierarchies from whom little could be expected at the best of times, but as the prophetic movement of believers who found in the gospel of Jesus Christ their grounds for being, their inspiration for struggle and their thirst for justice, is hardly mentioned. Inasmuch as individual Christians are mentioned, it is in terms of their leadership or their celebrity status. Their leadership is almost always divorced from their faith and they are seen in, and used for, their *political functionality* rather than their prophetic faithfulness.

This is true of both academics and politicians, and whether one reads recent histories of South Africa or studies the speeches of South African leaders, the results are the same. Not only is there an anxiousness to ignore history as it happened, there is a conscious, and constant, effort to rewrite history by omission and commission.

A people might forget their history because the horrors of their past are such that they cannot bear further contemplation. Psychologists have taught us that the pain of suffering is often (and easily) blocked out in a collective act of forgetfulness. The violence inflicted upon persons can no longer be borne, and remembering is a way of

---

[174] This is, of course, not to say that other faiths did not play a significant role in the inspiration of their members regarding their role in the struggle and I hereby want to acknowledge that with deep gratitude and respect. But an interfaith approach would take us too far. Our intention is to concentrate on the Christian faith only.

carrying the memories with you. It is a victimization that never ends. This can be true of the perpetrators too. They "forget" because they have an absolute need to forget, in a way which goes beyond mere denial. It is then not enough to say, "We did not know". Obliteration of the past is what is needed. As such, this is an act of suppression of memory, rather than simply "forgetting".

But we are not speaking of forgetfulness here. We are speaking of what I shall call *unremembering*. Unremembering is a deliberate political act for reasons of domestication and control. A people's history, or their memory, is falsified, rewritten or denied. This process is not a confluence of accidental political factors, neither is it the result of inevitable political "shifts". It is an act of appropriation. Although it may serve psychological ends, as an act it is deliberately ideological and serves a political agenda.

Since the beginning of South Africa's first decade of democracy a few remarkable things have been happening in relation to the church and its role in the struggle. First, the centrality of religious faith, especially in our struggle, has been all but ignored by the academic community. Second, apart from a few well-placed remarks during elections and on suitable occasions, the church's role in the struggle remained almost totally unrecognised by the leaders of government in South Africa. Third, the language of the church, to a remarkable degree, has been appropriated by the state; and fourth, space for critical, prophetic witness of the church is now, if not openly denied, nonetheless dangerously constrained. It would be worth our while to think a bit on this.

In the Name of Objectivity?

One of the foremost and most respected scholars of the Left in the United States, Eugene D Genovese, has raised the question of historians' acknowledgement of the centrality of religious faith in history in a recent study.[175]

"Until recently", Genovese writes, "we primarily had to contend with the illusion that a historian could proceed without a worldview and attendant political bias and somehow arrive at an objectivity that we might have thought only God capable of".[176] It may be impossible, some might argue, to keep value judgments from distorting our most determined efforts at objective analysis, but if that is the response to Max Weber's plea for ethical neutrality[177], that in itself should warn us against our own biases and admonish us to hold the inevitable distortions to a minimum. "We must", Genovese insists, "rein in our prejudices if we wish to do honest scientific work" (for) "we cannot escape the intrusion of a worldview into our work as historians".[178]

---

[175] Eugene D Genovese, "Marxism, Christianity and Bias in the Study of Southern Slave Society", in: Bruce Kuklick and D.G. Hart (eds.): *Religious Advocacy and American History* (Grand Rapids: Eerdmans, 1997), 83-95.
[176] *Op. cit.,* 83.
[177] Cf. Max Weber, *The Methodology of the Social Sciences* (Glencoe: Free Press, 1949).
[178] *Marxism, Christianity and Bias,* 84.

As illustration Genovese uses his own work, a major study of slave life in the old southern United States, a book that, in my view, has many followers, few equals and certainly no superiors.[179] During this study, Genovese says, he discovered, "in contrast to my own beliefs", two central issues without which the question of slavery in the US cannot be understood. First, the "vibrant culture under conditions of extreme adversity" that the slaves had forged, which would not have been possible without the "centrality of religion to that achievement" expressed in the "unique features of the black religious experience".[180]

Second, there were the political implications of this religious experience which tend toward the black nationalist interpretation of the black experience in the US, and thus the "call for serious qualification of the rival liberal-integrationist interpretation".[181] It is striking, he notes, how many "fine scholars" at least recognized the first, but have remained silent on the second, simply because it does not suit them ideologically to acknowledge this point.

For himself there really was no choice, although by his own admission, he found the results of his study disturbing. "The empirical investigations disturbed a historian with the biases of an atheist and a historical materialist who had always assumed, however mindlessly, that religion should be understood as no more than a corrosive ideology at the service of the ruling classes".[182]

Contrary to his expectations, religion emerged as a positive force in the book - "indeed as the centerpiece" - for in the end, the conclusion was inescapable:

> For while much went into the making of the heroic black struggle for survival under extreme adversity, nothing loomed so large as the religious faith of the slaves. The very religion that their masters sought to impose on them in the interests of social control carried an extraordinarily powerful message of liberation in this world as well as the next.[183]

The slaves did this by developing their own interpretation of Scripture and the Christian faith (a liberation hermeneutic we would say), and linking it with traditional African religious experience.[184] Not merely religion, as in a vague, general religiosity, but "the overpowering evidence of *religious faith*" (my emphasis) aroused in Genovese "a

---

[179] Eugene D Genovese, *Roll, Jordan, Roll: The World The Slaves Made* (New York: Pantheon, 1974).
[180] *Op. cit.,* 87.
[181] *Ibid.*
[182] *Op. cit.,* 88.
[183] *Op. cit.,* 88-89.
[184] Genovese is right. See, for example, the excellent study of Gayraud Wilmore, *Black Religion and Black Radicalism, An Examination of the Black Experience in Religion* (New York: Anchor Books, 1973; revised edition, Orbis Press, Maryknoll: 1983).

scepticism about the reigning tendency in academia to, as it were, sociologise faith out of religion - to *deny the reality of spirituality*".[185]

It is my contention that this is exactly what is happening in the writing of South African history and in the analyses of political scientists. Not only is the centrality of religious faith being denied by South African historiography, but (as a consequence) the political implications of that faith are ignored, because, in the words of Genovese, they "contradict our (i.e. historians') intentions". A historian has the duty "to make those implications clear". But simultaneously, they have the duty "to resist the imposition of (their) politics on the empirical record" by denying or ignoring the impact of faith on the political events and on the people who created them. Says Genovese with characteristic bluntness: "It is one thing to lay bare the political implications of our analyses; it is quite another to whore in some ostensibly worthy cause".[186]

Was God in the Struggle?

In three of the most recent, respected and widely read histories of the South African struggle against apartheid Genovese's point is clearly illustrated.[187] In these discussions the church is mentioned as a "non-governmental organization", an "organ of civil society" etc., but there is no serious analysis of, or engagement with, faith as source of inspiration of political action or of the role of the church as community of faith and conviction.

Anthony Marx, an American student of South African politics, knows only that Black Theology was a significant element in people's understanding of Black Power, and his comments are revealing: "Perhaps the way in which Black Power was most influential in South Africa was through the adoption of its derivative Black Theology by popular religious figures ".. However, he continues, advocates of Black Theology, inspired particularly by the writings of (American black theologian) James Cone, "emphasized spiritual rather than material oppression, and also healing".[188]

This is a statement of shocking ignorance. Marx seems to know nothing of the roots of Black Theology in South Africa, and has no knowledge of the inextricable link between Black Theology, Black Consciousness and Black Power, nor of the content of Black Theology as a theology of liberation, demanding a radical choice for the poor and the weak in society. He does not seem to know that Black Theology seeks an ethic of radical transformation and that the change we look for is a qualitative change;

---

[185] *Marxism, Christianity and Bias,* 88-89 (emphasis mine).
[186] *Op. cit.,* 88.
[187] Cf. Tom Lodge, *Black Politics in South Africa Since 1945* (Johannesburg: Ravan Press, 1990 4th ed.); Tom Lodge and Bill Nasson, *All, Here and Now. Black Politics in South Africa in the 1980s* (Cape Town: Ford Foundation and David Philip, 1991); and Anthony W Marx, *Lessons of Struggle, South African Internal Opposition, 1960-1990* (Cape Town: Oxford University Press, 1992).The same holds for the otherwise quite useful work of Jeremy Seekings, *The UDF, A History of the United Democratic Front in South Africa, 1983-1991* (Cape Town: David Philip, 2000).
[188] Marx, *Lessons,* 43.

that it deals with racism as well classism; that Black Theology within the context of apartheid did not simply look for unqualified "equality" with white people, but asked the question, "What does equality mean in *this* (racist, capitalist, misogynistic) society?" Black theology, we have said all along, must mean a search for a totally new social order. When we describe racism and economic and political oppression as "sin", it is not a "non-material" emphasis, as Marx claims, but the understanding that sin is not only personal, but also structural; that economic injustice is not just exploitation of the weak and the poor, but an assault upon the dignity of God.[189]

What does it mean then, that *this* theology, made popular by "popular religious figures", was spread among people who took their religious faith seriously? What impact did that have on the thousands who came to church, listened to our sermons, heard us preach at funerals and speak at rallies, read our books and pamphlets? What does it mean for a devout people when they are told that God is the God of the poor and that it is the call of the gospel for them to participate in the struggle for liberation?

Black Consciousness, as much as Black Power, was framed within the parameters of a Black Theological understanding of the struggle. To say therefore, as Marx does, for example, that non-violence was no more than a "useful tactic", or even, as he later states, "inconsistent with the (Black Consciousness) movement's basic ideological consideration",[190] is to ignore the serious debate about the use of violence and non-violence in the struggle in Black Theology that had raged from its inception into the 1980s, when it seemed as if the unbridled brutality of the state could call forth only one response: that of justified counter-violence.[191] At the very least, the continuation of the tradition of non-violence in the struggle in South Africa, in the midst of a climate of increasing violence from all sides, should be cause for some reflection on the sources of this critical hesitation.

Yet Marx suspects that there is more to this than meets the eye. "In this" he says, (meaning the choice for direct, non-violent action) "there was a conscious decision not to follow Franz Fanon on violence and also a disregard of the tradition of Marxist thought".[192] Surely this raises the intriguing question: "Why?" The allure of the violent ethic of Franz Fanon and some advocates of Black power was powerful, packaged as it was in the lyrical, poetic language that Fanon and Stokely Carmichael could employ so well. How could young, angry blacks not respond wholly and immediately to Fanon's ringing call to join the "Wretched of the Earth" in their urge to experience the "cleansing power" of violence? What about the attraction of the romanticising of the armed

---

[189] See e.g. Allan Aubrey Boesak, *Farewell to Innocence* (Maryknoll: Orbis Press), 1977, and the bibliography given there.

[190] Marx, *Lessons*, 47.

[191] Cf. amongst others, Boesak, *op. cit.,* James H Cone's classic, *Black Theology and Black Power* (New York: Seabury Press, 1969); Cone, *Speaking the Truth, Ecumenism, Liberation and Black Theology* (Grand Rapids: Eerdmans, 1986); Louise Kretzshmar, *The Voice of Black Theology in South Africa* (Johannesburg: Ravan, 1986).

[192] Marx, *Lessons*, 48.

struggle by both the African National Congress and the Pan Africanist Congress, using as focal point of the violent struggle for freedom no less a figure than that international icon of revolution, Che Guevara?

What was it that made so many young people in South Africa withstand that temptation? Or the temptation of vengeance, divine or otherwise? This is not to say that many did not turn to violence and that with a fury which sometimes stunned the mind and nearly drove us to despair. But even with hindsight it is hard to simply blame them. The violence that did occur in those years was sometimes shocking in its ferocity, but that is not the most important, or pertinent, thing one can say about that. The most important, indeed, the most astonishing thing is: why was there not much more of it? Why did the country not burn, and burn, and burn? For some reason Marx leaves it there. He inquires no further.

We encounter the same problem with Tom Lodge (1990), well-known and respected scholar and ANC expert from Wits University. In describing the context of black politics between 1945 and 1960, he begins by saying,

> The 1940s was a time when the proletarianisation and industrialization which resulted from a socio-ecological crisis in the countryside and the demands of a war-time economy created a vast new urban political constituency. The established political movements came to terms with it only hesitantly and in the meantime this new army of the urban poor dealt spontaneously with the immediate problems which confronted it … These new conditions combined to create a new political ideology; a fresh assertive nationalism which drew on two separate sources of inspiration, ethnic romanticism and working class radicalism.[193]

This observation is largely, but not entirely, true. Once again the politics of black South Africa is cast in an entirely secular mould. What inspired black political thinking was "ethnic romanticism" and "working-class radicalism". Seemingly nothing else. There is no mention of religion or the personal and communal convictions so decisive for public action that arise out of a radical understanding of the biblical message. There is no hint of any source of faith, otherwise so natural in the black experience, that inspires people to take such risks in their action against such overwhelming, terrifying odds. The "radicalism" is found only in the people as "workers", never in their embrace of the radical message of the gospel.

It is only much later that we get a hint that Lodge is not totally unaware of this. Writing about that decisive phase in the struggle in that period, the Defiance Campaign of the 1950s, Lodge cannot but mention that in the period of preparation for that campaign, "a mood of religious fervour infused the resistance", which was obviously sustained throughout the period. "When the campaign opened", he tells us, "it was accompanied

---

[193] Lodge, *Black Politics*, viii.

by 'days of prayer' and volunteers pledged themselves at prayer meetings to a code of love, discipline and cleanliness". *Manganos,* (women's church groups) wore their uniforms, clearly identifying themselves as Christians and *as such participating in the struggle,* and accompanied speeches with "solemn hymn singing".[194]

There is a tone of bemusement, even embarrassment, in the observation: "*Even* at the tense climax of the campaign in Port Elizabeth - where there were strong syndicalist undercurrents - people were enjoined on the first day of the strike to 'conduct a prayer and a fast in which each member of the family will have to be at home', and thereafter they attended *nightly church services*".[195] Those within the black Christian communities would not find this surprising at all. This type of action did not just signify a church-connectedness; it was the testimony of these Christian activists of their utter dependence on God in the struggle, which they could not pursue on their own.

This is a natural point of entry for a most meaningful discussion on the role of religious faith in the struggle for liberation in South Africa. Anyone who has read Ghandi or Martin Luther King, or the early leaders of the movement, knows the crucial place of faith, of religious discipline and the power of love in the struggle. In secular movement politics "discipline" is simply the unquestioning submission to the rules, decisions and leadership of the movement. Both Ghandi and King, however, as well as a long string of Christian leaders within the ANC before the interruption of exile, knew that "discipline" was firstly the discipline of spiritual commitment, one's inner connectedness to a Higher Power, and secondly the discipline *to be where one was needed* – sometimes on the streets, sometimes staying at home. Thirdly, it was finding the strength to resist, and rise above, the propaganda of the establishment, the threats and repressive actions of the state as well as the dictates of one's own immediate interests which include such basic things as the preservation of one's job, the need for food, to pay the rent, to send the children to school. All of them also understood that love was not an empty, foolish, sentimental notion, but the power to withstand the urge to retaliate, to force the adversary to come to terms with one's humanity, and thereby recognizing, and challenging, their own inhumanity.

Right through the 1980s we saw what that "mood of religious fervour" meant and what it could accomplish. It meant a determined acknowledgement on the part of ordinary people that first – since this is a struggle for justice and liberation, and God is a God of justice and liberation – God is in this struggle. The themes of the exodus and the liberation of God's people from slavery in Egypt are ancient themes, dear to oppressed people in their understanding of the Bible. The liberating deeds of God were revolutionary deeds, breaking the bonds of oppression and the power of the oppressor and calling God's people to the same deeds of faith.

---

[194] *Op. cit.,* 43-44.
[195] *Op. cit.,* 44 (my emphasis).

What, one wonders, does Lodge think they prayed for at the start of those hopeful, but nonetheless life-threatening, campaigns? What was said in those emotional outpourings of feelings so typical of the black church? Not much different, in fact very much the same, as the sermons preached by religious leaders some thirty years later, in another campaign of the same name, the Defiance Campaign of the 1980s, driven by the United Democratic Front.[196] What did they ask of God if it were not "the strength to love", as Martin Luther King would put it so much later? What did they plead for if not the boldness to face the powerful oppressor, his reprisals, his dogs, his prisons, his guns? What did they pray for if not the courage to face this adversity, to remain strong under pressure, to overcome this evil, to see victory? And what inspired them if not this certain knowledge: that their Lord Jesus had already faced the "powers and principalities" and had shamed, "unclothed" them and overcome them? And that therefore their struggle would not be in vain?

Anyone who has heard a crowd's ringing response to the words of Paul, "If God be for us, who can be against us?" (Romans 8:31, a favourite quote of Archbishop Tutu's), knows what it is that drives oppressed people to their knees and from their knees into the streets to face whatever enemy they have to face. They knew, with Elisha, that even though the enemy seemed strong and numerous, "Those who are with us are more than those who are with them" (2 Kings 6:16). They knew from the Bible that freedom is not cheap, that the price of liberation was high. They understood suffering from their own lives and the incarnation of God in Jesus Christ. They understood the meaning of the Cross, and they knew about giving oneself for the sake of the other, which is indispensable in any struggle for liberation.

When Lodge therefore discovers that during the Campaign, although some speeches were in the "strident tones of Africanism", "more typically" the verbal imagery involved "ideas of sacrifice, martyrdom, the triumph of justice and truth",[197] it does not surprise us at all. J B Marks, anticipating his arrest for breaking his banning order just before the campaign, speaks of his own conviction and to the heart of his supporters when he tells them, "This is the hour now. I am being crucified and I feel the weight of the cross".[198] They understood and responded, and it raised them up to yet another level of preparedness, because his words echoed the words of their Saviour: "If anyone would come after me, he must deny himself and *take up his cross, and follow me*" (Mark 8:34), and again, "Now my heart is troubled, and what shall I say? 'Father save me from this

---

[196] See, for example, Desmond Tutu, *A Voice in the Wilderness* (Johannesburg: Skotaville, 1984); Allan Aubrey Boesak, *Walking on Thorns, Sermons on Christian Obedience* (Geneva: WCC 1984); and AA Boesak, *If This is Treason, I am Guilty* (Grand Rapids: Eerdmans, 1987). There were reasons why "popular church figures" could draw crowds so much larger and more enthusiastic than others, and these reasons did not just have to do with oratory honed on the pulpit.

[197] Lodge, *Black Politics*, 44.

[198] *Ibid.* Even if JB Marks was considered a "syndicalist", his passionate references to the Christian faith showed either his clever understanding of the feelings of his audience, or refer to the ability of black South Africans to combine their socialist passions with their Christian faith, which is not as surprising as it might sound.

hour?' No, it was for this very reason that I came to *this hour*. Father, glorify thy name!" (John 12:27).

This is the biblical language our people have always understood. Not surprisingly, Lodge notes that those words "set the tone for much that was to follow".[199] That is so, not only because so many ANC leaders in those days were committed Christians themselves, but also because the people to whom they were speaking were Christians too, and these words resonated with a deep and unalterable sense of truth. The gospel, in all its fullness, was the inspiration for all of their lives and they could not conceive of a God who was not with them in their struggle, just as they could not conceive of a struggle for justice without this God. They could not conceive of *survival* without this God.

No wonder it was so utterly natural for Albert John Luthuli to say of this struggle, "The road to freedom is via the Cross".[200] These are famous words and Lodge, who knows about this too, recognizes that Luthuli's "religious faith and training brought into his politics a principled belief in non-violence and a remarkable optimism about the ability of whites to undergo a change of heart".[201] Unlike his predecessors and his fellow executive colleagues, we are told, "Luthuli still placed great faith in the moral impact of African struggle". In other words, what he believed in was in the spirituality of politics, in a politics fuelled not by greed for power nor inspired by the cries of human-made philosophies, nor by the dubious exigencies of nationalism, African or otherwise, but by the gospel of Jesus Christ. Luthuli's "remarkable optimism" about white people's ability to change was not just "optimism" but the conviction from the gospel that the love of Jesus Christ and the power of the Holy Spirit can overcome all sin, estrangement and alienation, can crumble the hardest heart, and break down the walls of enmity, whether they be race, class or politics. Faith in the power of Christ to reconcile people is a central tenet in the Christian faith, and has powerful ramifications for politics. But as to how this directed Luthuli and infused a spirit of reconciliation as biblically understood into the campaign - not a word. This despite the fact that Luthuli himself, like other African leaders, did not hide his faith and unashamedly proclaimed it the very basis of their involvement in the struggle for justice. Said Luthuli,

> It became clear to me that the Christian faith was not a private affair without relevance to society. It was, rather, a belief which equipped us in a unique way to meet the challenges of our society. It was a belief which had to be applied to the conditions of our lives; and our many works - they ranged from Sunday School teaching to road building - became meaningful as the outflow of Christian belief.[202]

---

[199] *Ibid.*
[200] Document in: Thomas Karis and Gwendolyn Carter, *From Protest to Challenge,* Vol. II (Stanford: Stanford University Press) 1973, 488, cited in Lodge, *Black Politics,* 61.
[201] *Ibid.*
[202] Albert Luthuli, *Let My People Go!* Cited in Kretzschmar, *op. cit.* 4.

Luthuli was even more explicit about this, explaining his inspiration for his part in the struggle and expressing his desire for the spirituality of struggle and of politics.

> For myself, I am in Congress precisely because I am a Christian. My Christian belief about human society must find expression here and now, and Congress is the spearhead of the real struggle. Some would have the Communists excluded, others would have all non- communists withdraw from Congress. My own urge, because I am a Christian is to get into the thick of the struggle with other Christians, taking my Christianity with me and praying that it may be used to influence for good the character of the resistance.[203]

These are words with the clarity of undiluted wine and it is as powerful a testimony to Christian participation in the struggle as one can hope for. Luthuli's prayer that the Christian participation might be "for the good character of the resistance" is precisely what it purports to be: a spirituality without which the struggle was sure to lose its way. Just as without that spirituality of politics which this book is pleading for, our democracy will stall, sputter and die. It was the realisation that democratic integrity does not lie in laws, plans and policies only, but in the *spirit* which is the driving force behind it all. It was the same Luthuli who set the tone for the struggle then and later, for the people who listened to him and for those of us who followed their lead decades later, when he said, speaking words he knew they understood, responded to, believed, and followed:

> Laws and conditions that tend to debase human personality - a God-given force - be they brought about by the State or other individuals, must be relentlessly opposed in the spirit of defiance shown by St Peter when he said to the rulers of his day, "Shall we obey God or man?[204]

But almost immediately Lodge set out upon a complete and entirely secular interpretation of the South African struggle. Z K Matthews is not mentioned for the Christian leadership he gave both to the struggle and to the World Council of Churches in subsequent years in its search for a "responsible society", but exclusively for his proposal for the summoning of a "national convention at which all groups might be represented to consider our national problems on an all-inclusive basis to draw up a Freedom Charter for the democratic South Africa of the future".[205] Again, what is pertinent is not the prophetic faithfulness of Christians in the struggle, Z K Matthews's foresight that for the sake of the integrity of the struggle, the Kliptown convention had to foreshadow the non-racial society we demanded and fought for, but merely his political functionality.

---

[203] *Op. cit.*, 10.
[204] In Karis and Carter, *op. cit.,* 486.
[205] Lodge, *Black Politics,* 69.

There is one, single, disdainful reference to "the American derived" Black Theology, as one of the "ideological stimuli which helped to distance black students from whites" in the years immediately before the Soweto uprising.[206] Apart from this negative and surprisingly superficial assessment, there is nothing about Black Theology or what impact it might have had on the thinking, and political praxis, of people as an expression of the theology of liberation.

In Lodge and Nasson reference is made to the South African Council of Churches as a "reinforcing factor in the revival of mass resistance … a supporter of militant anti-apartheid activity".[207] But how, and especially why, we are not told, although a simple perusal of the SACC resolutions at its annual conferences would have offered a wealth of historical information. Especially those resolutions dealing with civil disobedience, for example, would have been helpful. Nor are we told what "militant anti-apartheid activity" meant during the days of the state of emergency, at what costs such activity was initiated and maintained, and what inspired those activists to nonetheless continue their resistance. Nothing is said about the non-violent stance of the SACC, and in fact the way that sentence is framed one could as easily surmise that the SACC's "support" of "militant activity" meant support for violence.

The *Kairos Document* is recognized as the "most eloquent expression of the SACC position[208] and exposes the god of the state as anti-Christ, calls for rebellion against unjust laws, and preaches God as the God of the poor and the persecuted who takes sides in the struggle against the powerful and for the poor and powerless.[209] For a discussion of the political consequences of the *Kairos Document* both within the churches and on the ongoing struggle however (it was published only in 1985), one looks in vain in these books.[210]

Two glaring omissions in all these publications must be mentioned, and they are the Defiance Campaign of 1988-1989 and the *Call for Prayer to End Unjust Rule*, 1985.

The Defiance Campaign initiated and guided by the United Democratic Front was one of the most significant political events of the 1980s after, perhaps, the success of the election boycott campaign of 1984. The name itself was intended to call to mind the campaign of the 1950s, and it was much more than just an attempt to show the historical continuation within the tradition of the African National Congress, although that too, was important.

---

[206] *Op. cit.*, 323.
[207] *All, Here and Now*, 112.
[208] Actually the document was initiated by theologians associated with the Institute for Contextual Theology and others not officially linked with the SACC.
[209] *All, Here and Now*, 113.
[210] This whole discussion holds true also for Shaun Johnson (ed.), *South Africa, No Turning Back* (London: David Davies Memorial Institute of International Affairs, 1988), and Martin Murray, *South Africa, Time of Agony, Time of Destiny, The Upsurge of Popular Protest* (London: Verso, 1987). Surprisingly, it is also true of Mokgethi Mothlabi, *The Theory and Practice of Black Resistance to Apartheid, A Social-Ethical Analysis* (Johannesburg: Skotaville Press, 1984).

For me, and for the thousands of Christians who participated in this campaign, the religious fervour that was so fundamental for the Campaign of the fifties was once again the hallmark of our own participation. The campaign to challenge the government by breaking restriction orders, unbanning banned organizations ourselves, desegregating beaches and hospitals (*All God's Beaches for all God's Children!*), organizing marches and demonstrations, embarking on actions of civil disobedience, and generally "making the country ungovernable" through a non-violent revolution, must be seen as a political breakthrough of major proportions. At the international level, the campaign's call for trade and especially financial sanctions was a reflection of the resistance at home. It was intended to break the back of apartheid through sustained, non-violent internal resistance. And in a very real sense, it did. For radical Christians, it was a call in obedience to the gospel to "obey God rather than human beings" (Acts 5:29). It is no wonder that this campaign, like the one in 1952, started with a church service in the AME church in Hazendal, Athlone, near Cape Town.

In spite of the violence that at the time seemed to shake the world, this campaign was a sustained, disciplined, non-violent mass action. And it mostly remained so under the severest provocation. It emerged, most importantly, during the state of emergency designed to prevent any political action, let alone mass demonstrations. It was the state's grim determination to finally bludgeon the people into submission - over 30 000 were detained in the first months following July 1985, 40% of them children under 18 years old. Hundreds died as a result of police or military action, or torture in prison. And yet people somehow found the strength to continue, day after day.

In the 1988-89 report of the Foundation for Peace and Justice, I reported on the Defiance Campaign and spoke about the important elements of the Campaign: its non-violent character and the difference between our situation and that of the civil rights struggle in the US; the question of defying unjust laws; the importance of claiming the moral high ground and the realization of our ideals of non-racialism as seen in the growing participation of whites in the campaign. I ended with what I considered to be "the most important element of this phase of the struggle" namely, "trying to save the soul of the nation". For beyond liberation, freedom and democracy, that was the ultimate goal.

Throughout these times the leadership given by Christian leaders was prominent and our call upon the people was based upon and issued from our faith.[211] The words we spoke then were the words the people also heard from Christian leaders in the ANC, such as Rev. Calata, Professor D D T Jabavu, Albert Luthuli and the many others who took their faith out of the sanctuary into the streets. We were building on firm foundations and our words resonated because the people not only understood - the people *believed*. And their faith was deeply personal and therefore avowedly political. And they knew:

---

[211] Cf., for example, Jim Wallis and Joyce Hollyday (eds.), *Crucible of Fire, The Church Confronts Apartheid* (Maryknoll: Orbis Press, 1989).

God is in the struggle. The political consequences of that faith are awesome, and we have seen the evidence.

"The Call To Prayer" remains *the* turning point for the church in South Africa and the political consequences of our faith in the eighties. I say this not because I think that the challenge of the *Kairos Document* was less radical; far from it. But whereas the *Kairos Document* confronted the churches, the *Call to Prayer* invited the churches, on the basis of their own traditions, to participate in action they knew to be part and parcel of those traditions, namely the prayer for those in government, yet were not prepared to take seriously in the context of racist oppression and theological heresy that apartheid clearly was. The consequences for the churches were therefore greater than with the *Kairos Document,* which we presented not as an invitation to join a particular, and a particularly *ecclesiastical,* act (a prayer service), but as a theological challenge in general regarding the churches' stand on apartheid. It is in the nature of its *particularity* as an act of obedience and confrontation that the real challenge for the churches lay, and it is in the refusal of that *particular* call to obedience and faithfulness in which lay the failure of the churches. This is not the place to discuss those events and their theological and political ramifications fully. Suffice it to say that the call to pray for the downfall of the apartheid government presented the churches with a moment of decision that was quite unprecedented in our history.[212]

There was vicious reaction from the government, the white Establishment press, both Afrikaans and English, and condemnation from the churches, Afrikaans and English speaking. It was a rare moment of singular revelation: the rush of the so-called liberal English press to condemn the maker of the call and defend the government; the solidarity of white interests overriding the bonds of Christian community; and most of all, the power of radical evangelical action and its consequences for South African society, secular and religious. The "Call" split the churches of the SACC, the traditional "anti-apartheid churches", bringing forth the "most convoluted and agonizing statements" from their leadership. At the centre of the debate was the issue of whether the apartheid government was "legitimate" and whether Christians had the right "to pray them out of existence", but the heart of the matter was the *political consequences* for Christians in taking such a stand.[213]

We knew that this represented a moment in which the churches were called to turn from a theology of protest to a theology of resistance, a new form of commitment that knew that statements, resolutions or even the *formal* prayer for the government churches are called to were no longer enough. Charles Villa-Vicencio spells this out clearly. First, the theological rationale asks for more than a false piety which uses prayer as an escape

---

[212] I made the first call in 1978, and then again at the SACC Annual Conference in 1984. See Allan Boesak and Charles Villa-Vicencio (eds.), *When Prayer Makes News* (Philadelphia: Westminster Press, 1986). Also published as *A Call For an End to Unjust Rule* (Edinburgh: St. Andrew Press, 1986), it contains the primary documents chronicling the events, and the furore that followed, both in the churches and in secular society.

[213] Cf. *Call,* Introduction and *passim.*

from political responsibility; second, it is calling for liturgy and prayer that provide a basis for responsible social action, and third, this kind of prayer requires the churches to *engage in a new level of opposition to the state.*[214]

But it is more. It is, says Villa-Vicencio, a moment of truth, a kairos, which unleashes a power "not yet fully realised" by the churches. On the one hand, that is true. The churches themselves, so used to the ineffective blandness of Western theology and the lip-service value of church statements, and so accustomed to the anaemic quietude of their own prayer life, could not fathom the power unleashed by "the fervent prayer of the just". (James 5:16). We were of a people who did believe in the Christian adage that "Prayer changes things". That we not only believed this, but actually *acted* on it, was just too much for churches embarrassed by true evangelical fervour. On the other hand, I believe the church leaders *did* fully realize what that power could do in bringing about the radical changes the church has always prayed for, but never expected in our lifetime. Hence their vehement responses.

> It is a power which, judging from the response to the call to prayer from some institutional church leaders and the white establishment generally, many both within and without the church understand. This power, once unleashed, has something to do with that power against which, scripture tells us, the gates of hell will not prevail. To embrace this power is to take upon ourselves a terrible responsibility, the cost of which not all are able to bear. The political stakes in a country such as South Africa are high. The price being asked of the church is great.[215]

Such are the practical political consequences of the spirituality of struggle politics. Those who choose for the God of justice must "stand where God stands, namely on the side of the poor, the needy and the wronged" as the Belhar Confession of the Uniting Reformed Church in Southern Africa proclaims. Those who have decided to follow Jesus Christ must follow Him "into the streets of this country and into the face of the casspirs and the guns, and the water cannons, and the tear gas … (understanding) that the church's witness in this country today will stand or fall by our faithfulness in confronting the South African government and the evil it persists in doing".[216]

The political ramifications of such a faith that inspires hundreds of thousands of people cannot be ignored. Such was the case of the religion of the slaves, Genovese found, and such was the spirituality of the politics of struggle in South Africa, as it was the driving force behind the struggle for independence in India. This is not a question of pleading for a more or less formal recognition of the role of the church in the struggle. Our point is more direct: there can be no understanding of the struggle itself if this salient fact is ignored.

---

[214] *Op. cit.,* 22.
[215] Cf. Boesak in Wallis and Hollyday, *op. cit.,* 30,31.
[216] *Call,* 22.

It may well be that for some of the leadership and some of their followers it is true that what drove them was "ethnic romanticism and working-class radicalism", and I am certainly not saying that *everyone* who was active in the struggle was a Christian or that there were no other factors, no other sources of inspiration. But for any serious student of history, as John de Gruchy has observed, it is "obvious" that much of the leadership of the black nationalist movement was Christian, and that many of the leaders were ministers within the Christian churches. Their petitions and protests stemmed from Christian convictions. "African nationalism", he says, "depended heavily on educated Christian leadership".[217] The influence of Christian leaders such as Rev. James Calata, Dr A B Xuma and others, whose convictions inspired the struggle from the very beginning, is immeasurable.

To ignore the fact that millions of black people are Christians who take their faith seriously and who have discovered in the biblical story a powerful message of liberation, who believe passionately in God as a God of justice who calls them to seek justice with all their might, is to distort the struggle and is the height of both academic and political dishonesty. It is also a grave insult to those whose faith forms the heart of their life, including their political activity. Why is it so easy for academics to recognize the misuse of the Christian faith by oppressors of all kinds and all times, but they cannot acknowledge the power of the liberating gospel as reclaimed by the oppressed, even if the empirical evidence is there for all to see?

Once more Eugene Genovese makes the point:

> As we are tirelessly reminded these days, the history of Christianity has been strewn with blood, but, as we are rarely reminded, that same history has contributed a body of teaching that has made possible a line of resistance and counterattack.[218]

It is a matter of political and intellectual honesty.

"Apartheid is a Heresy"

In this regard we must raise yet another issue, namely that of the moral basis of apartheid. There were, basically, two reasons why Christian churches, and Christians individually, could play such a significant role in the struggle against apartheid. The first, and most important, was the convictions inherent in radical black Christianity and their political consequences. The other was the claim by the Afrikaner that apartheid could be morally justified as a Christian policy, and the importance of that claim for both the political leadership and their followers.

---

[217] JW de Gruchy, *The Church Struggle in South Africa* (Grand Rapids: Eerdmans, 1979), 48.
[218] Genovese, *Marxism, Christianity and Bias*, 94.

The intimate, interwoven relationship between the National Party and the white Afrikaner churches, and consequently, the relationship between Afrikaner *volk* (nation), Afrikaner nationalism and Afrikaner religion are well documented.[219] Veteran journalist and long-time observer of church and politics in South Africa, JHP Serfontein, mentions that the white Dutch Reformed Church, in the heyday of apartheid, was the biggest church among the ruling white minority (almost 70% of Afrikaans-speaking whites), playing a "special role" in the political, cultural and social life of the Afrikaners, comparable to the role of the Roman Catholic Church in some Latin American and European countries. Religion and the church are "interwoven" in the life of the Afrikaner and therefore of great importance. Most government leaders and Afrikaner politicians "are practising Christians, regular church goers, members of the NGK" who "constantly proclaim their obedience to God, their Christian beliefs, the Christian basis of government policies, and the God-given destiny of the Afrikaner".[220] This makes them "more sensitive than most to charges that (their) actions and racial policies are 'un-Christian' and in conflict with the Word of God".[221]

No wonder then, that observers have recognized that (therefore) "the highly religious orientation of Afrikaner society *all but required a theological basis to rationalize apartheid*".[222] That theological basis was indeed given by the white Reformed churches and became known as "the theology of apartheid", a sophisticated theological construction that went far beyond the rather crude "children of Ham", "mud races" theology so prevalent in the discussions about race in the history of the United States. And it was to become both the moral foundation and the cement that upheld Afrikaner nationalism and its most ambitious and precious spawn, apartheid.

Not only was the policy of apartheid the direct result of the "mission" policies of the white Dutch Reformed Church, the church did more than any other cultural or political body in the creation of apartheid. The role of the church overwhelms that of all other organizations in Afrikaner society in the preparation for and the birth of the apartheid state,[223] and the church was single-handedly responsible for some of the most notorious legislation, like the Group Areas Act, the Immorality Act and the Mixed Marriages Act. It was not without pride that the *Kerkbode*, official mouthpiece of the DR Church, wrote in 1948, after the National Party victory at the polls: "As a church, we have always worked purposefully for the separation of the races. In this regard apartheid can rightfully be called a church policy".[224]

---

[219] See, for example, JHP Serfontein, *Apartheid, Change and the NG Kerk* (Emmarentia: Taurus Press, 1982); Boesak: *Farewell to Innocence*, and Boesak, *Black and Reformed* (Maryknoll: Orbis, 1984); J Kinghorn (ed.) *Die NG Kerk en Apartheid* (Johannesburg, 1986).

[220] *Apartheid, Change and the NG Kerk*, 1.

[221] *Op. cit.*, 1, 2.

[222] Douglas Johnston, "The Churches and Apartheid in South Africa", in: Johnston and Cynthia Sampson (eds.), *Religion, the Missing Dimension of Statecraft* (New York: Oxford University Press, 1994).

[223] DP Botha, "Church and Kingdom in South Africa", in M Nash (ed.), *Your Kingdom Come* (Johannesburg: SACC, 1981).

[224] *Kerkbode*, September 22, 1948, 664-665.

Far more than merely a political philosophy and a socio-economic programme, apartheid became "an all-embracing, soteriologically loaded" philosophy,[225] underpinned by a theological rationale second to none.[226] As such it became a pseudo-gospel challenging the authority of the true gospel in the lives of the church and believers alike. As such, too, it was to function as a formidable cover for the atrocities of apartheid and a haven for the conscience of white South Africa, where their innocence could be protected. But it was, simultaneously, their Achilles heel, because apartheid's call on the gospel opened it up to, and made it vulnerable to, the critique of the gospel. The more they misused the Bible to bolster their theological and political construction, the more this construction was vulnerable to the dynamic power of the Bible to blow it apart. And this is what Christians who took the Bible seriously understood so well, as the devastating critique of apartheid theology by Douglas Bax so conclusively shows.[227]

The attack on the moral and theological foundations of apartheid thus had a multiple effect. It was an attempt to liberate the gospel and the Christian faith from the chains of apartheid abuse, but at the same time it stripped apartheid of the cloak of respectability. The erosion of the moral base of apartheid did have a devastating impact on the Afrikaner establishment's ability to continue to believe in apartheid, and it undermined their enthusiasm to defend it. That in turn opened cracks in the granite wall which would eventually render that wall incapable of holding back the flood.

This much was acknowledged by H W van der Merwe, who ascribed the "decline of apartheid" in no small measure to the "theological retraction" forced upon the white Dutch Reformed Church by persistent attacks on, and eventual victory over, the moral and theological basis of apartheid.[228]

Exposing the theology of apartheid as unbiblical, a pseudo-gospel and idolatry, proving conclusively that its claims on the Calvinist Reformed tradition were false, and finally to persuade the worldwide ecumenical community that apartheid ought to be declared a sin and its theological and moral justification a heresy, was the dynamite that did not in and of itself alone bring the system down, but rendered it forever vulnerable and unstable. What used to be a matter of pride in obedience to God, became a shame, not just in the eyes of the world, but in the hearts and minds of more and more Afrikaners themselves. Without it the struggle to conquer apartheid would have taken much longer. Afrikaners themselves knew this and implicitly acknowledged it. In the words of Dr

---

[225] Botha, "Church and Kingdom".

[226] See e.g. Boesak, *Farewell;* "Black and Reformed: Contradiction or Challenge", in Boesak, *Black and Reformed* (Maryknoll: Orbis, 1984).

[227] Douglas Bax, "The Bible and Apartheid", in: *Apartheid is a Heresy,* C. Villa-Vicencio and J W de Gruchy (eds.) (Cape Town: David Philip, 1983), 112-143.

[228] Hendrik van der Merwe, *Pursuing Justice and Peace in South Africa* (London: Routledge Press, 1989) argued this forcefully, but nonetheless found it necessary at the time to issue a warning: "While the decline of apartheid can be attributed in large part to the erosion of its moral and theological bases, this development should not necessarily be seen as a growth of altruism amongst whites". (p. 51). He might have been disappointed that the intellectual and political realisation of the end of apartheid did not lead to a change of heart towards black people.

Andries Treurnicht, former church leader of the Dutch Reformed Church, and eloquent spokesperson for the Far Right,

> I know of no other policy as moral, as responsible to Scripture, as the policy of separate development ... If the ... Christian Afrikaner can be convinced that there are no principles or biblical foundations for this policy of separate development, it is but a step to the conviction that it is un-Christian. And if we believe it is un-Christian or immoral, it is our obligation to fight it.[229]

And this is exactly what happened. When the moral foundations of apartheid and its theological pretensions were stripped away, all that was left was a naked lust for power, utter rapaciousness and greed, and the exposed nerves of an isolated people with a siege mentality; a fearful, tortured conscience, and guns. To be sure, not many actually turned around and *fought* it, but most had lost the will to *defend* it.[230] As a consequence almost none were willing to still die for it. And it remains true that this development proved to be a blessing for many in the DR churches and in the Afrikaner community in general, and released them to be far more courageous in speaking out than they otherwise would have been, perhaps because what we were able to do had been the convictions of their heart for years anyway.

The decision of the World Alliance of Reformed Churches in 1982 to declare apartheid a heresy was a theological decision, but the political implications were vast. "This is not an academic issue", says John de Gruchy, "but one of great practical significance. It is fundamental to the struggle against apartheid because it destroys any claim that it has a Christian basis. It is, in other words, not unrelated to the struggle for economic justice, the struggle between rich and poor, which many regard as the primary issue whether in South Africa itself or in the world as a whole.[231]

When one hears politicians like President Thabo Mbeki today speak of the inequalities within the worlds of the rich and the poor as a new, "global apartheid", one realises just how prophetic those words of de Gruchy had been. Villa-Vicencio says in regard to the Belhar Confession of the (then) Dutch Reformed Mission Church, which flowed out of the apartheid theology debate: "This statement is rich with political implications", and the churches would now have to spell out what that means.

---

[229] A P Treurnicht, *Credo van 'n Afrikaner* (Cape town: NG Kerk Uitgewers, 1975), cited in C Villa-Vicencio, "An All-pervading heresy" in: Charles Villa-Vicencio and John de Gruchy (eds.), *Apartheid is a Heresy*, 59-60.

[230] The tortuous debates in the white Dutch Reformed churches, followed by dissension and acrimony in their ranks, large-scale desertions and finally the break-away and establishment of the *Afrikaanse Protestantse Kerk,* are just some signs of this. The political consequences of these upheavals were, and continue to be, enormous, as is their psychological impact. But one must not try to deny, or belittle, the positive impact this has had on many in the DR Church.

[231] De Gruchy, "Toward a Confessing Church", in: *Apartheid is a Heresy*, 85.

> They will presumably have to say, in addition to much else, that any political or economic system which excludes anyone from full participation in any aspect of it on the grounds of race is morally unacceptable. When one takes the context of the Ottawa resolution into account and certainly when one reads the Confession of Faith of the N G Mission Church within the reality of the prevailing political situation in South Africa, one is quite justified in interpreting these pronouncements to advocate a vote for every person in one political system in this country.[232]

But the Belhar Confession concludes with words that echo the conviction of the Reformed tradition from Calvin to Beza and from John Knox to the Westminster Presbyterians, and show how conscious the synod was of the political context in which it spoke, even as these words portray simultaneously the historic continuity, the universal context and the prophetic understanding which distinguish a confession as a statement of faith from a declaration reflecting the politics of the day:

> We believe that in obedience to Jesus Christ, its only Head, the church is called to confess *and do all this, even though authorities and laws forbid them, and even though punishment and suffering be the consequence.* Jesus is Lord.[233]

It is these political consequences which Christians took seriously when they prayed and worshipped, and then took to the streets to demand their political rights and stake their claim on the land of their birth. It is this faith they took seriously when they faced the might of the apartheid military apparatus in the streets of their townships, when they withstood the guns, the dogs, the teargas, the torture in the prisons. It is not so much the cries of "*Amandla!*" which uplifted them; much less the philosophies of Marx and Lenin or the vague ideals of "democracy" or the "romanticism of working-class radicalism", whatever that may mean. It was not the fiery speeches of exiled leaders, whom they never heard and scarcely knew. (In truth, we find the ease with which these erstwhile Marxists have left their slogans behind now that they are in power and in sight of wealth unusually instructive.) It was for many thousands of activists the radicalism of the gospel which they had reclaimed from the stranglehold of apartheid at so high a price; a gospel which spoke of a God who identified with their struggle, a God whose resolute demands are for justice, liberation and peace.

It was this faith that inspired them when they marched and demonstrated and confronted an evil regime, and died in their hundreds, and in so doing gave renewed life to Luthuli's conviction that "the road to freedom is via the Cross". And because they were not afraid to bear that cross, they brought freedom to their country. That is a legacy this country and its people can ill afford to ignore, or squander, or deny. It is, I think, less than honest, and more than just a little arrogant, to now act, and expect of us to accept,

---

[232] *Op. cit.,* 70.
[233] Emphasis mine.

that apartheid was brought down by the armed struggle, F W de Klerk's *Realpolitik* and "Madiba magic".

"My Power and the Strength of my Own Hand ..."

For Christians all this is of much more than mere academic interest. Nor is it a question of being "recognized" by the state, now that it is "pay back time". For us it is a question of recognizing the presence and the power of God in history, and the obedient response of God's people to that power. It is, in other words, a question of *remembering*. It has nothing to do with wanting kudos for the church. It has everything to do with "the soul of the nation". The church lives, not by the glory of national achievement, nor by the approval or recognition of earthly powers, but in remembrance of the mighty deeds of God. This is the message of Deuteronomy 8, where Israel is reminded of the great liberating deeds of God for Israel's sake. Now that slavery has come to an end, the yoke of Egypt broken, the Red Sea and the Jordan crossed and the wilderness a thing of the past; now that there is prosperity and new-found wealth, the danger of forgetting the suffering in Egypt and the liberation from that suffering is great. "When you have eaten your fill and have built fine houses and live in them, and when your herds and flocks have multiplied, then do not exalt yourself, forgetting the LORD your God, who brought you out of the land of Egypt, out of the house of slavery, who led you through the great and terrible wilderness ... Do not say to yourself, my power and the might of my own hand have gotten me this wealth. But remember..." (8:12-17).

That is indeed the great temptation, and it is the calling of the church to make sure that the nation does not forget. For remembering where we have come from (the house of slavery and apartheid), who we were (enslaved and unfree) and who brought us where we are now (the God of liberation) is the surest way, the *only* way, of preventing us from falling into the trap of a new idolatry. Remembering the presence of God in the struggle will also help us to remember those closest to the heart of God, of whom Israel in that same Deuteronomy is so tirelessly reminded: the poor, the weak, the voiceless and the powerless, the needy, the widows and orphans, the stranger; those with "no name in the streets". To remember God is to remember those who are now, after liberation, so casually excluded from the secular covenant between the power elites in South Africa, whose gratification is now held up as the salvation of the poor. That is not a "new social contract", as we are told. It is a covenant with death.

But the church must make sure the nation does not forget for yet another reason. It was the extraordinary moral courage of South Africa's oppressed people that gripped the imagination of the world through all the decades of struggle. But what really fired the imagination of the peoples of the world was the even more extraordinary magnanimity of South Africa's people when they succeeded in their largely peaceful transformation from apartheid to democracy. Nelson Mandela called for tolerance, forgiveness and reconciliation. And the surprising thing is, the people responded. In the light of the horrific history of apartheid, this was a most astonishing thing.

How did South Africa's oppressed people do it, and where did Mr Mandela find the courage (the gall, some might say) to call upon them thus? He could, and he did, because Mandela knew he could draw from the deep well of spirituality from which his people have drunk for so long. He himself had *heard* AB Xuma, Albert Luthuli and ZK Matthews. He knew them personally. He was there at the time of the Defiance Campaign and saw with his own eyes the strength the people derived from their faith. He knows what and Who inspired them to take those risks, face those dangers, make those sacrifices. That is why his language echoed so much the language of the church: forgiveness, reconciliation, peace. Mandela, whether he acknowledges this or not, also knew what was at the heart of the struggle as it continued for all those twenty-seven years he sat in prison.

President Mandela's confidence was not misplaced. After all, the basic tenets of the struggle have been those very gospel themes Mandela called upon. Over and over again, spiritual leaders exhorted the people to remember that our struggle was not just for ourselves, but for whites also: "We are involved in the black liberation struggle" Desmond Tutu said, "because we are also deeply concerned for white liberation. The white man will never be free until the black man is wholly free".[234] The same theme was echoed at the launch of the United Democratic Front in Cape Town in August 1983.[235] And in this, too, we called not only on our faith but on our memory, echoing Dr AB Xuma when, in 1930, in an address to black and white Christian Student Associations, he pleaded for "bridging the gap between white and black in South Africa". "If the black man sinks," he said, "he will inevitably take the white man down".[236]

Reconciliation was seen, not as a clever trick to allay the fears of whites, or a tactic so as not to alarm conservative blacks, but as an indispensable end of the struggle. And it was linked intrinsically to that other great theme, namely non-racialism:

> We, therefore, must not allow our anger over apartheid to become the basis for blind hatred of all whites. Let us not build our struggle upon hatred, let us not hope for revenge. Let us even now, seek to lay the foundations for reconciliation between whites and blacks in this country by working together, praying together, struggling together for justice … The nature of our struggle for liberation cannot be determined by one's skin colour but rather by one's commitment to justice, peace and human liberation.

[234] As quoted by Donald Johnston, *op. cit.,* 190. This was a constant theme right through the struggle.
[235] "The time has come for white South Africans to realize that their destiny is inextricably bound up with our destiny, and that they shall never be free until we are free. How happy I am that so many of our white brothers and sisters are saying this by their presence here today". (Allan Boesak, in: *Black and Reformed,* 171).
[236] Karis and Carter, *From Protest to Challenge,* Vol. I, 218.

> In the final analysis, judgment will be made not in terms of whiteness or blackness, whatever the ideological content of those words may be today. But in terms of the persistent faithfulness to which we are called in this struggle.[237]

President Mandela had heard from us that the struggle is not just about victory, or freedom, and certainly not about "turning the tables"; it is also about "a movement deeper into God" (Tutu). He knew that we understood that it was about sacrifice. "So we find ourselves in a vulnerable situation" said Frank Chikane, "where we cannot do otherwise but, in fact, offer ourselves for sacrifice. I don't believe we as a church can now avoid the cross ..". And then, in an echo of Albert Luthuli: "For us to go into victory, we will have to go through the cross. Through that experience of the cross, I believe the system is going to be put down ..."[238]

It is this legacy of spirituality that Nelson Mandela could call upon, and which gave him confidence that his call would be heeded, even by those angry young people who, only a short time before, were exhorted to call for the death of whites as they toyi-toyed down the streets of the townships. The "Kill the Boer, kill the farmer" chant was a transparent, if emotionally effective, effort to reclaim some authority for the armed struggle. But Mandela, and with him the leadership, knew that when it came right down to it, they could not depend or call upon these atavistic slogans. They had to turn to something deeper, more meaningful and truthful, more humane; more expressive of the future than in tune with the past. And they found it in the spirituality of the struggle. If this were not so, if this were not the innermost traditions of struggle, there would have been nothing Mr Mandela could have hoped for or appealed to. Certainly, nothing in the legacy of Marxist-Leninist ideology could ever have prepared our people for the call for reconciliation, which for the Christian is rooted in God's reconciling work in Jesus Christ, who "emptied himself", and "taking the form of a slave, humbled himself, and became obedient to the point of death ..". (Phil. 2).

On the contrary, these are the very things Marxism despises. Karl Marx violently rejected Christian love, Christian social principles and poured scorn on the Christian concepts of love, forgiveness and justice. Christianity has done no good because it moves at a level of "fantasy" and "projection", which results only in justifying things as they are rather than changing them. Christian justice is warped, because even while "speaking of justice they preach cowardice, self-abasement, resignation, submission, and humility", while what the proletariat really needs is none of these, but "courage, pride, and independence, even more than it needs daily bread".[239] No, it is not in the legacy of Marx, nor in the radically atheistic, working-class consciousness of the black

---

[237] Boesak, *Black and Reformed*, 174.
[238] In Wallis and Hollyday, *Crucible of Fire*, 77.
[239] Karl Marx, "*The Communism of the Rheinisher Beobachter*" in Karl Marx and Friedrich Engels, *Werke*, Vol. 4 (Berlin: Dietz Verlag, 1959 – 1977), 200.

proletariat that the political leadership of Black South Africa found the astonishing willingness of South Africa's people to rise above themselves and deny their most basic human instincts for revenge and bitter retribution, and gave the ANC the opportunity to move so quickly into the seats of power. No, they found it in the rich memory of the powerful acts of God, in the truth of the prophets, in the life, death and resurrection of Jesus, and the joy of discipleship.

The people rejected the courage Marx spoke of for the strength that lies in once again giving themselves for the sake of others, willing to once again put on hold their own legitimate aspirations, deferring once again their dreams of justice, postponing once again their justly deserved rewards, forgetting once again their own sacrifices, for the sake of their trust in what they believed to be the greater good, thereby rising to a courage far greater than Marx ever dreamt of. By expecting, and accepting this, Mr Mandela and the ANC have done what should be done only sparingly and with great trepidation: they have taken upon themselves the burden of asking too much of people who have already given too much, and yet getting it. This trust dare not be betrayed. It is at our peril that our political leaders now ignore this truth, and act as if our transformation is the result of human effort only, stemming from our "working-class radicalism", our astuteness at the power-play of political compromise, and depending upon what the media call "Madiba Magic". It is a sin as heavy as the burdens our people are asked to continue to carry, and it will "cry to heaven" as surely as did the sin of Sodom and Gomorrah and the blood of Abel.

So the remarkable transformation of South Africa and the response which made Nelson Mandela an icon in the rest of the world are directly rooted in the tradition of spirituality which in turn is rooted in the faith of the oppressed people of South Africa. And *this* is what we are called to remember. We must not allow the government to forget, just as we cannot allow the church to forget. For if the spirituality of our struggle does not become the spirituality of our politics, we are doomed, for then we deny the mighty acts of liberation of God and we come to rely on the fickleness of our own devices. It is then that we fall into the trap Yahweh warns the people of Israel against: "It is *my* arm, *my* power, *my* hand ..."

In his search for the "African soul" through the "African Renaissance" President Thabo Mbeki has not once taken this history seriously. He sublimely sidesteps it as if it does not exist. Not once does he seriously consider our spirituality, both as historical legacy, present reality and hope for the future. Although this is not to say that he does not suspect that something deeper is at work here as he marvels at the ability of South Africa's oppressed people to respond to the call for reconciliation:

> Inspired by a wonderful wisdom, our people have fully grasped the concepts of reconciliation, nation-building and national unity. They have understood that unless we make a determined and sustained effort to achieve these objectives, we would both destroy the monuments of the magnificence of the human spirit and remove the conditions which enable us to build the new South Africa.[240]

But Mbeki leaves us somewhat confused. On the one hand, he knows that this wisdom (whose source he does not contemplate) is not at all as obvious or inherent as it may seem. "It is true," he admits, "that all this did not come about as the result of some spectacularly inherent wisdom of the people of South Africa".[241] Which begs the obvious question. But then, quite strangely, Mbeki ascribes the "South African miracle" to "the result of a set of historical circumstances which, in reality, left us all with no choice but to find a commonly acceptable settlement". So the "wonderful wisdom" of the people is the result of no more than "historical circumstances" which "left us no choice". But if "all this" is no more than the outcome of historical determination, the unavoidable result of having no choices, where is the "miracle" Mbeki himself repeatedly speaks of and South Africans proudly trumpet around the world? Historical determination needs no vision, as Mbeki calls upon his audience to have.[242] Indeed, historical determination negates the vision. It denies also the intense *spiritual* quality of the effort to forgive one's oppressor and to live in reconciliation with them. Historical determination does not move a people already burdened beyond belief to perform yet "more miracles". Yet this is exactly what Mbeki asks:

> As South Africans, we are called upon to perform new miracles. The miracles I speak of have nothing to do with the world of mystics or the supernatural. They are about the need for us to draw on the resources which enabled us to maintain our humour during the brutal years of the apartheid tyranny. *They are about the spirit which inspired us to be willing to sacrifice everything for the common good.*[243]

That is precisely the point we are trying to make. Here speaks a man amazingly out of touch with the spiritual traditions of his own people, and Mr Mbeki cannot have his cake and eat it too. What resources, what "spirit" is he talking of? What is it that moves people to sacrifice (his word) everything for an undefined "common good"? Has he forgotten what our people themselves thought what had sustained us through all these many years of trial and tribulation? Has he forgotten the great Sol Plaatjie's confession from 1916, that "The only thing that stands between us and despair is the thought that

---

[240] Thabo Mbeki, *Africa – the time has come,* 41.
[241] *Op. cit.,* 209.
[242] *Op. cit.,* 41.
[243] *Op. cit.,* 150.

Heaven has not yet failed us"?[244] Or that Meshach Pelem, the Bantu Union president in the Cape, in his 1919 presidential address reminded his comrades that our people were putting our struggle on "…an entirely new basis, after the principles which all faithful Christians realize are enunciated by the Lord Jesus Christ", and that he ended his speech by exhorting them to call upon their faith in a living, just God in their struggle. "In spite of our difficulties" he told them, "the time is not far distant when the poetic vision shall be realized". That vision he found in the words of the well-known hymn: "O Thou on Whom the nations wait … God, the Mighty and the just, whom all men must obey …"[245] Whatever is pretended today, *these* are undeniably the wells from which we as a people have drunk.

I contend that what amazes Mr Mbeki, and the world here, is a deeply *spiritual* force whose source is God, who enables us, against all odds and our own natural responses and desires, against the very dictates of our country's history, transcending the pain and the anger, to rise above ourselves, to seek reconciliation instead of revenge, to forgive as our heavenly Parent forgives us. These are undeniable, deeply-rooted Christian values that cannot be made to disappear by waving the magic wand of secular sacramentalism that South African politicians have become so adept at doing. Besides, Christians know that the "magnificence of the human spirit" which so enraptures Mr Mbeki is not nearly so obvious as he seems to believe. Human nature is selfish and self-centred, tends toward evil rather than good, is tainted by sin. It is not in our nature to forgive and to live in peace with others, especially those who have done us great harm. It is only when we are being enabled by something other, and greater, than ourselves, when we are able to reach deeper than merely into ourselves, that we attain those heights. What is good in us has to be drawn out, called forth, as it were. In other words, Christians would say, we need conversion, we need the liberating love and the enabling power of the Holy Spirit to come to confession, forgiveness, reconciliation and deeds of justice and love.

In his final "State of the Nation" address before Parliament on February 5th 1999, the year of the retirement of this remarkable man, Mr Mandela too did not give even a hint that the nation owes a single thing to this tradition of radical Christianity which helped secure both our struggle and its "miraculous" outcome. His reference to the African Renaissance was also in terms of "the rediscovery of our soul", which he described as "respect for life", the assertion of "our African identity" and, rather incongruously I thought, "making of our schools communities of learning".[246] By that one must presume that he, like the President, seeks a revival of Africa's intellectual prowess. The same is true of the speech Mandela gave in acceptance of the World Methodist Conference's Peace Award in October 2000.

---

[244] In Karis and Carter, *op. cit.,* Vol. I, 137.
[245] *Op. cit.,* 103.
[246] It might strike many as ironic that Mr Mandela speaks of the "RDP of the soul", while the Reconstruction and Development Programme, with its real possibilities for socio-economic impact on the lives of the nation, was the first government programme to be abandoned by his government.

And before the "Parliament of World Religions" which held its assembly in Cape Town in December 1999, Mr Mandela again spoke of the "contribution" of the church to the struggle. And again, he could not go farther than express appreciation for the education church-run schools gave leaders of the struggle without which he "would not be where I am today". This is a decidedly thin analysis of the role of religious faith in the struggle, and holds for leaders of Mr Mandela's generation only. Church-run schools, with few exceptions, were quickly phased out by the apartheid government in order to solidify the ideological supremacy of apartheid in the educational system of South Africa. Of the kind of admission made by Luthuli, for example, we hear nothing. This too, is a further step in the direction of the process of unremembering. To be magnanimous towards one's enemies is one thing. To deny God the glory is quite another.

I cannot say it clearly enough. As a nation we will live to regret this process. One must therefore be critical about the church's willingness to allow the government to appropriate the language of the church without the church's demanding that those words be filled with the biblical content they must have in order not to become mere ideological tools in much the same way as they had in the mouths of the apostles of apartheid. One must be critical of the church's lack of response when the government insists on speaking of "poverty", while we are called to present ourselves and the government with the *human reality*, and what Latin American theologian Hugo Assmann has called "the political face", of the poor. It is not enough for the government to call upon the church to "create a moral climate" to help in the fight against crime and corruption, as our political leaders have repeatedly done, while at the same time denying the church the critical space for prophetic watchfulness. And it is tragic that the church apparently expects the government to willingly *give* it that space. If the church does not *claim* that space, it will never be given.

"And Then Sunday Happens ..."

When forgetfulness is held before the nation as a patriotic virtue, and unremembering a proud achievement of the democratic revolution, it is the task of the church to call the people to an act of remembrance, and that act of remembrance may well become an act of resistance. Without the church's prophetic memory, our strength to continue to seek justice and peace will be lost; our icons, all those brave men and women and children who sacrificed their lives, will become idols; the creative fantasy with which we saw such marvellous visions will turn into the stultified utopias we have seen come and go with such depressing regularity. Without this active remembering our renaissance will remain empty and meaningless, because it might become a reawakening not rooted in our resurrection. We will merely awaken from death into death.

This is important, for when Luthuli speaks of the freedom that comes via the cross, and Chikane says that victory comes *through* the cross, they are really speaking of the resurrection, in which is rooted the final hope of the believer. We know that on the road to freedom there will be suffering, and pain and death, but we are already rejoicing in hope, for Good Friday is followed by Easter Sunday, and when Christ is raised up it is the final victory over death. That hope, and the joy it brings, was a constant fire in the hearts of our people, and burned brighter than the crucible of fire we had to enter every day. "Our cries and our joys and our bewilderments - all of those are taken up in this tremendous offering of our Lord and Saviour Jesus Christ ... Nothing can be more hopeless than Good Friday; but then Sunday happens".[247]

The resurrection of Christ is God's insurrection, God's *apanastasia*, God's rebellion against sin, inhumanity, death and destruction. It is God's rebellion against our resignation, our need for compromise with evil, and our tendency towards despair and hopelessness, against our willingness to sell God's dreams for God's people to the highest bidder in the name of "realism".

The open tomb is the surest guarantee against the enclosure of our soul, against the imprisonment of our spirit, against the interment of our hopes, which, if they remain in the grave of our own lostness, will surely and irrevocably be lost. The emptiness of the grave is the divine reversal of the emptiness of human history, re-creating it from a space of hopeless helplessness to the arena of God's life-giving power. To be raised with Jesus is to join God in that revolt against the forces of evil, whoever they may be and in whatever guise they may appear. And that is the rebellion the church is called to join, and at times it may be quite different from the rebellion Mr Mbeki has in mind. We join the rebellion for the African Renaissance *because of this rebellion.* That is whence we derive both our courage, our vision and our prophetic faithfulness. And this too, we have always known:

> South Africa belongs to all its people. This is a basic truth to which we must cling tenaciously now and in the future. This country is our country. Its future is not safe in the hands of people, white or black, who despise democracy, and trample on the rights of the people. Its future is not safe in the hands of people, black or white, who, to build their empires, depend upon economic exploitation and human degradation Its future is not safe in the hands of people, black or white, who need the flimsy and deceitful cloak of racial superiority to cover the nakedness of their racism. Its future is not safe in the hands of people, white or black, who seek to secure their unjustly required positions of privilege by repressing violently the weak, the exploited and the needy. Its future is not safe in the hands of people, white or black, who put their faith simply in the madness of growing militarism. For the sake of our country and our children, therefore, whether you be white or black, resist those people, whether they be white or black.[248]

There can be no compromise on this.

---

[247] Desmond Tutu in Wallis and Hollyday, *Crucible of Fire,* 69.
[248] Cf. Boesak, *Black and Reformed,* 175.

For all these reasons Christians must challenge the remaking of history in the thinking of academics as well as in the words and policies of politicians. Unremembering is not an innocent lapse of fact, nor is it a temporary amnesia from which the nation will in time recover. Without remembering we will deny the little people of God their true place in history, we will belittle their sacrifices, for their blood will have no binding call on our conscience, but will have merely served the rites of sacralised propaganda, "watering the tree of freedom" of which only the powerful will eat the fruit. Unremembering will deny their faith and it will replace Yahweh with idols of our own making, and as a nation we will repeat the folly of Israel:

> *"They exchanged the glory of God for the image of an ox that eats grass. They forgot God, their Saviour, who had done great things in Egypt, wondrous works in the land of Ham, and awesome deeds by the Red Sea".* (Ps 106:20-22)

We will deny the people not only the truths from their past, but also their hope for the future, for unremembering burdens us with a closed, pre-determined history from which we can never learn nor draw inspiration. American church historian Eldon Ernst speaks of the study of history as a "mind-blowing and heart-wrenching experience". Without the recognition that people of faith can, and did, "unleash forces that help to overcome evil in the world", history is empty, and ceases to be a source of hope. What Eldon Ernst says about the history of American Social Christianity is equally true for South Africa. Lessons from history can help us to retain that hope,

> But without something of [Martin Luther] King's "cosmic companionship", something of [Dorothy] Day's sense that "Christ is with us today", and something of [Walter] Rauschenbusch's experience that "our consciousness of God is the spiritual counterpart of our social consciousness", hope finally might elude us. Do not we Christians believe that the time between Christmas and Easter - a time already past yet a time that still happens in history until the end of time - provides us with the realistic courage, the "strength to love" and the idealistic hope to persevere in social ministry and mission?[249]

These are the roots of South African (black) politics and the deepest source of our spirituality of struggle. The mess of potage of secular ideologies or the accidents of historical pre-determination are too cheap a price to pay for an experience so dearly gained, sacrifices so willingly and painfully made, a faith so wondrously wrested from those who sought to betray it by using it as a tool for our destruction. Again, this is not open to compromise. It may well be that reclaiming, regaining and celebrating our memory, yet another conscious act of remembering, may entail yet another struggle. But our new democracy is nothing if it is not rooted in the memory of our people. Neither is it an end in itself. The end remains the total freedom of our all people

---

[249] In a personal communication to his students and to the writer.

and the glory of God. "We still have a mission", Robert Sobukwe reminded us, in a strong speech at his graduation ceremony, which today rings as true as it did then, "a nation to build, we have a God to glorify, a contribution to make towards the blessing of mankind".[250] And like Albert Luthuli, we are called to "pray to the Almighty to strengthen (our) resolve … (in) striving, for the sake of the good name of our beloved country … to make it a true democracy and a true union in form and in spirit, of all the communities in the land".[251]

This unashamedly religious bent, this incorrigible faith, this search for the glory of God in politics, the unshakable belief that the "handle that turns the wheels of the universe is in the hand of God" and because of that hand "a new world is about to be begotten", as expressed by Rev. James Calata, president of the Cape African Congress in 1938,[252] is not just the fancy of one or two persons who happened to be leaders in the struggle for justice. It lies deeply rooted in the very soul of African people. It is indelibly written by every step of defiance, every march in protest, in every blow struck for freedom, by every single drop of blood shed for liberty. To search for *that* soul, and in the process seeking to cut out *that* memory, is to re-create a mutilated African. Our efforts will fail. Thus, to paraphrase African-American theologian Gayraud Wilmore: black pride, black power, African nationalism and the struggle for black freedom, dignity and the African soul, had no past without the religious faith of African people and the prophetic church, and without them it may well have no enduring and meaningful future.

---

[250] In Karis and Carter, *From Protest to Challenge,* Vol. II, 332.
[251] *Op. cit.,* 489.
[252] Karis and Carter, Vol. II, 131.

CHAPTER FIVE

CRITICAL SOLIDARITY?
The Role of the Church in post–apartheid South Africa

The Incarnation of God

A local church newspaper informs me that in early 2004 Finance Minister Trevor Manuel had occasion to speak to a gathering of church leaders. In that address the Minister expressed his disquiet at the inactive role of the church after 1994. "What worries me the most of the church in the past ten years", Trevor Manuel confesses, "is that it became silent. The challenge to the church for the next ten years is to incarnate God in the context of South Africa".[253] Trevor Manuel is one of the very few Cabinet members who knows what he is saying when he speaks of the role of the church in the struggle. He knows how the church led, inspired, guided our people during those difficult decades. He knows, too, that the presence and active participation of the church brought to the struggle a spirituality that gave it a unique quality without which our struggle, and its outcome, would have been very different. He knows that the church's role was a prophetic one, challenging the might of the apartheid state in all its forms; a kingly one, in holding before the government and the people the demands of the Kingdom of God, holding before the people as well the unshakeability and irreversibility of the dream of God for our liberation during the darkest hours; and a priestly one, in which we lived, strived, struggled, bled, suffered and hoped with our people, knowing always that the God of justice is with us. And that that God shall call us to account. Therefore he hopefully knows what he is saying and what to expect if the church does rise up in obedience to God in South Africa today.

I have heard the Minister clearly, and with deep appreciation. Indeed, his concern is shared by a great many of us in the churches today. In this chapter we shall endeavour, within the framework of the above, give a response to the Minister's challenge and desire. I, too, long for the church to become again what we were, with the same humility and passion, the same commitment and obedience to God, the same deep longing to discover once again the meaning in democratic South Africa today of the portentous words of Mr Manuel: to "incarnate God in the context of South Africa".

In order to give our discussion a better contextual understanding, a short historical excursion is necessary. From the founding of modern South Africa, the Christian church was destined to play a significant role, for good or ill. The church came to South Africa

---

[253] This remark I found in *Helderstem,* monthly journal of the Dutch Reformed Church Helderberg, Somerset West, No. 8, September 2004, 3.

very much part and parcel of the colonialist project and its role was more or less that of the established churches in Europe. The church served as the spiritual counterpart of the state, a state that very much saw itself as "Christian" for which the theology of "throne and altar" was natural. As the church of the colonists, it was the spiritual home of those who brought light to this dark continent, and the conquest of the land and its peoples was as much a Christian endeavour as the conquest of the African soul. In fact, the colonial victories were God's victories, and the land, and the wealth within it, were just as easily seen as a right, a gift and a reward: God's recompense for a pioneering people who brought with them the Gospel of salvation for the savages of a dark continent, and who were, in fact, God's own people. In the words of Cecil John Rhodes, "God's ideal type, his own Anglo-Saxon race".[254]

There was, therefore, no thought of a "prophetic" calling, no "critical distance" from the state, and no critical presence of the church in society. The church identified wholly with the colonial project and could not conceive of a vision divorced from the vision of the imperial power, whether that vision was expressed by Jan van Riebeeck or Cecil John Rhodes, Willem Adriaan van der Stel, or Lord Charles Somerset. The criminal appropriation of the land, the genocide of the Khoi and the San, the destruction of whole cultures and the enslavement of people, indigenous and imported, all this was not only permissible; it was unavoidable, absolutely necessary for the colonial project, and therefore the will of God.

In the early history of colonial South Africa, therefore, the prophetic instance was created, not by the institutional, established church, but by the Christian missionary societies, or rather, by their representatives in South Africa. More specifically we will have to think here of the London Missionary Society and the names of James Reed, Dr Robert Moffat, Dr Johannes van der Kemp and especially Dr John Philip. They, who worked among the indigenous people of South Africa, were the first to recognize both the inhumanity of the system of slavery and its dehumanising impact upon the people who were its victims. They were the first, too, to recognize the racism of South African society for the evil it was. And it was from them that the prophetic critique came, not from the established churches, who continued to find biblical justification for slavery and South African society's racism.[255]

With this, it seems that a pattern was set that would emerge again and again in South Africa's history: not the established church as an institution, but the church as a *prophetic minority* would acknowledge itself compelled and convicted by the gospel to create the prophetic instance, and challenge society in terms of the radical claims of the gospel. As it is, the abolition of slavery (as the suffrage of women later) was far more the result of the work of radical, unorthodox Christian groups, humanitarians and "political saints"

---

[254] Cited in John W de Gruchy, *The Church Struggle in South Africa* (Grand Rapids: Eerdmans, 1979), 34.
[255] An interesting example of this is a report written by a certain Rev. M C Vos , DR Church minister at Tulbagh at the beginning of the nineteenth century; see Boesak, *Farewell To Innocence*, 104-105.

such as Wilberforce rather than the efforts and convictions of established, mainline churches either in South Africa or in Britain.[256]

These missionaries became the bane not only of the settlers and their governments, but of the "settler church" (de Gruchy's phrase) as well. The hostility was visceral. Because they married indigenous women, they were called "immoral"; because they took up the cause of the oppressed and exploited native peoples, they were accused of "meddling in politics". Because they enlisted public opinion overseas and sought to influence government decision making, they were called "traitors". Because they were passionate about justice and unflinching in the exposure of injustice, they were called "one-sided". An irate Janssens, then Governor of the Cape colony, spoke words that would be echoed almost word for word by representatives of white governments in South Africa about turbulent priests and *dominees* through three centuries:

> If the harm that missionaries have done in the Colony and its surroundings (with the exception of the Moravian Brethren in Genadendal) is weighed against the good they have done, it will be found that the harm is very serious and the good amounts to nil. Most of these missionaries (rogues) should be sent away with the greatest possible haste, and those who may be allowed to stay - if there be any - should be given entirely new instructions.[257]

Unlike the settler churches, English and Dutch, established or non-conformist, they did not serve the needs of the white farmers and settlers, nor sought good relations with the settler governments as their first priority, but identified rather with the indigenous peoples and their struggles for dignity, justice, rights and land. This was true for the Cape as well as much later for the Boer republics in the north. There the thorn in the flesh was not an Englishman but a Dutchman, Rev. P Huet, who lashed out with prophetic indignation at the way black people were treated by white Christians. Huet knew what he was witnessing:

> God knows, and I myself know, what indescribable injustices occur in these parts! What gruesome ill treatment, oppression, murder![258]

Not all missionaries were the same, of course, but the more "mission work" became the domain of settled settler churches, the more they conformed to the norms of white society rather than those of the gospel. The "missionary minded" Rev. M C Vos is just one blatant example. The faults of the missionaries were many, and the fundamental

---

[256] See Ernest Marshall Howse, *Saints in Politics: The Clapham Sect and the Growth of Freedom* (London: George Allen & Unwin, 1973).

[257] Cited in Jane M Sales, *The Planting of the Churches in South Africa* (Grand Rapids: Eerdmans, 1971) 51. See also Ido H Enklaar, *Life and Work of Dr J T van der Kemp 1747-1811, Missionary pioneer and protagonist of racial equality in South Africa* (Cape Town/Rotterdam: A A Balkema, 1988).

[258] P Huet, *Het Lot der Zwarten in de Transvaal*, full quote cited in Boesak, *Farewell*, 34.

critique of black people about the exchange of the land for the Bible cannot just be pooh-poohed. And if one should argue that the imperialist venture should not have reached Africa at all, and that therefore the missionaries, as part of that venture, merely tried to clean up the mess they themselves had made in the first place, then the point is moot anyway. And true, the more the indigenous people came to understand the gospel *themselves,* and the more they sought their own, indigenous, contextual understanding of that gospel as it pertained to their own lives, the more they understood also the shortcomings in an interpretation from the missionary side that was well-meant but nonetheless in many ways inadequate. Missionaries were sympathetic, but they were, after all, colonial whites from Europe, and there were limits to their understanding and interpretation of the gospel for the world of political, economic and human subjugation and alienation in which the Khoi and other blacks had to live.

A poignant example of this truth is the 1884 poem of the blind and gifted John Ntsikana, catechist and the first African on the subcontinent to compose Christian hymns in the African languages. Just how much he, spiritual child of Johannes van der Kemp, wrestled with this painful discovery is perhaps reflected in the fact that he published this poem not under his real name but using the pen-name *Uhadi Wase-Luhlangni,* "The Harp of the Nation":

> *Some thoughts till now never spoken*
> *Make shreds of my innermost being;*
> *And the cares and fortunes of my kin*
> *Still journey with me to the grave.*
>
> *I turn my back on the many shams*
> *That I see from day to day;*
> *It seems we march to our very grave*
> *Encircled by a smiling Gospel.*
>
> *For what is this Gospel?*
> *And what salvation?*
> *The shade of a fabulous ghost*
> *That we try to embrace in vain.*[259]

Here we hear already the first sounds of a yet unborn Liberation Theology, the first expression of a hermeneutic of suspicion. For it is the struggle with Ntsikana's "fabulous ghost", that shredding of the innermost being by the "many shams", the cares and fortunes of our kin and that vain embrace that would give birth to Liberation Theology as Black Theology on the African continent. But here, in the words of our blind and anguished poet, we can already hear the announcement of that birth. Nstikana discerned clearly what was true and what was "sham" in the gospel he heard from missionaries.

---

[259] Quoted in Es'kia Mphahlele, *ES'KIA, Education, African Humanism & Culture, Social Consciousness, Literary Appreciation.* (Johannesburg: Kwela Books, 2002), 298.

He understood also the inexpressible paradox: being encircled by a "smiling gospel while we are marched to our graves", in other words a gospel from which he could derive no understanding, no sharing of the pain, no comfort for his tortured soul. Here is not just the discovery of pain and sham, but also a sense of betrayal and outrage. And already Ntsikana understood the difference between the power of the gospel and the presentation of that gospel by those who did not share your pain. The full theological articulation of that realisation would come with a new generation, understanding the hermeneutical significance of being black in a white racist world, and understanding the radical message of the gospel for that world, a full century later. Then the black Christian would see no reason any longer for turning our back on the shams that paraded as truth in the name of the gospel. We would, rather, face and confront them, unmask them. Then, Ntsikana's "fabulous ghost" would take on flesh and bones in the reality of the black Messiah.

But even given all that, it would be less than honest to deny the role these missionaries did play, the foundations for prophetic protest they did lay down in those early years, and the prophetic traditions they did uphold. And even if it is true that the resilience of the true gospel message guarantees that the gospel always asserts itself, despite human manipulation, it is equally true that this never happens without God using an instrument, opening an eye to see the truth, and opening a mouth to speak that truth. That the instrument may prove to be imperfect does not matter. It is the perfection of God's truth that matters.

It is from the early missionaries, however imperfect they may have been, that the South African church first learned the power of the gospel as inspiration for social action. It is from them we learned that preaching the gospel and fighting for justice belong together, that calling upon the name of the Lord means championing the cause of the oppressed, the poor and the weak. De Gruchy observes, and he is right, that "the church's struggle against racism and injustice in South Africa only really begins in earnest with their witness in the nineteenth century".[260] It is from them that the church in South Africa inherited its prophetic legacy, its understanding that there is something irresistibly powerful, undeniably liberatory and joyously rebellious in the gospel of Jesus Christ. And that, I submit, is no small thing.

The Ambivalence of Paternalism …

As can be seen from even the one example cited above, the role of the church in South African society was always a complex matter. During the first three decades of this century, the so-called English speaking churches were far less vocal than they were during the apartheid era. This is not to say, however, that they were not critical of the South African situation. They spoke out on the race problem, land distribution and African education. They called for better housing and living conditions and for consultation with Africans on matters affecting them. In 1915 the Synod of the Church

---

[260] De Gruchy, *op. cit.,* 13.

of the Province asked that the Native Land Act of 1913 be "immediately repealed until such a time as *more generous and comprehensive* legislation is forthcoming".[261] The social witness of the other English-speaking churches was more or less the same. They placed extraordinary reliance on resolutions, addressed in reasonable, patient, respectful tones to the government, even though it became clearer and clearer that the white government had no intention of listening or responding. So, although they attempted to speak what de Gruchy calls "the prophetic word", when that word remained unheeded, unheard and unaddressed, they could not do more, although they clearly knew that more was needed.

But De Gruchy[262], in his otherwise very helpful analysis, does not dig deeper than the prevailing atmosphere of "paternalism", "white guardianship" and the lack of black leadership, and he is undoubtedly correct as far as it goes. But there must be a deeper, more profound reason, I believe. The English-speaking churches, although the majority of their membership were black, were essentially *white* churches. They, under the tutelage of their white leadership, were firmly and comfortably ensconced in the warmth of the ruling establishment, very much aware of "the white man's burden". In spite of the tensions between Afrikaner and English-speaking South Africa during the decades following Union in 1910 and World War I, de Gruchy reports, "relations between the DRC and the English-speaking churches were cordial, and attempts were made to foster cooperation between them".[263]

This close relationship was felt also in the political field. The political power of the English-speaking South Africans was dependent upon cooperation with Afrikaners. The common thread then, as in the beginning of the colonial project, was the need for white solidarity to secure white supremacy. "Thus, while the English could dominate much of Parliament, they were always in need of Afrikaner support". De Gruchy mentions this in the context of an excuse: "Yet, it should be remembered that the English could never govern South Africa alone".[264] But for us it makes perfect sense. The church wanted "more generous" laws, "more comprehensive" legislation, "more consultation". In short, the church asked of the government what, as a *white* church, it thought black people needed, or wanted, or deserved. But there was no thought of fundamental justice, of full and meaningful participation that would mean black majority rule. The protest was always within the boundaries of "white guardianship" and the need for white supremacy. Which is one reason why it took those churches so long to accept black leadership and even longer to abide radical black leadership. The relationship with the government, as with the white Dutch Reformed Churches, was of greater import than the issues of justice the blacks were clamouring for. What divided white South Africans, and conversely what united blacks and whites *in Christ*, however

---

[261] *Op. cit.*, 37 (my emphasis).
[262] *Op. cit.*, 39.
[263] *Ibid.*
[264] *Op. cit.*, 36.

significant both might have been, was never significant enough to break the bond of common white interest.

It did not take black people long to find this out. Already in 1883 SN Mvambo had perceived that white solidarity is not hindered by either language, ethnicity or denominational affiliation.

> In fighting for national rights, we must fight together. Although they look as if they belong to various churches, the white people are solidly united when it comes to matters of this nature. We blacks think that these churches are hostile to one another, and in that way we lose our political rights.[265]

How true. Ntsikana's "fabulous ghost" would continue to haunt the church. One hundred years later, in the crucial and excruciating debates on civil disobedience, the World Council of Churches' Programme to Combat Racism, sanctions, and especially the active participation in the struggle, we would truly discover the truth of these words and how very little things had changed in that regard. Also, though, the English-speaking churches spoke to a white government in which they had more faith than the situation warranted. But then again, the government was *their* government, the upper crust of English South Africans who held positions of power and who served in Parliament were *their* members, who were protecting *their* interests, and those interests did not coincide with the interests of the oppressed black majority. The voice they truly heard was the voice of power and mutual white interest. They implicitly trusted the government, not because there was any promise of justice, but because it was a *white* government with which they could identify more than with their black brothers and sisters. The gap between what de Gruchy calls "synodical resolve" and "congregational involvement", or in other words, between saying and doing, had *social, economic, and political* roots. It is important to remember that white, racial solidarity guaranteed white political hegemony, which in turn guaranteed white economic superiority. That early creation of a platform of wealth remains one of the most potent factors preventing genuine black economic empowerment even today.

It is, ironically, the same affliction – the credibility gap between knowing and doing - that crippled the Dutch Reformed Church in the nineteenth century during the long and tortuous debate on racism in the church, centring on baptism, the Table of the Lord and the presence of Christians who were not white. The church knew the demands of the gospel, but could not withstand the social, economic and political pressures of white society. They too, were caught between what "Scripture teaches" (which they knew and acknowledged), and what the church called "the weakness of some", meaning the racism of the whites. Here began what was aptly called "the history of a heresy".[266]

---

[265] *Op. cit.,* 51.
[266] Chris Loff, "The history of a heresy", in: *Apartheid is a Heresy*, 10 - 23. The relevant discussion is on 17 - 20. Loff calls this a "sinful predisposition" nurtured by a "deluded theology".

In the end, the need for white solidarity toward the common goal of white supremacy rendered the English speaking churches more helpless than they had wanted, or intended, to be. If they were ambivalent, as de Gruchy points out[267], it was the ambivalence of the accommodation to race, to social custom, to the very ambivalence of power itself. In the end also, the victims were the oppressed and the gospel. The pattern we saw in the beginning would repeat itself. The torch of prophetic faithfulness was kept alive by the prophetic minority, linked forever to the name of Father Trevor Huddleston, who in *his* evangelical fervour for justice, incurred the wrath of both the government and his church authorities.[268] The church sleeps, was his judgment, although it "occasionally talks in its sleep".[269] In stark contrast, the very public and activist stand of the white Dutch Reformed churches as institutions, regarding the issues of race, economic justice and political participation, and their engagement of the state, was therefore all the more remarkable.

... versus the Advocacy of Conviction

The white DRC took strong exception to the relatively weak political and economic position of the Afrikaner community *vis-à-vis* the English-speaking political and economic establishment. The fact that the English needed the Afrikaner to stay in power was seen as an injustice in itself: the Afrikaner could not just help the English to stay in power. The Afrikaner themselves *needed to be in* power. As long as the goal of white supremacy was served, English-speaking South Africans would just as easily support *them*. The once-despised idea of Anglo-Saxon chosen-ness and manifest destiny as expressed by Cecil John Rhodes was stormed, conquered and appropriated with astonishing ease as it was now articulated by Dr DF Malan, Dutch Reformed minister and Nationalist leader:

> Our history is the greatest masterpiece of the centuries. We hold this nationhood as our due for it was given us by the Architect of the universe ... The last hundred years have witnessed a miracle behind which must lie a divine plan. Indeed, the history of the Afrikaner reveals a will and a determination which makes one feel that Afrikanerdom is not the work of men but the creation of God.[270]

The church considered it a grave injustice that this calling from God could be thwarted, and calling upon its Reformed heritage rooted especially in Calvinist political activism, railed against this situation in sermons, public statements and publications. It did more. The church called for, and organized so-called "congresses of the people" (*Volkskongresse*), where the people were rallied, informed and inspired by their leaders,

---

[267] *Church Struggle*, 37

[268] Cf. De Gruchy, *op. cit.*, vii, 60.

[269] *Op. cit.*, vii.

[270] *Op. cit.*, 30, 31.

intellectuals and preachers. The question of white poverty was translated into an economic plan; what was seen as political subjugation was turned into a programme of political empowerment, and the whole was captured in a Christian nationalism which brought together all the strains of politics, economic empowerment, theology, faith and (Afrikaner) nationhood.[271]

This all-encompassing programme found expression in one word: *apartheid*, and became the *Leitmotif* of South African politics after the 1930s. No area of Afrikaner life was left untouched: religious life, education, politics, economics, culture. Up front were the spokespersons, the intellectuals, the preachers. Behind the scenes was the sinister *Broederbond*, a secret society of carefully chosen men in leadership positions from all walks of life, planning, envisioning, manipulating.[272] Nothing was left to chance. And driving it all, its deepest source of inspiration, were the white DR churches. Without the churches all this would have been unthinkable. In fact, Afrikaner intellectuals have recognized that the role of other organizations in the Afrikaner community "faded into insignificance" next to the crucial role of the church in preparing the Afrikaner for a socio- political programme that would "revolutionize" South African life, according to Rev. DP Botha.[273] The preparation Botha was speaking of was the preparation for the victory of the National Party at the polls in 1948 and the official adoption of apartheid as state policy. And historian GD Scholtz was equally grateful: "Without hesitation it can be said that it is principally due to the church that the Afrikaner nation has not gone under …"[274]

Never before has South African history seen such an all-embracing, ambitious, life-changing phenomenon, planned so meticulously, and carried out so swiftly. It caught the English establishment by surprise and brought its political power, if not its economic power, to an effective end. And as Christian nationalism was all-embracing, so was apartheid. The apartheid measures of the English-speaking governments (for apartheid was, to state an oft-observed truth contrary to popular English propaganda, *not* the invention of the Afrikaner, but a result of the racism of the English) were taken, honed, perfected and brought to their full logical, and quite horrifying conclusion.[275]

Now the struggle was no longer against colonialism as such, for in contrast to the English, the Afrikaners considered themselves as part of Africa, as they had no other

---

[271] See, among many studies and the literature mentioned there, *Kerk en Stad, reports commissioned by the DR Church* (Stellenbosch: DR Church:, 1948); RTJ Lombard, *Die Nederduitse Gereformeerde Kerke en Rassepolitiek* (Silverton: D R Church Publishers, 1981); J Kinghorn (ed.): *Die N G Kerk en Apartheid* (Johannesburg: Macmillan, 1986).

[272] Cf. JHP Serfontein, *The Brotherhood of Power - An Expose of the Secret Afrikaner Broederbond* (Johannesburg: 1980), 272.

[273] Rev. DP Botha, "Church and Kingdom in South Africa", in M Nash (ed), *Your Kingdom Come*, SACC (Johannesburg: SACC, 1980), 273.

[274] In De Gruchy, *op. cit.*, 31.

[275] The infamous Land Acts of 1913 and 1936, which robbed the indigenous peoples of their land, were the brainchild of English-speaking governments, and much of apartheid as political policy to ensure white supremacy was the legacy of Theophilus Shepstone, one-time governor of Natal.

home "to go back to". That fact would become one of the single most important factors in determining the ferocity of the struggle and the determination of whites to stay in power. It would characterize our struggle in ways that no other struggle for liberation and independence on the continent would be characterized. Indeed, today South African political leaders may speak of our "transformation" and some may even use the word "liberation", but none of them speak of "independence", as do the Africans to the north of us. The impact of this fact on South Africa's post-apartheid reality is massive and, in some ways, tragic.

The fact also that Afrikaner nationalism was so intimately interwoven with their religious faith would add a unique dimension to the struggle in South Africa; even more so, since the Afrikaner's faith was expressed in terms of the Calvinist Reformation. Here was none of the ambivalence that so marked the theology of Luther with its "two Kingdoms" theory. Calvinism was, and remains, decidedly a theology for the public square, a call to establish the reign of Christ over all areas of life, in a world that was meant to be the "theatre of God's glory". It is a political theology that inspired both institutional and individual participation in politics and public affairs, and that not just as a consequence of status (i.e. as a member of the nobility, for example), but as a matter of conscience for all believers. The theological confession that all human beings are sinners before God and in need of redemption immediately had social, economic and political consequences. That confession guaranteed the equality of all human persons before God and called upon the Calvinist "to kneel before no one". Calvinist politics has always been radical politics. It was a radicalism that struck fear into the heart of the establishment, for it did not bow down to status or privilege, feared not revolution, was in fact decidedly militant, and showed a revolutionary commitment that the modern world had not known before.

> Reformation must be universal… reform all places, all persons and callings; Reform the benches of judgement, the inferior magistrates… Reform the universities, reform the cities, reform the countries, reform inferior schools of learning, reform the Sabbath, reform the ordinances, the worship of God… You have more work to do than I can speak… Every plant which my heavenly Father hath not planted shall be rooted up![276]

Such was the language of the Calvinist reformation, and such was the language, and the attitude, inherited by the Afrikaner Calvinist. And that link with religion and the Calvinist tradition, by the same token, determined the role of the church in the struggle. In a strange way the Afrikaner's insistence that apartheid was a Christian policy, indeed a *church policy* according to the official mouthpiece of the DR Church *Die Kerkbode* (September, 1948, which we quoted in the previous chapter), would make the policy

---

[276] From a sermon by Rev. Thomas Case, Puritan preacher, before the House of Commons in 1641; cited by Michael Walzer, *The Revolution of the Saints, A study in the origins of radical politics* (London: Weidenfeld & Nicholson, 1966), 10, 11.

vulnerable to the critique of the gospel itself. Dr Koot Vorster, DR church leader of the sixties and seventies, spoke with a confidence which must have sounded reassuring to those who listened to him in 1970:

> Our only guide is the Bible. Our policy and outlook on life are based on the Bible. We firmly believe the way we interpret it is right. We will not budge one inch from our interpretation [in order] to satisfy anyone in South Africa or abroad. The world may differ from our interpretation. This will not influence us. The world may be wrong. We are right and will continue to follow the way the Bible teaches.[277]

The self-confidence of the erstwhile Dutch Reformed church leader was breathtaking, but he spoke with the certitude of the chosen. Nonetheless it was a false confidence wrapped around the gospel, totally inappropriate to the gospel, and not even twenty years later the power of that very same gospel would blow the structures of the moral and theological justification of apartheid apart. This is, I think, what that important phrase from the Reformation, "the Scriptures interpret themselves", means. Scripture resists manipulation, however clever; it rebels against abuse, however pious; it asserts itself, not as a philosophical or ideological tract or a scroll of wisdom, but as the Word of God, "living and active, sharper than any two-edged sword, piercing until it divides soul from spirit, bone from marrow …" (Heb 4:12). To "follow the way the Bible teaches" is precisely to oppose apartheid, to expose it as pseudo-gospel, a blasphemy and a heresy, and therefore not to rest until that ungodly system would be no more. The apartheid establishment did not know it then, but in falsely claiming the gospel they were nurturing a fire in their laps. God will not be used, nor mocked.

We cannot truthfully call this involvement of the church in the empowerment of the Afrikaner "prophetic", because it was an involvement for the sake of one group only, at the cost of the rights, indeed the humanbeingness, of others. It served not justice, but a partial, racial justice; it sought not God's truth for all, but a particular, selected truth to serve their own ideology. They sought justice not for the poor, but for the *white poor*, and found it at the cost of justice for the black poor. They struggled not for all God's children who were needy, weak and oppressed, but created first a narrow, exclusive, white *volk*, who sought their freedom in the oppression of all others who were not white. They deliberately rebuilt the walls of partition Christ had broken down and in so doing enacted a *reversal* of the way of Jesus, who sought to establish God's justice and liberation across the barriers of gender, race, ethnicity and nationality.

In their efforts they called not upon the God of the prophets and the God of Jesus, but bowed down to an idol of their own making, a white god made in the image of white, Afrikaner Christian nationalism. It was not the Word of God and its demands that they responded to, but rather the dictates of race, blood, passion for their own group

---

[277] *Sunday Times*, 8 November 1970, cited in C Villa-Vicencio, "An All-pervading Heresy: Racism and the English-speaking churches", in: *Apartheid is a Heresy*, 59.

interests and the insatiable greed that comes with power that became their guiding light. Nonetheless, it was a Herculean, if totally misguided effort, and one cannot help but wonder what South African history would have been like if the Afrikaner Christian had put all that energy and conviction into the liberation of *all* God's people in this country instead. I believe this remains true even for today, if Afrikaans-speaking Calvinists can re-harness all that energy, conviction and vision, not out of a sense of enforced guilt, but from a renewed sense of destiny; not apart from, but together with, the rest of the nation.

The Crucible of Fire

This is what American activist pastor and author Jim Wallis called the apartheid years and the struggle of the church against that system.[278] The role the white Dutch Reformed churches played during the apartheid era was the role of a virtual state church. Just as the English-speaking churches provided justification for, and lacked critique of, the imperial endeavour, so the Afrikaans churches actively provided justification and protection for the apartheid state. It remains amazing how, despite all their differences, in this regard those two groups of churches were exactly the same. It was a role in which the church was at ease with the existing powers. Its language was no longer the passionate language of the prophet, but the careful reasoning of the court theologian. It concentrated on the "good intentions" of the policies and remained oblivious to the realities of their outcome. Its professed sympathy for the victims of apartheid was always tempered by, and therefore obliterated by, its solidarity with the *volk*. Within the given and hallowed framework of "separate development", "guardianship" and "mission work", its catchwords were "realism", "pragmatism", "charity" and "obedience".[279]

That was a realism which knew that things could not be changed, since we live in a "broken world" where the power of sin has totally overwhelmed the liberating power of the gospel, and where unjust structures and inhumane relationships are "creationally given" and divinely ordained, and therefore untouchable and unchangeable. That pragmatism was the kind that people so easily learned to live with in the skewed realities of power, and in the words of Jeremiah, they "aided and abetted the oppressor in his oppression", instead of letting justice "roll down like waters and righteousness like a mighty stream" as Amos demanded. The charity so proudly exhibited was a charity that soothed the conscience, because it had totally replaced the love for the neighbour and the justice which is what the LORD requires. The charity that "tithe mint, dill and cumin" [but] "neglected the weightier matters of the law: justice and mercy and faith". (Mt 23:23)

---

[278] Cf. Wallis and Hollyday, *Crucible of Fire*, cited above.

[279] These are constant themes in the theology of apartheid and in the official reports of the DR Church. Cf. Lombard, *op. cit.*, 79-90 and *passim*; Kinghorn, *op. cit.*, especially chapters 5 and 6; JC Marais, *Die N G Kerk en die Regverdiging van Apartheid* (Sovenga: Stofberg Theological Seminary, 1986), especially chapter 2. See also WA Landman, *A Plea for Understanding, A Reply to the Reformed Church in America* (Cape Town: Dutch Reformed Church Publishers, 1968). Landman, interestingly enough, works these themes out in political, rather than theological terms. See especially the *Annexes*.

The blind obedience so alien to the gospel, and so far from the liberating fantasy of Jesus (Dorothee Sölle), which demands of the oppressed person meek acceptance of whatever suffering is meted out to them because it is "God's will". That obedience which allows the security policeman to imprison, torture, maim and kill and return home to his family, knowing he was "only doing his job", which was also God's will. The obedience that demands that women "be silent" even in the face of the denial of her humanity and physical and psychological battering.

But again, there was a small minority who would not reconcile themselves with the political and theological stance of their church and who kept on raising before the DR Church the demands of the gospel. Foremost among those was Prof. BB Keet of the Dutch Reformed Seminary in Stellenbosch. "My Bible teaches me", he told the church, "that God is no respecter of persons and that His compassion is for the miserable, the underprivileged, the neglected children of the human race".[280] He spoke clearly, published widely, and challenged the white churches at every opportunity. His leadership inspired others, notably his colleague from Pretoria, Prof. Ben Marais, whose book *The Colour Crisis of the West,* showed such remarkable insights for the time, and later Rev. Beyers Naude whose prophetic life and witness gave such strength to two generations of Christian activists, within and outside the church. In time there were others, but they remained a largely ineffective minority and the vast majority of them, as time went by, found the strain of choosing between the truth of the gospel, the demands of an ever more radical black leadership, and their critical solidarity with the Afrikaner people, increasingly hard to bear. They, too, could not move beyond the written word, and hence active solidarity with the oppressed largely eluded them till the very end.

But second, there was the role played by those churches close in mindset to the white DR Churches. They were also white, racially divided from their black constituents, conservative in outlook and fundamentally satisfied with the apartheid system. Among them were the Apostolic Faith Mission Churches, and also the Baptists who, maybe because of their mainly British origins, had completely forgotten the evangelical fervour with which American Baptist Walter Rauschenbusch had pursued social justice as a consequence of his faith. Theirs was a passive conservatism (different from the active, aggressive conservatism of the white DRCs) that sought refuge in religious quietism and political pietism, enjoying the fruits of apartheid and never allowing the consequences of those choices to dampen their evangelical fervour.

They accepted the status quo as divinely ordained and saw no role at all for human intervention in history. Whatever happens, both on earth and in the heavens above is, it seems, the business of God. All we have to do, on earth, is prepare ourselves to go to heaven. And it calls on Christians to concentrate, not on their lives on earth, but on the life beyond. It remained blind to the evil of apartheid, the suffering it caused, or any sense that this naked oppression of even their own black members was against the will of God. As long as their white comfort was untouched, God remained undisturbed. It

---

[280] Cited in De Gruchy, *Church Struggle*, 58.

was not surprising at all when black members from these churches, under the leadership of clergy, such Rev. Frank Chikane and Dr Japie Lapoorta, broke the silence, joined other Christians in the struggle and found themselves in fierce opposition not only to the government but also to their white-controlled denominations.

Thirdly, there was the conservatism that found a home in a fundamentalist messianism that arises out of the conviction that the status quo, no matter how conservative it is, is not sufficient and, in fact, is unable to bring about the kind of society that they have in mind. Scorning the revered pragmatism of the realists, or the realism of the pragmatists, they are rather guided by a set of firm, not to say inflexible, beliefs grounded in the past and driven by a vision from the past - a vision that seeks to establish a society that will resurrect what they call "values" from the past which they seek to establish in society. They do not shun direct political involvement and they are driven also by that peculiar sense of certitude that comes from the knowledge of an exclusive calling. As so graphically illustrated in the quotation from Dr Vorster, above, they and they alone understand the will of God.

These are the newly arrived "Charismatic" churches that did not disturb the apartheid status quo, but nonetheless have had a strong "Christian" right-wing agenda, working not only in South Africa but in the front-line states as well. They have emerged visibly in the post-apartheid era, *ex nihilo* as it were, as if they have no political history before 1994, some making new alliances with the ANC-led government, others seeking to play much the role in South Africa that the Christian Fundamentalist Right seeks to play in the United States. Their connections with powerful right-wing Christian groups in the US and Germany, for example, are well known.[281] In our post-apartheid society some of these churches are seeking to redefine their role, becoming more activist according to the importance of the issues for their membership. It will be interesting to continue to observe both their astounding growth and their chosen role in post-apartheid politics in South Africa, and how differently that role is perceived by white-led Charismatic churches, on the one hand, and black- and coloured-led churches, on the other.

Fourthly, there was the role the so-called liberal, English-speaking churches in South Africa played. As we have indicated, Afrikaners have often pointed out the immense hypocrisy of these churches, and the communities they represent, in acting as if apartheid were not only the brainchild of the Afrikaner, but that the Afrikaner alone benefited from it. The white membership of these churches, too, enjoyed the fruits of the system, were loath to identify too closely with the liberation struggle, and made sure their criticism remained within the bounds of acceptable reason. Journalist JHP Serfontein tells the story of how avowedly "liberal" newspapers on whose staff he served managed to suppress stories about church actions that were regarded as too

---

[281] The Research Institute for Christianity in South Africa report on *The TRC and Faith Communities*, makes the point that it is disturbing that these groups, in spite of the role they played during the apartheid era, all failed to make submissions to the Truth and Reconciliation Commission, despite repeated invitations to do so. *RICSA Report*, 37 (Cape Town: UCT, 1996).

subversive to publish, thereby proving their own slavish submission to the apartheid government's wishes.[282]

Some English-speaking theologians have known this as well, and did not try to hide the flaws within these churches. Charles Villa-Vicencio spoke of racism in these churches as an "all-pervading heresy",[283] and took that even further in his more recent publication, *Trapped in Apartheid*, which explores the dilemma of the English-speaking churches in South Africa during the apartheid years.[284]

This is not to deny that the English-speaking churches criticized government policy and sometimes quite severely. It was when the Nationalist government in the late 1950s promulgated a bill virtually banning racially mixed church services in so-called white areas that Geoffrey Clayton, Anglican Archbishop of Cape Town, wrote his famous letter to the Prime Minister:

> The Church cannot recognize the right of an official secular government to determine whether or where a member of the Church of any race … shall discharge his religious duty of participating in public worship … We feel bound to state that if the bill were to become law in its present form we should ourselves be unable to obey it or to counsel our clergy and people to do so.[285]

The passing of the bill by a huge majority caused Clayton to write in a pastoral letter read to all the congregations that "before God and with you as my witnesses, I solemnly state that not only shall I not obey any direction of the Minister … but I solemnly counsel you, both clergy and people, to do likewise".[286] This was a rare prophetic instance created and seized by a church leader that would only be matched years later when the leadership of the churches were black. Other churches followed this example, although always with much debate and agonizing, and then only in the wording of their resolutions, not in the actual decision for civil disobedience. Condemnation of apartheid in synods and conferences became common cause, but as both Villa-Vicencio and John de Gruchy pointed out, there was always a considerable gap between word and deed that bedevilled these churches.[287]

The English-speaking churches never endeavoured to justify apartheid morally or theologically and in terms of doctrine and principle they could not be faulted, "but it is in the general practice that the English-speaking churches are found wanting" says Villa-Vicencio, and de Gruchy comments that black church leaders have remained sceptical about the "seriousness of the churches in combating racism".[288] These churches, in the

---

[282] Serfontein, *Apartheid, Change and the N G Kerk* (Emmarentia, Taurus Press: 1982) 2, 3.
[283] In: *Apartheid is a Heresy*, 59 - 74.
[284] Cape Town: David Philip, 1994.
[285] Cited in Villa-Vicencio, in: *Heresy*, 65.
[286] *Ibid.*
[287] *Op. cit.*, 67.
[288] *Ibid.*

eye of a rising storm in South Africa, have chosen to remain "moderate" and "realistic", with a "laissez-faire" outlook on politics, and this, "perhaps more than anything else ... has caused other churches ... not to take the English-speaking churches too seriously".[289] This not only caused serious tensions within those churches, but also had a decidedly negative impact on their public testimony. As with the white Dutch Reformed Churches, one has to ask what would have happened if the English-speaking churches had been half so critical of English-speaking governments *before* the apartheid era, or had truly combated the racism they knew to be the plague of South African society. Or was it really too much to ask of them: to uproot the tree whose seeds they had planted, which the Afrikaners have watered and nurtured, and under whose shade they all sat?

But this observation leads us to something else not so readily discussed in the great and ongoing church and apartheid debate. In an almost bizarre way, the black Dutch Reformed Churches (for Blacks, Coloureds and Indians) mostly stood on the sidelines throughout the first three decades after 1948. They were, as the "missionary products" of the white DRC, totally subservient to the white "mother church". Missionaries from the white church were their pastors and administrators, their spokespersons and their teachers at their separate, racially divided, and scholastically inferior theological schools. The theology of these churches was an unbiblical mixture of orthodoxy and pietism that hardly bore any resemblance to the robust, world-formative theology (to use Nicholas Wolterstorff's term), the Reformed tradition inherited from John Calvin, so that these churches had very little, if any, social consciousness. There was not a hint of the radical biblical and theological interpretations that so inspired the white DRC during the first four decades of the 20th century and articulated so forcefully by DF Malan, for example - these they carefully kept from their teaching in these churches. New perspectives would be brought by a few younger teachers from the white DRC, but the fundamental change in these churches would come only with liberation theology, and a completely new understanding of both the Bible and the radical nature of their Reformed, Calvinist heritage.

Their preachers, who received their training from white professors who were themselves "missionaries", remained theologically impoverished and undernourished. They heard nothing of John Calvin's holy tirades against the wretchedness of the poor and the greed and complacency of the rich.[290] Nor did they hear Calvin say that the whole human race is united by a sacred bond of fellowship.[291] Their theology did not include Calvin's insight that a just and well-regulated government will be distinguished for maintaining the rights of the poor and the afflicted.[292] Their hermeneutical key was shaped and cut by the white church, and could not open the door to the proper understanding of

---

[289] Villa-Vicencio, *Trapped*, 14. Because of this, he says, "the contribution of these churches to the South African conflict can only be minimal".

[290] See, for example, Calvin's commentary on Luke 16:14, *Opera*, 46, 406.

[291] *Op. cit.*, 45, 613.

[292] *Op. cit.*, commentary on Ps 82:3.

Scripture these churches so sorely needed. Theirs was truly a theology of subservience and enslavement.

Especially the "coloured" Sendingkerk continued to suffer from the shock and indignity of being kicked out of the (white) church and forced into a separate church formation in 1881. The church was paralysed, caught up in the longing to "return" to the (white) fold, its lack of identity, its insensitivity to the socio-economic and political situation of its own people, and above all, its inability to forge a theology responsive to the situation in which it found itself and reflective of its Reformed traditions and its own understanding of the Scriptures. Its difficulty in creating its own identity was partly the result of its theological paucity, but also a reflection of the political and psychological dilemma in which the "coloured" people as a whole found themselves, and with painful irony still do.

The strong and overbearing presence of "missionaries" (within this context an utterly incongruous term if ever there was one) on its pulpits, in its church meetings, conferences and synods guaranteed that debates were overshadowed by, and infused with, the ideology of the white church. That presence also spelled out the financial dependence of those churches on the white church, and by the same token the fear of upsetting the existing relationships. It took a long time for those churches to make the link between the iniquitous political and economic policies of the apartheid regime, the consequential poverty of the vast masses of black people and the central role of the white church in upholding the government, preparing the ground for the most nefarious laws on the statute books, providing moral justification for their own oppression and guaranteeing the status quo.

To be sure, the *Sendingkerk* did speak on the question of apartheid after 1948. It was forced to by mainly three things. First were the laws that prohibited mixed marriages and sexual relationships across the colour line. These laws were experienced as an indescribable insult, an assault upon the dignity of a people whose very existence was evidence of the mixing of the races, and the church could not but respond to this. Second came the infamous Group Areas Act through which the coloured people were forcibly removed from newly proclaimed "white areas" and lost their land, their homes and the churches which had been theirs for generations. It is tragic, but unusually instructive that the most powerful argument for this group, namely their being descendants from the Khoi and San as the first nations of this part of Africa, never featured in the debates about land. Third was the rebellion in the church led by the Rev. Isaac Morkel and which led to a breakaway and the establishment of a new church, the Calvinist Protestant Church in 1950, when the white leadership of the *Sendingkerk* refused to comply with Morkel's request to declare apartheid an un-Christian policy which should be rejected by both church and state.

The protest from the *Sendingkerk* was muted at best though, and made no impression at all on either the government, the white church or the people. Because the leadership of the church was white, sons from the white DR Church and loyal to the National Party regime, their words reflected that reality. Besides, while words of protest were spoken on occasion, the reality was that the *Sendingkerk* enjoyed some privileges afforded it by the government by virtue of its relationship to the white church, but mainly because of the underlying sense of loyalty to the government. While protesting against the Group Areas Act, for instance, the *Sendingkerk* was only too willing to cooperate with the government in helping to create the new "coloured" areas.

The breakaway by Rev. Morkel was similarly ineffective, since the new church was no more than yet another coloured church that suffered from the same ailments that afflicted its "mother". The political promise of its birth was never fulfilled. The Calvinist Protestant Church therefore never played any significant role in either sensitising or conscientising the coloured community, neither did it make its mark in the struggle against apartheid. Nor did it follow the lead of the *Sendingkerk* in the 1980s, when it declared apartheid a sin, a blasphemy and its theological justification a heresy. In those crucial years it never joined the South African Council of Churches nor supported any of the church-sponsored public actions against the apartheid state. The one or two brave preachers who remained in the *Sendingkerk* and spoke more boldly than their church, identifying with the Christian Institute, were hounded both out of the church and the country.[293] But it has to be said that the bulk of the "coloured" pastors in this church before the late 1970s never found the will or the courage to challenge apartheid, in society or in the church.

The parting of the ways, both between whites and blacks within multi-racial churches, and for black and white churches, came with the years following the Soweto uprising in 1976, and especially the 1980s - the coming of Black Consciousness and liberation theology, the growing radicalisation of Black Christianity and the active participation of Christians in the hurly-burly of the struggle against apartheid. More specifically, there were the debates and decisions on civil disobedience, church support for sanctions and the call to pray for the removal of unjust government.

For most blacks in the Christian church, the gap between words and deeds became too much when we saw just how much that gap was being filled, not with air but with the blood of thousands of youths, women and men. Then the liberal, conciliation politics so typical of the English-speaking churches, and the hesitant, anaemic politics of the white-controlled black Dutch Reformed churches which sought to please both sides of the divide could no longer be borne. Theirs was a role that was critical of society, but not really convinced that radical change was needed or necessary. Interaction with the powers that be, trusting them to (eventually) do the right thing, rather than challenging or confronting them, was their model. Theologically they had no foundation, and politically they had no cogent analysis to help them in this situation. They drank from

---

[293] The Rev. John George Plaatjies had to leave the country under pressure from the government and without a peep of protest from his church, and Rev. Isaac Theron of the Paarl Zionskerk congregation was suspended from the church under dubious interpretations of church law. He finally formed his own, independent church and died a tragic and disconsolate figure.

theologically polluted wells, their understanding of their own tradition too shallow to equip them for the hard battles apartheid forced on the oppressed in every walk of life.

As Villa-Vicencio and De Gruchy have pointed out, English liberal theology was just as easily exposed as totally inadequate in the face of the growing conflict. Racism, for most in these churches, if they thought about it at all, was a regrettable attitude, a psychological aberration, for some maybe even a personal sin, but not structural, systemic or indispensable for the ongoing economic exploitation of our people. The violence of the state in suppressing dissent, physical and systemic, if it was even recognized, was sometimes acknowledged to be shocking, but nonetheless understood as legitimate, and not nearly censured as harshly as the counter-violence from the liberation movements or the spontaneous violence from the people in the townships. Fearful of anything that might vaguely sound like "extremism", they were too comfortable with the art of compromise, too anxious for reconciliation at any cost.

Too conscious of the good intentions of the government (which former President F W de Klerk argues till this very day!) and too fearful of possible chaos, they could not see the havoc wreaked daily by apartheid on our lives, and too afraid of change they could not see our suffering nor understand our willingness to suffer for the sake of liberation. Too beholden to the white power structures, too pampered by enjoying white privilege without having to take responsibility for it (like the Afrikaner had to), they did not know, nor did they want to know, the risk and the joy of what the Danish pastor and leader of the resistance against Nazism, Kaj Munk called "holy rage", which is that "recklessness" which comes, he says, from the knowledge of God and the knowledge of humankind. Too much captive to centuries of white solidarity, our black pain was too deep to be articulated by their white voice.

It is in this context that we speak of the prophetic role of the church in South Africa. It is not a role chosen by the institutional church as a whole, let us hasten to say once again. It finds, as it did at the beginning of our history of state and church in this country, its expression in the convictions and the actions of a minority who find themselves overpowered by the gospel, driven by an overriding concern for justice, convinced that justice will be achieved only through radical transformation of both the lives of people and of society. It is a role that the church does not take upon itself: it is always thrust upon the church by the compelling truth of the gospel the church seeks to proclaim.

It does not deliberately seek, but certainly does not avoid, confrontation with the powers that be. Disobedience to the government is not a duty - obedience to God is. The realisation that the struggle is ultimately not for a cause, but for people; living, breathing human beings in whom the image of God longs to find expression is what sustains this prophetic reality. By the same token, that realization frees us from the paralysis of apathy and from the anxiety of mindless activism. It liberates us from the tyranny of relativism and from the yoke of cynicism. It lives from a vision of the future, rather than from an idealized past, and it is guided by its solidarity with the poor and the oppressed, the weak and the voiceless, and what it believes to be the radical demands of the Scriptures. It knows that its strength lies not in connections with the powerful, but in its weakness in identifying with the powerless.

Farewell to Innocence

It was really the decade of the 80s that saw both the harshest oppression in the history of apartheid and the full bloom of that prophetic movement. That happened in a number of ways. First of all, the 1980s brought a full and painful understanding of what began as the loss of our innocence in 1976, when the state turned the full wrath of its violence against the defenceless and unprepared children of Soweto. The revolt, and the violent reaction it called forth, spread across the country and in the Cape found a dismal climax in the death of the children in Elsies River, which for the coloured communities of the Western Cape carried the same symbolic weight as Soweto. We were then made to see and experience just how far the South African government was willing to go, and how much it would make us pay, to maintain the system of apartheid. Simultaneously, we learned just how indifferent most of the Western world was to the suffering of poor and oppressed people who are not white. We came to understand more than ever before that on one level the struggle was not just against the might of apartheid; it was against international white solidarity and all the power that reality represented.

Secondly, this understanding, this loss of innocence was given flesh and bones by the coming of age of liberation theology.[294] Liberation theology was not just about our own liberation, spiritually and physically; it was also about the liberation of the Bible from the hands of the oppressor, changing it from a tool of subjugation and ideological exploitation into a source of inspiration for justice and freedom for all people. This last was important, since liberation theology, if it wanted to be biblical and authentic, and meaningful for our South African situation, could not simply be the black counterpart of white, Afrikaner Christian nationalism.[295]

Thirdly, there was the realization that the struggle against apartheid would, in a very real sense, remain significantly crippled unless the moral and theological underpinning of the apartheid system, as espoused by the white Dutch Reformed Churches, was not exposed, attacked and destroyed. This was not just a political strategy based on the extraordinary vulnerability of the apartheid establishment because of its insistence on wanting apartheid to be a Christian policy. It was, first and foremost, the direct result of the resilience and rebelliousness of the gospel itself. The living, liberating God of the Scriptures could never be remoulded into an idol of oppression and ethnic glorification. This was also for our own sake: after all, how could one remain Christian if the Christian faith could so easily be turned into an instrument, and justification

---

[294] It was for a reason that my own work on liberation theology has the title *Farewell to Innocence*. (Maryknoll: Orbis Press, 1977). See the Introduction, 1-7.

[295] See M Buthelezi, "The Ethical Questions Raised by Nationalism", in T Sundermeier (ed.) *Church and Nationalism in South Africa* (Johannesburg: Ravan, 1975); and also Boesak, *Farewell*, Chapter 4.

of, one's oppression? What kind of a God were oppressed people worshipping? In the peculiar set of circumstances, for black Christians who were also Reformed, the question was even more acute.[296] And it was in this regard specifically that the black Dutch Reformed Churches discovered their special calling, their destiny, and in a very real sense their redemption.

Fourth, it became clear to us, not just through the dictates of our own worsening situation, but indeed the demands of the Scriptures, that the realization of our faith meant transforming words into action, and that that was what the LORD required. Participation in the struggle, we discovered, could no longer mean just bold words on Sunday morning and carefully crafted statements on Monday afternoon. It had to mean the active decision to commit our bodies and our lives to the cause for justice for the sake of the oppressed. One could not, on Sunday morning, exhort the government to be the servant of God from Romans 13, in order not to become the beast from the sea from Revelation 13, but then on Monday say "No" to those who ask you to lead a march because one thinks of the tear gas, of prison, or one's family, or one's life. One could not avoid taking an active stand, taking the church and one's faith to the streets, as it were, even if that meant confrontation with both the authorities of the state and of the church. That was a point of no return which could no longer be avoided or postponed. The struggle for justice could no longer be seen as "added to" our faith; it was at the heart of our discipleship.

During that time too, the conviction grew that the church should take more direct responsibility for leadership in the struggle. The reasons were clear. In a sense the government had left us no choice. By the mid-eighties the state of emergency was fully in place, most of the organizations of the people were banned, and hundreds of individuals who had played leading roles were "restricted". Activists had gone into prison in their thousands and the apartheid regime, in its unrestrained violence, raged like a wild beast. The churches remained as the last bastion of the struggle, a true sanctuary, and were thrust into an activist role that many in the churches, especially their leadership, were not prepared for and did not want.

But there was more. It was also a logical, historical development. For a very long time the struggle in South Africa had been rooted in Christian faith; its spokespersons, like Rev. Calata, Chief Albert Luthuli, ZK Matthews, Steve Biko and a host of others had unashamedly claimed their faith as source of inspiration for struggle and sacrifice and hope. The oppressed people of South Africa are irrepressibly religious. Their faith was never, as was so easily the case in white Christianity, totally divorced from their daily experiences of suffering and hope. Though many, out of fear and sheer despair, accepted a pietistic, escapist religion, most did not and saw no dichotomy between their faith in a liberator God and their struggle for freedom. In their thousands they attended the funerals of those murdered by the regime, packed our services on Sundays and

---

[296] This is what we tried to address in speaking of "Black and Reformed: Contradiction or Challenge". See Boesak, *Black and Reformed* (Maryknoll: Orbis; Johannesburg: Skotaville, 1984).

during the week, flocked to special prayer services and ecumenical gatherings where political themes were not shied away from.

They believed passionately that the God of the exodus, who brought Israel from slavery and raised Jesus from the dead, would help them cross that sea into freedom, would raise them up as they fought for justice. The God of the Bible was the God of justice they prayed to in the silence of their homes, called upon in the midst of suffering, and relied upon in the heat of confrontation. They understood, in spite of the mammoth efforts of white Christianity in this country, the liberating and radical call of the gospel in terms of justice and freedom and human dignity. What African American scholar Gayraud Wilmore writes of their black counterparts in the United States, was also true of the oppressed people in South Africa. Notwithstanding the perversion of the Christian faith by whites, he says, black religion and the black church,

> discovered at the core of the Christian faith, something which had been obscured by white Christians: a radical predisposition for liberation and justice which stood in stark contrast to the benign conservatism of the white church and its sanctification of the Euro-American hegemony.[297]

That discovery is precisely the discovery of the biblical story - the story of the God of the exodus, the prophets of social justice and radical conversion, and of Jesus of Nazareth - and the difference that story makes *in* the human story. That discovery negated, and replaced, the ideologically-loaded theology white Christianity had sought to impose on them. It negated white domination as a God-given right and black oppression as a divinely ordained condition. It affirmed in them their irreplaceable status as children of God and freed them to see God's vision for them and their children. In dark and lean years, through veils of tears and suffering, in the most appalling situations of fearsome adversity, they drank from this well. And out of all this they fashioned a spirituality that infused the struggle, turned their weakness into strength and their fears into courage, their despair into a wellspring of hope. In calling upon the church to fulfil its prophetic role, therefore, the people did no more than call the church home, and thereby to truthfulness, and thereby to faithfulness.

Critical Solidarity or Prophetic Faithfulness

By the beginning of the 1990s there already were disturbing signs that the churches, which had briefly risen to the occasion and moved from formal protest to open challenge in 1988 and 1989,[298] were beginning to reconsider their stance. There arose a new and

---

[297] Gayraud S Wilmore, Black Religion and Black Radicalism, 231.

[298] After the banning of the last few UDF organizations in February 1988, and after the white elections of 1989, the churches took a united stand in their resistance to apartheid. The march, led by 25 church leaders in 1988 was unique and without question a highlight in the church's understanding of its role in the struggle. For a fairly accurate record of this see Wallis and Hollyday, Crucible of Fire, The Church Confronts Apartheid (Maryknoll: Orbis, 1989).

rather vigorous debate within the churches. On the one hand, churches who had been in the forefront of the struggle were now publicly thanking God that their "political role" was now over, and that they could now "return" to their "proper" roles. Some were propagating the view that the church is called merely to preach the "universal values" of love, peace, justice and what the white Dutch Reformed Churches used to call "neighbourliness". Anything else would make of the church a political party.

From different points of view, both groups came to the same conclusion and were seeking some safety in the very risky situation churches now thought they found themselves in. Both found this safety in the vagueness of a new pietism: one in the "proper" role of the church (saving souls?) and the other in hazy philosophical formulations based on a revitalized, but still misunderstood, "sovereignty in its own sphere" theology.

In response to this debate, we then wrote:

> We believe that the church still has political responsibility in the sense that we should continue to seek the Lordship of Jesus Christ over every area of life. The prophetic task of the church is not yet over and must be fulfilled at least as vigorously now as in the past. Moreover, when a new government is in place we shall have to be as clear as we tried to be *vis-à-vis* the white minority regime. The watchword here is "prophetic faithfulness". We shall also have to continue to respond to calls from the community to act with them in order to address the wrongs in our society.[299]

It is now clear that the churches have not responded well, neither to the new political situation nor to the calls of the community to continue to address the wrongs. The Minister, whatever his motivations, regretfully, is right. There are really no signs that the churches are nearly as ready to be as watchful, or (dare we say it?) as faithful as we were in confronting the apartheid regime with the truth of God's Word.

There has been no significant church or ecumenical action regarding some of the most burning issues in South Africa today. On the issues of poverty the institutional churches have remained largely silent. The lone voice to be heard is that of Anglican Archbishop Ndungane. The questions of the new government's insistence on the continued, and indeed growing, involvement in the manufacturing and sales of arms have been raised more insistently by others, whose own Christian commitment has compelled them to force the churches on board. Neither the growing gap between rich and poor and the rapid creation of a new, wealthy black elite, nor the non-existence of South Africa's commitment to human rights in our foreign policy have been addressed at all.

The voice of protest and challenge has come, rather, from smaller ecumenical groups and non-governmental organizations who have sometimes managed to get the churches

---

[299] Director's report, Foundation for Peace and Justice, 1989-90.

to co- sign a press statement. But of a church-initiated, theologically grounded, public challenge there is hardly any sign. The raging debate on the issues surrounding the Truth and Reconciliation Commission and its controversial Amnesty committee has been left to others, and there was virtually no meaningful theological debate or contribution to these crucial issues facing South Africa. There are many who share the bitter disappointment of former ANC MP and Ambassador, Carl Niehaus, who found himself "ashamed as a Christian" that the churches contributed very little theologically during the transitional phase of negotiations in this country, "except for a vague call for peace and reconciliation". On all significant matters, he says, "the church was confused and silent".[300]

There may be very good reasons for the silence of the church at this crucial juncture in South African history.

Φ Some may argue, as I have noted, that since "liberation" has been achieved, the church's public role is now over and the church should now revert to its "proper" calling.

Φ Many of the issues that the churches have raised are now being recognized, and addressed, by the new government. In fact, the special commissions set up by the government - commissions on human rights, gender equality, land, truth and reconciliation - are (or were initially) either headed by prominent church persons or have many persons of faith on their staffs. In that sense, the work that the church was forced to do in this regard has now been taken over by the government, and for that the church can only be grateful.

Φ Now is not the time for confrontation. The nation as a whole is called upon to participate in a process of (re)conciliation and dealing with the present and ongoing injustices means dealing with the legacy of the past. This can only open old wounds and make it harder for people to realize the ideal of the "rainbow nation".

Φ Nation-building is a difficult and sensitive process and in South Africa, with its terrible past, its black/white as well as its rich/poor divide it is doubly so. The churches, and religion in general, have been accused of playing a divisive rather than a unifying role in the past. It is now time for others to do what is necessary to secure our young democracy. Admitting this reality, the churches would do better to modestly step aside and let the "democratic forces" do the job.

Φ Many of us, the descendants and remnants of the struggle tradition in the churches, regard the liberation movement as "our" movement. The government is now "our" democratically elected government. They epitomise our own political and personal achievements. The policies they espouse are the crystallised ideals we fought and sacrificed for. Or so we would like to believe. Besides, we do not want to be identified with what most of us consider hypocritical and unnecessarily strident opposition politics.

---

[300] Quoted in Lyn S Graybill, *Truth and Reconciliation in South Africa* (Boulder CO, USA & London: Lynne Rienier Publishers, 2002) 26.

These arguments might in fact sound reasonable and plausible, and from one point of view very understandable. But it depends on where one stands when they are made. From another point of view, these are arguments from those in this country who have already "arrived"; they have crossed the Jordan of their "previously disadvantaged" status. They are already pitching their tents in the Promised Land. Those for whom very little, if anything, in life has changed, who still suffer daily from the legacy of apartheid and the benign neglect of the present rulers, find these arguments difficult to stomach. They are still, in the words of one old man from the Karoo who cornered me at a filling station in Three Sisters, just north of Beaufort West, and with whom I had a rather distressing conversation, "on this side of the red Sea". For them, in a very real sense, liberation has not yet come and they live in mortal fear that they will be forgotten even as they see the walls rising between themselves and their former comrades. Unlike the new black elite, these people have not yet arrived, and the church cannot act as if we all have.

On this point I would rather be led by the Belhar Confession of the Uniting Reformed Church in Southern Africa, which calls on the church "to stand where God stands "and is always to be found, namely on the side of the poor and the oppressed, the weak and the excluded. The issue for prophetic faithfulness is never who is in charge, but what they do while in charge. The quality of our liberation in 1994 for those who have done well, who have become the new billionaires and millionaires of economic transformation, is decidedly different than for the vast majority of our people, who remain crushed under the heavy burden of chronic poverty. South Africa's one-sided new-found sea of prosperity has created a divide amongst our own people. If the church does not speak for those who are being left behind, who will? If the church, identifying with the new elite, believes that we have already arrived, who will hear their voice from across that sea?

If the poorest of the poor have not arrived, if they cannot sit "each under his own vine and his own fig tree", the vision of justice from which the church lives has not been fulfilled. The fact that the new government has heeded the church and is taking human rights seriously is reason for gratitude, and the fact that the government has turned to individuals nurtured by faith is laudable. It does make us feel more like a partner in the national process than we ever were. But the price of this close relationship is high and the call is for eternal vigilance. The clamour of American politics, for instance, has never been more "Christian" than now, but the voice of the poor, and therefore the voice of God, has never been more effectively silenced than now.[301]

South Africa is a country of deep and disturbing inequalities. Those inequalities make the notion of a "rainbow nation", if not laughable, then at least suspect. For those who truly care, however, it is not an unattainable dream. But dreaming dreams and running with visions is not the same as living with the politics of delusion. Because the church lives the dream of God - that dream that envisions the inverted order of life: where

---

[301] See Jim Wallis, *The Soul of Politics* (New York, The New Press, Maryknoll: Orbis, 1994) especially Part Two: "The Broken Community".

the last shall be first, the poor filled with good things and the rich sent away empty-handed; where the bow of the mighty is broken and the feeble gird on strength; where the powerful are scattered in the confused thoughts of their hearts, but the poor are raised from the dust of the earth - many write off the church as unrealistic and "other-worldly". But they are wrong. The church sees this dream, not in the clouds, or the cards, or the market, but in the promises of God as these are reflected in the faces of the poor, the courage of the weak, the hope of the downtrodden and the joy of the oppressed.

The church knows that reconciliation can never become a reality without confrontation of the past and the wrongs of the present. And the price of reconciliation can never be the continued suffering of the voiceless. The church should know, better than most, that the expectations of the oppressed are not extravagant, nor unrealistic. They are basically universal: good and responsible government that knows the difference between right and wrong, justice in the courts, safety and peace in their neighbourhoods, equality before the law and equal protection *under* the law; gainful employment and a decent wage, decent housing and decent education for the children. Is it wrong that the people expect the government to address these needs urgently rather than to spend over R30 billion on weapon systems the country does not need?

The people who continue to raise these questions are heightening tensions in our young democracy, we are often told. It is not the people who heighten the tensions; it is government that causes the tensions by ignoring and neglecting their needs. Telling the government this in no uncertain terms would not be betrayal, as if the church had crawled into bed with a hypocritical opposition. The betrayal lies in not speaking up for the poor, in ignoring the plight of the needy, in denying both the gospel and the Lord of the church, in not opening our "mouth for the dumb". The betrayal lies in the breath-taking callousness of Parliament in proposing a 7% raise for themselves just after the hard and acrimonious battle of teachers, nurses and police to scrape together 6,2% from a government that did not just fight them on the issue, but humiliated them at just about every level.[302] We cannot be silent in the name of discretion. If the opposition uses the witness of the church for its own political ends, it will stand condemned by its own history. If the government condemns the church for its honesty, then it has much more to fear than just losing an election. Besides, the church knows of a higher loyalty; it is called by a higher power.

Deep down, I suspect, there is another matter. In fact, there may be several. Can it be that our churches which fought so hard against apartheid now feel more responsibility for the government than we should? After all, we have fought for them, called for the release of the political prisoners and the return of the exiles. We have defended them in our sermons and in our publications, praised their policies and exalted their ideals. We have preached at the funerals of their followers, who had shown such indescribable courage in the face of the apartheid might, and their young foot-soldiers who, heeding

---

[302] See *The Cape Times* and *Die Burger*, 7 October, 2004.

their call, set aside all else, picked up a gun and paid the price. We have visited those who were tortured, comforted their loved ones, encouraged them in the face of adversity and suffering.

We contrasted their ideals with the harsh policies of the apartheid regime; held them up as caring, compassionate and just. We hailed them as heroes and their leaders as touched by the hand of God. When the moment called, we went to prison for them and shed our own blood for their cause, which was also ours, risked our lives for what we, and they, believed in. Is the identification too close? Is it that when *they* falter, *we* fall, and when *they* fall, *we fail*? Is critique of government too much *self-critique*? Is this the price for having been so *right* in the struggle?

In a quiet, remarkable way, the government has acquired – no, *appropriated* – the language of the church to encapsulate the politics of the land. It's not just that they quote from the Bible as Thabo Mbeki so often does. Apartheid politicians did that all the time. But because they are ours and took *us* so seriously when we spoke of these things with them, in those secret meetings long before it became fashionable to organise Dakar safari's to "talk to the ANC", we hear them differently. They speak of peace and justice and truth and reconciliation, and they call upon us to defy the cynics and to believe that we can perform "new miracles". They talk about our "spirit that inspired us to sacrifice everything". Even though from time to time our politicians seek to de-spiritualise their speech according to their audience, these words call forth, as they are surely meant to, a deep spiritual resonance in people of faith such as we are, and they know us to be.[303] Often they shame us, for they speak of gender equality, gay and lesbian rights, and ecological responsibility in a way the church knows it should have, but did not have the courage to. On these issues, the liberation movement seems to have understood the Scriptures better than many of us in the churches, and that shames us - as it should.

For some reason we seem to think that if *they* say it, we don't have to. And because *they* said it first, we don't know *how* to. And so, out of a curious mixture of pride and shame, embarrassed joy and saddened hindsight, ownership and dispossession, we stand aside, made dumb by our own unwatchfulness. We are wordless while the debates rage, speechless while the words of our faith are filled with meanings alien to the gospel. That, I believe, more than the sometimes vituperative reactions of politicians to the hesitant critique the church has dared to utter, has robbed the church of the space to create and claim the prophetic instance. There is no alternative here: we must reclaim it. Just as under the apartheid regime, the church cannot allow the speech of the church, the words of Scripture, to become the words of political expediency, the phrases of media propaganda, or the unthinking, bloated verbosity of what passes for parliamentary discourse.

There is, of course, the grave danger that the church, in our desire to be part of the building programme for the new nation, is caught and trapped by our own naïveté. It

---

[303] On several occasions, Thabo Mbeki waxes lyrical on these issues. See his *Africa*, 150 and *passim*.

may well be that, just as some of us were not theologically and politically equipped to deal with the challenges presented by apartheid, we may once more find ourselves in a similar position in democratic South Africa. Let me try to illustrate.

On 12 July 2004 President Mbeki was the featured speaker at the Triennial Conference of the South African Council of Churches.[304] The President began by giving credit to the churches for their "enormous contribution" in the struggle by "joining" with the masses "to rid South Africa of the yoke of the white minority regime". Then Mbeki raised the question of what the churches should be doing regarding the task, "within the context of a democratic South Africa", of "ensuring that the dreams of the people are realised as speedily as possible". To this question the president suggested two responses he expected from the SACC.

First of all, the President addressed the same issue that former President Mandela did in 1996, and with the same directness. "It is clear," he said, "that it has become fashionable among some in our society, including some who claim to have contributed to the democratic victory, to position themselves as what are called watchdogs or advocacy groups". The president concedes, unlike Mr Mandela in 1996, that this "may be perfectly legitimate" and "may very well be a necessary task in ensuring that the democratic victory does not lose its way and betray the hopes of the millions who fought for the liberty we all enjoy". He made clear, however, that while it may be legitimate, it is not preferable. The "temptation" to assume this role, the president added in words disturbingly reminiscent of the PW Botha era with its "Foreign Funding Act", and of President Mugabe's railings against his political opponents whose money comes from "abroad", "is enhanced by the availability of foreign funding for those who would be watchdogs". Even though Mbeki admits that the SACC would probably not be satisfied with just "observing, analysing and assessing the actions of those who continue to act as agents of change, content merely to criticize or approve what others are striving to achieve", he clearly does not see this role for the SACC, and therefore for the church in South Africa. That, he says emphatically, "is not the principal task of the Council".

The principal task of the churches is "to play its part among the forces in our country that have defined themselves as actors for the progressive reconstruction and development of our country", as understood in the "social contract" that the ANC promised the people in the 2004 elections, "to create jobs and fight poverty". *That* is the "national agenda" which the churches have to understand and support, within the framework of the concepts traditional to African social practice of *letsema* and *vuk'uzunzile,* in other words the spirit of volunteerism and "standing to do things for yourself", (rather than expecting the government do them for you).

This spirit, which the churches must embrace, informs their participation in the national agenda which Thabo Mbeki describes as "taking our destiny into our own hands". He summarises the national agenda in six points:

---

[304] The speech is available from the SACC in Johannesburg.

Φ The fight against poverty and underdevelopment which stands "at the centre";

Φ The growth and expansion of the economy, which must ensure raising the standard of living and the quality of life of the poor and the more equitable sharing of wealth;

Φ Better safety and security for all, which include the transformation of the social conditions of the poor;

Φ South Africa should continue to occupy its place among the global pace-setters in the challenge to create a non-racial and non-sexist society;

Φ The "great importance" the government attaches to the issue of national cohesion;

Φ The last point of the national agenda is the mobilisation of our people to sustain their role as their own liberators, which they played as we fought for our liberation from racist oppression and exploitation. "The task of these masses today is to join the people's contract for a better life for all".

This is the national agenda the people, as well as the churches mobilising the people, must carry out.

Clearly, the agenda, being the ANC's own political programme as set out during the election campaign, has already been set by the leadership. This the churches must affirm and join, in the spirit of volunteerism and self-help, avoiding the "temptation" to see their role as one of "watchdog" over the government, its policies and practices. Immediately the newly elected President of the SACC, Prof. Russell Botman, responded that the churches understood quite well what the President had spoken about, and that there was agreement that there was indeed no role for the church as watchdog, but rather as "partner" in achieving the national agenda.[305]

The first question to arise is obviously whether it is up to the president to tell the churches what their role should be in society, or whether it is the responsibility of the churches to explain to the president their biblical mandate *vis-à-vis* matters of public interest. Secondly, I think the churches of the SACC, in their understandable desire to be a partner of government in the very worthwhile project of nation building and the achievement of the "national agenda", may have made a fundamental mistake which may cost us dearly. In my view, I discern three profound failures in the uncritical response of the SACC to the invitation of the president.

The first is a failure to learn from the lessons of history, the second is a failure to see what is in the text, and the third is a failure to see what is behind the text. My reference to history is not in regard to the days of apartheid, although much is doubtless to be learned from the church-state relationship at that time. My example is more immediate. Pressures to toe the party line and not be too critical of the leadership of the movement and its decisions came quite soon in our new democracy. In fact, it was former president Nelson Mandela who first led the attack on those bodies and organs of civil society who

---

[305] According to Prof. Botman on SABC's *PM Live* that same day.

seek to "play the role of critical watchdog" over the movement and serve as channels for grassroots communities to voice their grievances and wishes[306]. Mandela was quite harsh, describing such efforts as posing an "illegitimate challenge" to the leading political role of ANC. So from the start the ANC had made it clear that under its watch civil society, which in their understanding includes the church, should play a supporting but apolitical role in South African society. The ANC leads, as the slogan goes, and any challenges to that leadership are *a priori* "illegitimate". Legitimate political leadership can only come from the movement.

Indeed, "civil society" in general seemed to have accepted this, as was clearly demonstrated by the *2001 Civil Society Initiative,* organised by former National Party politician Roelf Meyer and attended by national and international leaders including former presidents Mandela and Bill Clinton.[307] "The theme of the conference, as well as the overall initiative," writes US academic Krista Johnson, "was one of encouraging the spirit of volunteering and self-help, promoting social partnerships between government and civil society organisations, and defining an apolitical role for civil society organisations as assistants to government in service delivery".[308] Johnson quotes Roelf Meyer:

> The CSI holds the view that in South Africa civil society forms part of a social partnership with the state and with business. It works alongside government and business to further the common national interest *in a non-political arena.*[309]

In other words, the church is expected to support the government in its initiatives to formulate and implement policy, but will not be allowed to critically engage government on the wisdom of those policies, or the manner of their implementation. The church is to be a junior partner, which I am not sure the church must be, not a "watchdog", let alone a "critical voice over against" the government, as I believe the church must be. And this is the second failure we detect. The SACC seemed not to have understood that the President was inviting them to merely accept what government has already determined to be the "national agenda". We are not invited to critically help fashion the national agenda, merely to accept and support it. The national agenda itself as defined by the President is something the churches cannot fail to support. But that is not the point. There are issues here that need ongoing, serious debate. It is not just a matter of the nation "taking our destiny into our own hands"; *that* we heartily applaud. The question is *how.* For example, the way the economy grows now is through our submission

---

[306] *Report of the President of the African National Congress, Nelson Mandela,* 5th National Conference of the ANC, December 16, 1997, Mafikeng. The problem at issue here was the abolishment of the UDF and the unhappiness of many about that decision. And one in which I personally was involved. But that important debate would take us too far from the point we are trying to make here.

[307] Cf. Krista Johnson, "Liberal or Liberation Framework? The Contradictions of ANC Rule in South Africa". *Journal of Contemporary African Studies, 21, 2, May 2003,* 321-338.

[308] *Ibid.,* 337.

[309] Johnson, at 337.

to the relentless demands of globalization, which has cost us millions of jobs instead of creating more. The economy expands at the cost of the poor and the needy and the government is saying, "There is no other way". The effects of that same process of globalization are preventing the wealth of the country from being equitably spread, creating a small, enormously rich black elite, but in fact widening the gap between them and the ever poorer masses.

Uplifting the social conditions of the poor is another issue we agree upon, but then there must be open debate on issues such as priorities in government spending, about the huge waste, for instance, in the endless experiments – from the type of housing the poor are being offered, to those in education over the last ten years that have brought us no closer to a solution. There is an enormous contribution the churches can and must make to the debate about "national cohesion", which includes the questions of racism, reconciliation and justice. But on all these issues the churches are waved aside, relegated to *letsema* and *vuk'uzenzele*, not allowed to critically help shape the debate and the policy, bringing to bear those arguments fashioned and informed by the churches' own understanding, inspirations and convictions, which did so much to give identity to the struggle and help gain the democratic victory the president seems to be so grateful for. And it is really not good enough for Thabo Mbeki to say that the struggle against apartheid is over, that therefore in the new democratic South Africa the critical witness of the church is no longer needed.

It is in this regard that we must discuss the third problem, namely our failure to read *behind* the text. Why is it that Nelson Mandela, and after him Thabo Mbeki, are so adamant that the church should not challenge the government, or the leadership of the ANC which at this particular time in our history amounts to the same thing? Especially on those issues we agree must be our national goals, when we agree on the principles of our national agenda? Why are they so anxious to put this "vanguard of the masses" during apartheid (as Mbeki calls the churches) on the sidelines of political activity in the new democracy?

We gain a better understanding of this phenomenon when we read the careful analysis of Krista Johnson in that same piece we have quoted above.[310] Johnson shows how much, on these matters, the ANC has been influenced by the philosophical arguments of Lenin. Lenin, like Marx, believed in the participation of the masses in the struggle for the "democratic revolution". However, Lenin argued that, given its lack of cohesiveness and limited focus, the working class required (a Communist) vanguard leadership to control the spontaneous and "decentralised" actions of the masses. Advice may be

---

[310] The point Johnson wants to make is different from ours but it remains extraordinarily helpful. Her argument concerns the ways in which, ironically and paradoxically, the Marxist-Leninist way of thinking of the ANC is so very like the liberal, Western approach when it comes to "leadership" and the role of "the masses" and other role-players in society. For liberalism and Leninism alike, there was agreement on who would be qualified to lead the struggle. Liberals saw leadership in its intelligentsia and bourgeoisie. Leninists saw it in the "party" or the "collective" leadership. In any event, the agreement was that the "people" could not lead. The masses, the rest, could not be trusted with this process. Hence the "contradictions of ANC rule" in her title.

given from the bottom up, but decisions are taken at the top. In the unified, hierarchical structure, decisions, and therefore guidance, from the top down are regarded as the most efficacious. That principle is called "democratic centralism". For a political programme to be successful, the leadership must be "the vanguard". In this thinking the task of political transformation could not be left to ordinary people, but required a select group of the political elite to plan and execute the process. Along this line of Leninist philosophy, a select group of intellectuals have the task of thinking and acting on behalf of the masses.[311] Johnson then shows how, despite many practical adaptations in other matters (such as the switch from Marxist economic policies to neo-liberal capitalism), the ANC as an organization consistently held onto this principle during its period in exile, as well as after its return to South Africa in the 1990s.[312] Persistent is the theme, from Oliver Tambo in 1969 to Nelson Mandela in 1996, that *the primacy of the political leadership is unchallenged and supreme, and all revolutionary formations and levels (whether armed or not) are subordinate to this leadership…"* [313]

For the ANC *anno* 1996, the boundary between the state (the supreme revolutionary leadership) and civil society is just as clear, as are the vanguardist notions of an inviolable separation between the role of the leadership and that of the masses. For the ANC it is a question of "the combination of the expertise and professionalism concentrated in the democratic state and the capacity for popular mobilisation that resides within the trade unions and genuinely representative non-governmental popular organisations… The democratic state therefore has the responsibility to ensure that this independent and representative non-government sector has the necessary strength to play its role in ensuring that the people themselves… become conscious activists for development and social transformation".[314]

In other words, Johnson goes on to explain, and I agree, the author ascribes to the state the role of knowledge producer, able to develop policy and set the agenda for social transformation. He restricts the role of civil society organisations (among which the ANC numbers the churches) to that of mobilisation and implementing directions from above. He attempts to make a clear distinction between the government or party experts who "know" and the mass of people who are only supposed to apply this knowledge, leaving out of the equation the capacity of the average citizen to act and form his or her own opinion.[315]

Within Alliance politics, of course, there are those who, because they know it so well and could recognise it earlier and easier than the churches, could discern more quickly what was happening. To be fair, their recognition came sooner because it is their

---

[311] *Op. cit.,* 325-326.
[312] *Op. cit.,* 327-331.
[313] *Op. cit.,* 329 (Partial emphasis mine).
[314] From an ANC document, 1996, the author of which is widely believed to be Thabo Mbeki himself. The document shows clearly that "democratic centralism, tight internal discipline and strong central co-ordination continue to be the main organising principles of the ANC". (Johnson, 335).
[315] *Ibid.*

ideological heritage, so to speak. Thus SACP intellectual Jeremy Cronin rang the alarm bells at what he and the SACP described as the "Zanufication" of the ANC.[316] It is not that Cronin meant that South Africa was becoming like Zimbabwe and that the chaotic situation in that country would soon be duplicated here. This interpretation was more the rather desperate attempt of the mainly white opposition party to score some badly needed political points. It was also more than just "bureaucratisation", which put the power within the ANC in the hands of a small clique ("Mbekiites", Cronin calls them), who would presumably drive through whatever Mr Mbeki wants, against the will of the majority of the ANC membership whom, Cronin believes, are in support of the ideological positions of the SACP which Mr Mbeki has discarded. These masses, according to Cronin, see the Communist Party, "in a moral sense, as some kind of guarantor that the revolutionary, radical credentials of the ANC haven't disappeared, haven't debacled".

But Cronin had something else in mind, I think. His attack was in fact focused on his perception that Thabo Mbeki himself is becoming more and more of a dictator, a more sophisticated version of Robert Mugabe, stifling any criticism or meaningful debate within the ANC and the Alliance, isolating himself not only from the masses who support the ANC, but also from those in the leadership (presumably the SACP) who disagree with him. In Alliance jargon, Thabo Mbeki is displaying "Stalinist" tendencies, a term Cronin does not shy away from in this interview. Apart from the fact that some may see irony in the fact that a leading Communist is accusing the president of being "Stalinist", there are serious implications to this accusation and the resultant angry response from the ANC was not unexpected. With these issues in full public debate, the church cannot plead the false innocence of political naïveté. We do not necessarily agree with Jeremy Cronin in his judgement of Mr Mbeki, but it is helpful to at least take heed of the warning signs that have caused such turmoil within the leading political partnership in the country. This is important, for another part of the workings of "democratic centralism" dictates that once the leadership has debated an issue, had taken into account the input "from below" and made a decision, there can be no public dissent. Even if an individual wishes to differ in private, S Bronner tells us in "The Political Theory of Rosa Luxemburg",[317] he or she would have to support that same decision in public. That is precisely the decision taken by the 2003 ANC Conference in Stellenbosch, Western Cape. Such a decision, needless to say, has immense consequences for Christian public witness when one is a member of, or in alliance with, the African National Congress.

This is "democratic centralism" and this is the philosophy behind the tensions whenever the church, or any other group, seriously seeks to engage the ANC leadership or the government in fundamental debate on issues regarding governance or the state of our democracy. The government's emotional reactions to questions regarding the R30 billion

---

[316] The transcript of Cronin's interview with Irish academic Helena Sheehan was made available by the ANC leadership.
[317] In *New Politics,* 1,4:1771-187, cited by Johnson, *op. cit.,* 324.

defence expenditure is a case in point. This, I submit, has serious consequences for our democracy as well as for the witness of the church in our democracy. For those of us who discovered all this only belatedly, it was a bit hard to swallow. Of course we read Fanon's *Wretched of the Earth* in which he so eloquently warned anti-colonialist movements against this disastrous distinction between the party and the popular-democratic organs, or the leaders and the masses. But in our revolutionary fervour and passionate naïveté we never thought we would be confronted with the same phenomenon. But it does make certain things better to understand: the irritation with which government treats trade unions who threaten to, and do, go on strike; why teachers and other civil servants speak of "arrogance" in their dealings with their Minister; the spiteful silence on the issues of HIV/AIDS when government is confronted with the activism of the masses; the offensive manner in which a Minister tells a Christian activist to "come off his moral high horse", when that person wants government to answer questions about the arms deal in court. It has serious ramifications for the role of the church as well, not as "watchdog", but as the representative of Christ, the community of Jesus, or, as Trevor Manuel correctly, although perhaps unknowingly, called it, the incarnation of God.

This volunteer, non-political support-role we are expected to play, whilst true knowledge and expertise reside in the leadership of some political party, may indeed be acceptable to Roelf Meyer and the "organs of civil society", but the church is more than that. And the President deserved to have heard this at the SACC conference. The church is the bearer of the vision of the Kingdom of God, and in its mission the charge of Isaiah 61 and Luke 4 remains central. It is given its mandate not from society in general, which tolerates it as just another sociological phenomenon or a partner in the NGO sector, nor from the state, which expects from it submissive support but not critical engagement, and which regards it as a distribution centre of welfare grants *for* the poor but not as the genuine voice and partner *of* the poor. The church receives its mandate from God to Whom it owes its highest responsibility and deepest loyalty. We have learned too many painful lessons from Africa's post-colonial experiences, and from our own apartheid past, to allow a new Constantinianism, as American theologian Stanley Hauerwas calls it, to take hold in South Africa again. Besides, for Christians from the Calvinist tradition the Lordship of Jesus Christ remains central in our thinking about and our doings in the world. There is not one inch of life that does not fall under the sovereignty of Christ. No matter how sovereign nation states or other political entities might regard themselves to be, ultimate sovereignty belongs only to God. There is thus no way in which a government can determine the boundaries of the testimony of the church, or dictate the public actions of the church. For the church to speak publicly on behalf of the poor, the silenced and the dejected, and for justice, peace and equity, is a biblical mandate the church dare not ignore or forget. We learned our commitment to justice and the poor not from Marx or Lenin, but from the torah, the prophets and Jesus of Nazareth. We have inherited our passion not from political slogans and ideological philosophising, but from the Psalms and the revolutionary songs of biblical women like Hannah and Mary, the mother of Jesus.

The church of Jesus Christ is not just another non-governmental organisation, however much the government would like to classify us as such. The church cannot be relegated to the sideline activism of volunteerism, charity and apolitical cheer-leadership, especially not at a time when critical engagement with our elected government is crucial in facing issues such as globalization, economic justice, HIV/AIDS and nation building, and the voice for public justice is so burningly necessary. This is especially glaring in the light of the historic role of the churches in the anti-apartheid struggle and the benefits the liberation movement is now enjoying as a direct result of the churches' political participation in the struggle.

There is of course much value in the critical reminder that the church has made many mistakes, and that its own history is full of shame as regards the issues of human freedom and dignity, on which it has betrayed both the people and the gospel. The church should take that seriously, and it should cause us to stand in humility both before God and the world. But it is less than honest to speak of the church, when it suits the occasion, as if it were one monolithic bloc, and as if the history of the Christian church of the West is the same as history of the church in Africa, for example; or as if the churches that created and benefited from apartheid are the same as those who suffered in the cause of ridding our people from the yoke of apartheid. And humility in acknowledgement of our failures and sinfulness does not mean silence in the face of injustice and inhumanity wherever they may occur. We, the children of slaves who believe in Jesus Christ as our Saviour, who are the singers of the Psalms of rage and longing, and the inheritors of the gospel of liberation, should not allow ourselves to be burdened with, and paralysed by the sins of the colonialist church, as an excuse for our voice to be silenced and our public witness to be impugned.

But there is a still deeper, and at some level for me personally, far more disturbing question, and I raise it with trembling and hesitation. Can it be that the churches knew that the apartheid regime, in its perverse insistence that apartheid was Christian, had opened itself, against its will, far more to the appeal of the gospel than the ANC government is able to do? That because they called upon the name of the Lord, they could not avoid hearing the voice that spoke in that Name? And even if in hearing they did not *listen*, that that Name would still wear them down? The name of Yahweh spells justice and liberation, wholeness and humanbeingness, is filled with holiness and awe. In that Name Moses invoked the plagues upon Egypt and called on Pharaoh to let his people go. In that Name Israel crossed the Red Sea and saw the death of evil on the sea shore. In that Name the prophets spoke, and Elijah made Ahab tremble, Amos called for justice to roll down like waters, and Jeremiah faced the rage of Jehoiakim. In that Name Jesus was baptized, claimed and glorified, and in that Name Peter stood before the Sanhedrin telling them that he would obey God rather than human beings. Those who call upon that Name cannot prevent being overpowered by that Name. So the apartheid establishment denied the gospel while preaching the gospel, betrayed the Name while calling upon the Name, but all the while, inexorably, unavoidably, eroded their ability to resist the power of that Name. Are we afraid that, because the ANC ignores the Name, is not in awe of its power, not overcome by its presence, there is no common ground of appeal, except for those vague and well-worn political slogans others have laid claim to, and they themselves seem no longer to believe in?

Fleeing from a worse tyranny

In 1994 the South African Council of Churches called an ecumenical consultation to ponder the role of the church after apartheid. Aside from the fact that issues such as poverty, gender equality or ecology were scarcely mentioned, or the fact that women, even then, were severely under-represented, the report raises the issue of the relationship to the new government. That relationship ought to be one of "critical solidarity". That in itself is not the problem, for as John Calvin has taught us, government is not the "natural enemy" of the church and certainly one cannot blame the churches in expecting a different response from an ANC government than we could have from the old apartheid regime.

The problem is that nowhere is the critical, prophetic role of the church mentioned. It is almost as if the consultation could not foresee a time when the church and the state might differ on priorities or policies, or that the nature of politics would itself be redeemed by the mere fact of the participation of the African National Congress Alliance. As if the ANC itself would not be in need of critique or correction or redemption. The subsequent silence of the church in the public arena seems to validate this conclusion. This is a grave mistake, and one we have seen before with those "critical minorities" in the white Dutch Reformed churches. In the end the critical solidarity with their white churches and with the regime precluded genuine solidarity with the suffering masses, and prevented them from that full commitment that was so needed in the struggle. The very real pain this dilemma caused them was, however, not as deep as the pain caused us by their inability to give themselves fully to the struggle for justice. Their hearts may have been in the struggle, but their bodies never were. One need not be a cynic to understand the truth in Lord Acton's famous dictum about power and the power of its ability to corrupt. Neither does one need to be a Calvinist to heed Calvin's warning that "kings are pleased with their own greatness and wish their own pleasure to be treated as an oracle" and that "their obstinacy utterly perverts justice".[318]

The voice of black theologian Molefe Tsele echoes that same critical hesitation and ought to become the voice of the church as a whole. "We need", he asserts, "to test the significance of our time and our new democracy, and ask in spite of the litany of social ills that followed in its wake, whether we can say that something new, opportune, creative and authentic is taking place here; and further that, unless we grasp the moment, we may risk relapsing into a worse tyranny than we have known".[319]

---

[318] See Calvin's commentary on the book of Daniel.
[319] Molefe Tsele, "Kairos and Jubilee", in H Russel Botman and Robin M Petersen, *To Remember and to Heal, Theological and Psychological Reflections on Truth and Reconciliation* (Cape Town: Human and Rousseau, 1996) 71.

That same Molefe Tsele said something else the churches cannot afford to neglect, or forget, and his brave voice admonishes us in no uncertain terms:

> We must run away from an incestuous co-habitation with government, for to do so will be suicide to our mission as the church... To be in alliance with a persecuted political movement is one thing, but to become its ally in government is another... Are we useful tools for the ANC's agenda of ascendancy to power, remembered only when needed, or do we have our own agenda?[320]

That, I submit, is the challenge. Spoken in 2001, and with Molefe Tsele now in the structures of the SACC as their Secretary-General, those courageous, prophetic words, almost predicting the dilemma of the SACC three years later (including the very word "agenda"!) take on added significance and power. Leaving the state to its own devices is not forgivable. It deprives the state of understanding its vast possibilities and its own limitations; the exciting heights its power can achieve and the fearsome boundaries beyond which its power cannot, dare not, go. It deprives politics of the wholesome confrontation with spirituality and the call to radical conversion. It deprives politicians of the always necessary reminder that they are not God, but servants of God for the good of the people. It deprives, most of all, the powerless and the voiceless of their voice and their future. In the end, it will deprive the nation of the redemption of its soul.

The church in South Africa is called still by God to be a prophetic, healing, critical, eschatological presence. No political sea change can change that. Now, as then, we are still called to be the voice of the voiceless. Now, as then, it is no easy task. In reminding ourselves of that, we may do well to remember what we said to ourselves in the darkest days of our struggle:

> *We are not called to be fearful, we are called to love;*
> *We are not called to be perfect; we are called to be faithful;*
> *We are not called to be fearless, we are called to be obedient;*
> *We are not called to be all knowing, we are called to believe;*
> *We are not called to claim, we are called to give;*
> *We are not called to be victorious, we are called to be courageous;*
> *We are not called to lord it over others, we are called to serve others.*

---

[320] Cited in Nico Koopman & Robert Vosloo, *Die Ligtheid van die Lig, Morele oriëntasie in 'n postmoderne tyd* (Wellington: Lux Verbi, 2002), 46.

For it is in serving that we shall reign;
It is through courage that we shall find victory;
It is by giving all that we shall gain all;
It is in believing that we shall find certainty;
It is in obedience that we shall overcome;
It is in faithfulness that we shall find perfection;
It is in loving that we shall dispel fear;
It is in slavery to Christ and his justice that we shall find freedom;
Now and forever, for ourselves, and for the world.[321]

---

[321] Allan Boesak, Presidential Address, World Alliance of Reformed Churches, Seoul, Korea, 1989, *WARC General Council Report* (Geneva: WARC, 1990) 154.

CHAPTER SIX

"A NATION AT PEACE WITH ITSELF"
Reconciliation, Justice and the Building of the Nation

The Quest for Reconciliation

It is time to turn to yet another crucial element in our efforts to mould the African Renaissance, namely reconciliation. It is crucial, because it is at the heart of what South Africa is striving for, and therefore essential in its own understanding not just as a nation but as the nation giving leadership to the African renaissance as the "search for the African soul". We have already taken note of the judgement of Dr Ibbo Mandaza from Zimbabwe as he speaks of "the ideology of reconciliation". We shall have to see whether this negative assessment is justified.

"We had no option but to create the Truth and Reconciliation Commission" admits Adv. Johnny de Lange, Deputy Minister for Justice in an address entitled "The Historical Context, Legal Origins and Philosophical Foundation of the South African Truth and Reconciliation Commission".[322] The reasons are many – from the political stalemate (the "equilibrium in the balance of forces" he calls it), to the destructive capacity of the outgoing, illegitimate white minority regime; the choice for a negotiated settlement instead of a revolutionary take-over; the need to deal effectively with the oppressive past and the gradual establishment of a constitutional state, to name just some of them.

The ANC government had set for itself the goals of "reconciliation, reconstruction and development". These, the "kernel of the social transformation project", could best be reached by the "attainment of the twin goals of socio-economic justice and the restoration of moral order in our country".[323] Of course, the international community expected South Africa to deal with the past in a way that would derive its legitimacy and morality from international human rights practices, and that, in turn, would determine the new regime's legitimacy and acceptability in the international community. The answer to that demand would be found in a truth commission, "rather than" Nuremberg-type trials or even worse, people-driven vigilantism. And even though there is in South Africa a constitutional commitment to reconciliation and nation-building, and a need to create a "common memory" that can be recognized and acknowledged, "our call for a truth commission did not come from the constitution or any law, *but from our morality as people*

---

[322] In Charles Villa-Vicencio and Wilhelm Verwoerd (eds.) *Looking Back, Reaching Forward* (Cape Town: UCT Press, and London: Zed Books, 2000)14-31.
[323] *Op. cit.*, 16, 17.

who want to heal our nation, and restore the faith of those in our country and the international community in our common future".[324]

For De Lange, as for most ANC representatives initially, these ingredients were the makings of a quite unique situation, even though South Africa's TRC was by no means the first such commission to be set up.[325] This uniqueness stems from "our morality as a people", the "unique epilogue" of the South African Constitution,[326] and the "win-win" situation of the "South African way", that is, how to "achieve both justice and reconciliation – not just one or the other", to rise above narrow, party-political interests to a "higher, nobler goal for our divided country as a whole to emerge from a shameful past as the winner".[327]

The question of justice is important, and De Lange refers to it "in the broadest sense" – "collective justice, social justice, a restorative justice that seeks to address and deliver to the collective – that is aimed at nation building and reconciliation". It is a justice that "focuses on the future rather than the past; on understanding rather than vengeance; on reparation rather than retaliation; on *ubuntu* rather than victimization".[328] In order to "avoid the constraints of retributive justice" De Lange writes, South Africa had to broaden its perception of justice "beyond punishment". In his view the country had succeeded admirably, since in the process,

> justice is not only being done, it is seen to be done. It is restorative justice in its essence, but also contains essential elements of retributive justice in that the truth is told, lies are exposed and the perpetrators are becoming known. It may not be perfect justice – justice does not exist in its perfect state and compromises have to be made for the greater collective good.[329]

---

[324] *Op. cit.*, 18 (my emphasis). The development of a "collective memory" and "shared memories of the past" was considered part of the "mandate" of the TRC, and is important in weighing the value of the TRC for South Africa's national life. Cf. Ruben R Richards, *Truth, Lies and Public Discourse: In search of a collective consciousness about the past through the work of the South African Truth and Reconciliation Commission.* Paper prepared for the 13th Baptist World Alliance Congress, Durban, South Africa July 1998.

[325] There have been at least 18 such commissions world-wide before South Africa's TRC, including Uganda (1974), Bolivia (1982) Argentina (1983/84), and Chile (1990/1991), to name only a few.

[326] Under the heading *National Unity and Reconciliation,* the Constitution states, among other things, "The pursuit of national unity, the wellbeing of all South African citizens and peace require reconciliation between the people of South Africa and the reconstruction of society." Prof John De Gruchy adds another element. While other commissions were "just" truth commissions, "ours was chaired not by a judge or a lawyer but by an archbishop, a pastor and father confessor". *Reconciliation: Restoring Justice* (Cape Town: David Philip, 2002), 41. This fact gave rise to a whole new set of problems and arguments, which we shall discuss.

[327] *Op. cit.*, 23.

[328] *Op. cit.*, 24.

[329] *Op. cit.*, 25.

This means that the perpetrators will be given amnesty if they "disclose the truth" about their misdeeds, and the victims will have the satisfaction of having "heard the truth", and of reparations by the government. Those perpetrators who have not disclosed the full truth will be prosecuted through the "normal" judicial system, even though that process does not hold out much hope for justice in the courts when it comes to the prosecution of persons responsible for apartheid criminal acts. Referring to the unsuccessful prosecution of former Minister of Defence Magnus Malan who refused to apply for amnesty and whose defence was paid for by the state, De Lange complains that the legal system "at the time" suffered from a "serious crisis of credibility, legitimacy and efficacy" and "competent, honest, professional investigations (and) prosecutions" could hardly have been expected.[330]

The unsuccessful trial of apartheid scientist Dr Wouter Basson is another such example. The point, however, is that this trial took place six years into the new democracy and in many ways the same critique can still be made of the judicial system in South Africa and, indeed, has been. The new Minister for Justice, Bridget Mabandla, at her first public appearance bemoaned the "untransformed" nature of the system and black Cape High Court President Judge Hlope has lashed out publicly at white colleagues on the bench whose racist attitudes make it hard for black judges to function and for the bench to perform with credibility.[331] The point is simply that ten years after democracy the situation is disturbingly the same and victims of apartheid abuses will not see prosecutions for apartheid offences and do not see any hope of meaningful reparations either. So those "compromises for the greater good" shall have to be made in the first place by the victims.

ANC intellectual and former Minister of Education, Kader Asmal, and others also speak of the "need" for "genuine reconciliation".[332] Reconciliation, the authors argue, does not mean "painless forgetting". Rather it means restoring friendship between people. The "heart" of reconciliation is not the "manufacturing of cheap and easy bonhomie". It is the facing of unwelcome truths in order to harmonize incommensurable world views so that inevitable and continuing conflicts and differences stand at least "within a single universe of comprehensibility". In this rich sense reconciliation (as envisaged by the work of the TRC) is thus a "real closing of the ledger book of the past".

The authors emphasize the moral import of reconciliation for the nation. It is part of the "revival of the South African conscience", the "flipside" of forgiveness". Thus genuine reconciliation involves moral and political restitution in the sense of the German term *Wiedergutmachung*, to make good again. It must do more. It must "bring about a rupture with the skewed ethics of apartheid and so upset any possibility of smooth sailing on a

---

[330] *Op. cit.,* 29.

[331] *Rapport,* 10 October 2004. "Of course there is racism on the bench" said Deputy Minister Johnny De Lange in parliament. Cf. *Die Burger,* 29 October 2004. The implications of this remain deeply ominous for the justice system and for democracy.

[332] Kader Asmal, Louise Asmal and Ronald Suresh Roberts, *Reconciliation Through Truth, A Reckoning of apartheid's criminal governance* (Cape Town: David Philip, 1996) 46ff.

previously immoral course". We cannot allow yesterday's immorality to govern today's processes of moral repair.

They warn that we must not be too disturbed by those who will want to deny history. What matters is not merely the fact that we remember history, but the way in which we remember it.[333] The TRC is expected to help South Africans in this process of creating the collective memory we have spoken of before, even though in our case it might prove extraordinarily difficult. Hence the hope that is invested in South Africa's reconciliation process and the "new environment" the new democratic reality will help create:

> So often it appears that history teaches only despair; cynicism can seem to sweep all before it, as it did in the old South African governance. But in a new environment, one that takes unflinchingly the full measure of the past, South Africa can become a safe place for idealism, the sort of place and time when hope and history rhyme.[334]

President Thabo Mbeki too had spelled out his own understanding of reconciliation. Reconciliation is the "twin" of transformation, and national reconciliation and national unity "had to belong among the principal results of the resolution of the South African conflict".[335] Without that reconciliation the conflict would never come to an end, and it would never be possible to embark on the programme of reconstruction and development. Hence the need for the TRC to discover the truth about apartheid abuses, to enable those involved to obtain amnesty and those affected to receive reparation. But Mbeki stresses that "reconciliation that merely sought to reassure the former rulers by forgiving them their sins and legitimizing their positions of racial privilege could never be sustained... reconciliation also had to be situated within the context of a vigorous process of transformation".[336] Reconciliation is both political and the result of a political process.

And yet Mbeki knows that reconciliation is more than just politics. There is an unavoidable personal element which South Africa sorely needs:

> The challenge ahead of us is to achieve reconciliation between the former oppressor and the formerly oppressed, between black and white, between rich and poor (who, in our conditions, are also described by colour), between men and women, the young and the old, the able and the disabled... South Africans seeking to reconcile ourselves with one another... moved to act together in pursuit of common goals, understanding that we cannot escape a shared destiny...[337]

---

[333] *Op. cit.*, 216.
[334] *Op. cit.*, 216.
[335] *Africa – the time has come*, 63 and 40ff.
[336] *Op. cit.*, 63.
[337] *Op. cit.*, 41.

Despite the biblical language however, ("South Africans reconciling themselves to one another") Mbeki is adamant that we should not confuse him with a preacher even though he is aware of the Christian understanding of reconciliation which dominates the minds of most people in South Africa:

> Certainly, in our case we could not approach the matter of reconciliation purely on the basis of the biblical injunction to love thy neighbour as thyself, as a voluntary outpouring of goodwill by a multitude of individuals who happened to be moved by the spirit. Reconciliation has and had to be based on the removal of injustice. This is precisely why, in our case, it is impossible to achieve reconciliation, an accommodation of different interests, without effecting fundamental transformation.[338]

There is a tone of slight but unmistakable disdain in this remark which at some level is understandable. There is among the ranks of the ANC leadership a morbid fear of sounding "Christian", even though in our South African circumstances that can hardly be avoided. Both Thabo Mbeki's and Trevor Manuel's frequent forays into the Hebrew and Christian Scriptures show that and those forays are not at all always sarcastic. But it also has to do with the subject under discussion. The word "reconciliation", since Paul wrested it from classical Greek in his second letter to the Corinthians, has become a biblical term that can no longer be divested of its theological meaning. It is so central to the Christian faith that it is totally impossible to be a Christian without being confronted with the demand for reconciliation.

But it also reflects a fundamental misunderstanding. Thabo Mbeki is persistent in his demand that reconciliation without fundamental transformation of society is empty and meaningless. That it is not a simple matter of "forgiving perpetrators their sins", but that it must challenge the bitter realities of poverty and social stagnation, and that it must become meaningful within the framework of the nation's commitment to equity and justice. And he is absolutely right. But the President thinks that the Christian understanding of reconciliation has nothing to do with justice, indeed, undermines it. He believes that the biblical injunction to "love your neighbour" is an inadequate, vague concept that agitates against a vigorous commitment to justice. But he is wrong. The biblical call for neighbourly love is precisely embedded in the love of God which finds its deepest meaning in justice. God is a God of justice and the love God calls for is a love that transforms relationships, societies, indeed the world, so that "justice and peace can embrace" (Ps. 85:11). This is a theme to which we shall return. Suffice it to say for now that it is a great pity that Thabo Mbeki seems so thoroughly convinced by the Marxian understanding of Christian love which we have alluded to in Chapter 4, that the evidence of the practice of that love during the struggle as we understood it evidently makes no impression. In our view reconciliation *is* transformation or it is nothing at all, as Herman Wiersinga has taught us, and that it is so not only at the

---

[338] *Op. cit.,* 55.

personal level. It transforms, let me say it again, towards humanity and justice all of society and the world.

What we have discovered in our discussion up till now are a number of things. First of all, expectations of the work of the TRC were high. Reconciliation was indeed considered the "kernel" of our social transformation, as Johnny de Lange put it. Secondly, reconciliation is understood as a process of transformation beyond the TRC. Thirdly, there is a remarkable effort to claim the process of reconciliation for the sphere of secular, political activity, indeed as a result of this activity. But fourth, if these and other spokespersons of the ANC understood this kind of reconciliation to be the goal of the period of reconstruction, whether political, social, economic or otherwise after the negotiated settlement, for former President Nelson Mandela it was far more. It was, in his view, the "fundamental objective of the people's struggle" preceding negotiations, settlements and political compromises:

> The quest for reconciliation was the fundamental objective of the people's struggle, to set up a government based on the will of the people, and build a South Africa which indeed belongs to all. The quest for reconciliation was the spur that gave life to our difficult negotiation process and the agreements that emerged from it... The search for a nation at peace with itself...[339]

Reading these words, one can already detect the change in emphasis from the words Mandela spoke in parliament in 1999 and the subsequent discussions about the TRC and its work thereafter. And at this point I am not referring to the acrimonious political debates, the litigation actions and the academic critique that befell the TRC in the years following its report. I have in mind something entirely different. For De Lange and a growing number of ANC interpreters reconciliation was the necessary outcome of the negotiated settlement, the obligation placed upon South Africans by the "unique" wording of the Constitution, the result of the careful consideration of the "balance of forces". Even though he cannot but use words like the "healing of the nation", reconciliation is primarily a "national process" embedded in the "social transformation project during the transition", as we have seen. For Mandela on the other hand, reconciliation was the "spur" that "gave life" to negotiations, in other words, that had driven the process, given it its true meaning, because it was at the heart of the struggle *all along*. It was not something that the ANC created after exile during its deliberations on and preparations for negotiations, it was the legacy of the spirituality of struggle that the ANC had *inherited from the people*. Mandela, in speaking thus, calls to mind the words of Chief Albert Luthuli, that Christian ANC leader *par excellence,* who provided in his words and in his life that life-giving inspiration towards reconciliation that Mr Mandela was so aware of when he responded to the TRC Report:

---

[339] Speech in special session of Parliament, accepting the Report of the TRC, 25 February, 1999.

> From the beginning our history has been one of ascending unities, the breaking of tribal, racial and creedal barriers. The past cannot hope to have a life sustained by itself, wrenched from the whole. There remains before us the building of a new land, a home for men (*sic*) who are black, white, brown, from the ruins of the old narrow groups, a synthesis of the rich cultural strains we have inherited.[340]

Clearly Mr Mandela's interpretation is one that leaves more room for the spiritual inspiration for our reconciliation process than the purely political interpretation of De Lange and others, and the difference is not unimportant. It has become, in fact, the cause of heated debate in the interpretation of the value of the Truth and Reconciliation Commission and its work for South Africa's politics.

Pathologizing the Nation?

The literature on the response to the TRC, its work and its report has become vast and it makes for fascinating reading. It is not our intention to revisit those arguments here, except for where in the course of our own argument we cannot avoid it. Instead, we would like to focus on the issue that our discussion thus far has led us to. It centres on the question of whether the TRC has failed (and for some it has), because it gave in to the temptation of what has been called "excessive spiritualization", and, furthermore, whether that same "spiritualization" threatens the success of the national project of reconciliation and nation building. Are we aware enough of the "grave dangers" if reconciliation is understood not as a *secular,* political process, but as a spiritual, even religious process, as the *event* of the TRC certainly seems to have been. In this regard words such as "idealistic", "abstract" and "romanticizing" are used regularly.

Dr Charles Villa-Vicencio, Executive Director of the Institute for Reconciliation and Justice, would rather speak of "political reconciliation" as the correct designation for what is happening in South Africa.[341] He warns that political reconciliation is necessarily a "modest concept". Moral demands that are too high, "romanticised notions of repentance, forgiveness and restitution" are often "politically unhelpful". Villa-Vicencio seeks to keep the process of reconciliation clear of these notions, since political reconciliation is "not dependent on the kind of intimacy that religious and some forms of individual reconciliation may demand. Rather, statecraft and politics require peaceful co-existence. Forgiveness may come later… after the building of trust". Villa-Vicencio knows that reconciliation is "more than theory". He is even willing to say it involves "grace", though one must presume that this is the grace of "magnanimity" rather than the grace of God. The furthest he is willing to go is to agree with a Mozambican woman who acknowledged that reconciliation is "more than anyone of us can bring to the

---

[340] *Let My People Go!*, 231.

[341] In a brochure on Reconciliation, as yet unpublished at the time of writing. It will be made available by the Institute in Cape Town.

table… It is a gift that comes from the spirit of the ancestors". Villa-Vicencio concurs: "It is a celebration of the human spirit".

I am not one for cavilling, but in the context of this book I think we are entitled to ask: what does this mean, the "spirit of the ancestors"? Is this a statement of faith or of political correctness? And is this call upon the "spirit of the ancestors" not as much a "spiritualization" than a call upon the Holy Spirit of God to lead us in all truth in our oft tortured search for reconciliation in South Africa?

Nevertheless Villa-Vicencio has a point. The dynamics of political reconciliation may not be the same as the act of reconciliation is in the church. But I question his neat dichotomy between what is "political" and what is "personal". It is never that simple. People are not just political animals, they are human beings, with bodies and souls, with memories of the past and hopes for the future, they are spiritual beings with their own relationships with God or whatever gives them spiritual guidance. And they bring all of that into the sphere of their political activity. Here it is wise to recall the adage of Dutch theologian, H M Kuitert, that "everything is politics, but politics is not everything".[342]

I would rather also stand with Rev. Frank Chikane, who in his reflections on this debate has this to say:

> It seemed to me that the concept of reconciliation was being equated with negotiations, political settlements and so on. This, I believe, robs the word reconciliation of its deeper meaning, one which includes the concept of healing. Negotiations can result from political pressures or from a mutual decision by parties to avoid a war because the costs are too great. This does not necessarily mean the parties have had a change of heart – they are simply relocating the battle ground to the negotiating table or parliament. For me, the deeper and more critical meaning of the word reconciliation goes beyond this simplistic understanding. It involves people being accountable for their actions and showing a commitment to right their wrongs. Ideally, South Africa needs voluntary disclosure – and I use this phrase in place of the theological term 'confession'. From the religious point of view, the recognition of truth is akin to confession, which must lead to repentance, and then to conversion. Only such a trajectory merits forgiveness.[343]

Chikane hits the nail on the head. The debate *is* about reconciliation being "equated" with negotiations. It *is* about reconciliation not simply being a "relocated battleground", a "site of struggle". Reconciliation is not just secular political settlements. It is about "healing". It is not the Christian understanding of reconciliation that confuses the issue.

---

[342] In a captivating little book of the same title (Ten Have: Baarn, 1986).
[343] Cited by Mahmood Mamdani, Reconciliation Without Justice, *Southern African Review of Books*, Issue 46, November/December 1996.

What is "confusing" is the simplification of the issue by those who seek to radically secularise it, thereby trying to domesticate it, bringing it under (their) political control, by the same token robbing the word not only of its meaning but of the radical nature of its appeal.

One of the foremost proponents of the "secular pact" idea is well-known academic Prof. Jakes Gerwel. He has made his views known in a well-argued contribution provocatively and unambiguously entitled "National Reconciliation: Holy Grail or Secular Pact", in the same publication of the Institute for Reconciliation and Justice in which Johnny De Lange's article can be found.[344]

We must avoid, Gerwel argues, confusing politics and theology in defining and determining the contours of national reconciliation. We must not "pathologize a nation in relatively good health", which is what he fears the "spiritualization" of reconciliation will do or is doing already. South Africa is not an "unreconciled nation" Gerwel asserts, because "it is not threatened by imminent disintegration and internecine conflict". Moreover, the absence of external mediators, sponsors or guarantors during our negotiations signified "a national confidence based on a particular self-definition". Gerwel contrasts the conflicts and wars which preceded the Union of South Africa with our own democracy, which averted a predicted civil war. Gerwel is very much afraid that a "spiritual" or theological understanding of the reconciliation process is not able to see this, because it is asking for "more", reminding us of Villa-Vicencio's reticence about moral demands that may be "too high" to appreciate the gains made by political reconciliation. Gerwel argues that,

> It is wrong to suggest that South Africa is a wholly or predominantly unreconciled society because it contains within it a number of residual and enduring contradictions... South Africa is grappling to come to terms with these and to grow as a nation in relation to such realities. Despite conflict, a sense of political co-existence and civility is beginning to emerge in South African politics – nothing should distract from the remarkable progress the nation has already made.[345]

It is in this context that Gerwel expresses his fear of what "spiritualization" can do. "The appeal is that we do not pathologize a nation in relatively good health by demanding a perpetual quest for the Holy Grail of reconciliation".[346]

South Africa is, after all, not "imagined communities". There is, in a sense, a "solid history to the materiality of the South African nation. There exists tangibly a political basis to a united South African nationhood".[347]

---

[344] *Looking back, Reaching Forward*, 277-286.
[345] *Op. cit.*, 285.
[346] *Op. cit.*, 286.
[347] *Op. cit.*, 282.

> Divisions, differences and conflicting interests of various kinds, levels
> and intensity occur throughout our society – and while many individual
> victims and perpetrators of gross violations of human rights are not
> reconciled, and group-based memories of discrimination will probably
> remain for a long time, the country has progressed far on the road of
> political reconciliation.[348]

Gerwel insists that we should recognize that the idea of national reconciliation is not
new; just like the concept of non-racialism, it was always embedded in the struggle.
"Positive, future trends" were already manifest in the "perverted past". This explains
the "miracle" of our transition and "demystifies" it. As such, reconciliation was not a
new process waiting to be initiated in a situation threatening large-scale disintegration,
and neither is it a "spiritual notion" that primarily acts amongst individuals. The TRC
focused on selected, specified categories of killings which had to "symbolically carry
the burden of that entire past of division, strife, conflict, suffering and injustice".[349]
The "pure horror" of those narratives focused attention on the deeply personal and
emotional levels at which people in this society "should (also) reconcile". And it is
that which directed attention away from the "formal, statist view" which seemed to
dominate during and immediately after the negotiation phase.[350]

Gerwel explains: "In this phase reconciliation was predominantly understood and
celebrated as the mutual search amongst erstwhile political foes for and the formal
attainment of the political and constitutional unity of the country". But there was a
"subsequent spiritualization of the TRC and of the understanding of reconciliation
itself" brought about by "subjective factors such as the dominant presence of
religious personalities and a general liberal-Christian perspective in the Commission"
which "significantly contributed to the subsequent amplified spiritual approach to
reconciliation".[351]

"The genesis of the TRC, though, is to be found in the *sober politics of accommodation*
borne out of a historically conditional sense of shared South African nationhood".[352]
And this is where it properly belongs, since the "current usage of the concept of
national reconciliation" (i.e. its "spiritualization") not only contributes to "a discourse
of division", it also espouses notions of "idealism" and "obfuscation" completely
implausible for our contemporary society:

---

[348] *Op. cit.,* 282-283.
[349] *Op. cit.,* 278-279.
[350] *Ibid.*
[351] *Op. cit.,* 280.
[352] *Ibid.* (my emphasis).

> It is, put in perhaps over-simplistic terms, unrealistic to expect everybody in such a complex organization as a nation to love one another. Human social reality is intrinsically contradictory, and a late 20th century society with the history of South Africa no longer seeks for such idealistic denial or obfuscation of contradiction. Institutionalized commitment to consensus-seeking, cultivation of conventions of civility and respect for contracts have become the mechanisms of solidarity in contemporary society, replacing the organic idiom of 'love for neighbour' that might to a greater extent have made older, less complex societies cohere.[353]

We have come across this argument before, namely with Thabo Mbeki. Mr Mbeki rejects the notion of "love for the neighbour" because he believes it is an impediment to genuine transformation. Prof. Gerwel does the same, but on the grounds that the Christian injunction to love the neighbour as one loves oneself belongs to a time and in societies of primitive simplicity, which in our complex modern South Africa serves only division, obfuscation and a misplaced idealism. What will save us, and our process of reconciliation, is building on the solid secular foundation of sober accommodation politics. We shall have to try to respond as carefully as we can.

Searching for the Holy Grail?

We must immediately make the point that reconciliation means much more than just the fact that there is no "conflict, strife or internecine wars". That is the kind of minimalist interpretation we must avoid. We must repeat what we said twenty years ago with regard to justice and peace. Peace is not the absence of war, but the active presence of justice.[354] The same holds true for reconciliation. Without justice and a whole lot more, all talk about reconciliation becomes either empty, pious prattle or deceitful political demagoguery. Whether one links this kind of "reconciliation" to God or to the "political balance of forces", it is misleading and meaningless, and certain to continue to victimize the victims of injustice.

It can certainly be argued that as negotiations went on, the parties focused increasingly on common interests and destinies rather than differences, contradictions and antagonism, as Hein Marais has pointed out.[355] And that undoubtedly was good for the process and the country. To say, however, as Prof. Gerwel does, that the "genesis" of the TRC, and therefore of South Africa's reconciliation process, was the politics of accommodation, "borne of a historically conditioned sense of shared South African nationhood", is only partly true. There is still "the other shoe". I remember well the time when the National

---

[353] *Op. cit.,* 283-284.

[354] Allan Boesak, "Jesus Christ, the Life of the World", address before the WCC Assembly, Vancouver Canada,1983, in *Black and Reformed,* Ch. 14.

[355] Hein Marais, *South Africa: Limits to Change: The political economy of transformation* (London: Zed Books and Cape Town: UCT Press, 1998), 89.

Executive Committee of the ANC discussed the question of how to deal with the past. It was not just a matter of white South Africa's apartheid past, but also the ANC's past, namely the issue of what happened in the camps that operated in exile, which became such a burning question in the reports of Amnesty International. It eventually gave rise to the establishment of the Motsuenyane Commission of inquiry into human rights abuses in those camps. A report was presented, the allegations confirmed, the perpetrators named and the organization accepted collective responsibility for those actions and expressed regret to the families of those ANC cadres who had suffered those abuses.

In September 1993 the NEC, after the pattern of the work of other truth commissions elsewhere, notably that of Chile, took a policy decision to call for such a commission for South Africa. Our discussions were interrupted by a request from then President F W de Klerk. The National Party was not happy with the term "truth commission". It felt strongly that South Africa would be better served if the commission was to be a "truth *and* reconciliation commission". De Klerk argued strongly for that addition, and the ANC, mindful of Albert Luthuli's dream of "the building of a new land" which we quoted a while ago, finally conceded. That proved to be a critical point and it would indeed make our commission "unique". And while the idea for some of us resonated with the strongest spiritual elements in the history of our struggle, it resonated likewise with those who thought that it would be a handsome political tool in the quest we had set on ourselves: nation building.

I was not against the idea. In fact, in the light of my own Christian convictions which I upheld publicly right through my own participation in the struggle, I welcomed it. I felt it wise, however, to sound a note of warning. The issue was not reconciliation; it was, rather, our understanding and interpretation of it. I argued respectfully that I thought I knew the mindset of the Afrikaner better than anyone in that room, most of whom were just back from exile. I did not have much faith in the National Party's declarations and I strongly suspected that we should here not just look at the *political* motivations of De Klerk and the National Party, we should seriously be considering the *religious and theological* motivations as well, since in the Afrikaner mind these always go together. From experience in the church as well as in politics we knew how the Bible was used in Afrikaner politics, and how the radical message of the Bible was made servant to ideology, domesticated for purposes of subjection and control. I feared that this was what was at play here. The NP needed the word "reconciliation" for political purposes for which the theological cloak of reconciliation was a perfect cover. It would appeal to religious people, white and black and by far the majority in the country, and it would give the NP a weapon the ANC did not understand. Mr De Klerk and his party did not intend to allow reconciliation to confront the country with the demands of the gospel, but to blunt the progress of radical change and transformation. And this is what Thabo Mbeki discovered only belatedly. Only it is not the gospel he should blame, but the ANC's own inability to listen when some of us raised questions.

Indeed, the New National Party's, and Mr De Klerk's, personal vociferous opposition to, and visceral enmity towards, the consequences of the TRC's work are ample proof of this. Neither De Klerk nor his party had tried to move a finger to help whites understand, support and become part of the process of reconciliation in the country. The "truth" alone about apartheid would be too confrontational, too merciless an exposure of what the NP had hoped would remain hidden for ever. Adding the "soft" touch of reconciliation with its gospel imperatives of forgiveness and acceptance would in turn allow the softening of that truth, should the country ever be confronted with it. The ANC may not have thought of the consequences of those gospel imperatives, but Mr De Klerk did, and he knew that that was what millions of South Africans would hear.

And it is here that Jakes Gerwel's "historically conditioned shared sense of nationhood" loses me. It may well be true that the ANC and the purest streams of the struggle had always had the desire for nationhood, unity and a reconciled people. But I submit that it never was true of the National Party or for most whites, Afrikaans or English speaking, and that the politics of accommodation did not make them share that dream; it merely accommodated a political agenda that was not in sync with the ANC's hopes on this point. As a result I find Gerwel's notion of a "historically shared nationhood" more wishful thinking than political reality. The truth of the matter is that FW De Klerk did not introduce the notion of reconciliation because he "historically" shared the dream of nationhood which so inspired the oppressed people of South Africa in their struggle. He did so in the hope that the superficial theological understanding of reconciliation he knew many South Africans had would allow him to get away with his now infamous "let bygones be bygones" politics the moment the emerging truth would be too hard to handle.

It is difficult, too, to follow Gerwel in light of President Mbeki's insistence that South Africa's enduring problem is a two-nation problem, one white and rich, the other black and poor. More than Mandela ever did, Mbeki has exposed the racism still rampant in South African society, and even though it is costly, both for his popularity in the white community and for the political debate, he is adamant that he will continue to do so. White editors and white people castigate him for "playing the race card", black editors and black people applaud him for his honesty. "I pray", Mbeki said according to a newspaper report, referring to his white political opponent, "that (people of your sort) would one day find the intellect, courage and humanity to acquaint yourselves with the pain, anger and aspirations of those who know the meaning of racial oppression".[356]

The "room for democratic redress" that Prof Gerwel sees is another case in point. Where is this room, when more and more people feel themselves excluded from the democratic process, as seen in the large numbers who did not even register for the last elections, let alone bother to vote? Is this "room" in the courts, perhaps, where racism

---

[356] Willem Jordaan, in *Die Burger*, "Politieke debat moet tog meer inhou as net rusies", 27 October 2004.

still dictates judgement in too many instances, and where transformation has not yet taken any meaningful hold? Or in the Constitution, when the government can with impunity afford to ignore a judgement of the Constitutional Court as in the *Grootboom* case, because it concerns justice for poor people who do not have the means or the power to pursue the matter? I am not saying that there is not room for redress. I am suggesting that it might exist if one has the means, the time and the energy, and that for the people who really matter, the poor and the voiceless, it is already harder to find than we would have thought. In this, and with other issues as well, he is more into romanticising than those of us who understand the need for our reconciliation process to be profoundly spiritual in order for it to make any sense at all in our efforts to heal the nation and to give genuine leadership in our quest for a renaissance.

Throughout Gerwel pleads for the "secularity of the Commission's work", but cannot himself avoid the spiritual essence of the Commission's labours. He himself gets caught up in the language as he speaks of the TRC as an "event of story-telling, confessing and forgiving, presenting a unique moment in the country's history" even as he hastily (but too late) adds "within a quasi-judicial framework". Gerwel is caught up in the same dilemma as the President. The very nature of reconciliation as a biblical demand and reality makes it impossible to avoid the language of the spirit. Asmal and his co-authors are caught in the same bind. "The TRC", they write, "might bring the possibility for the victims to fulfil a *civic sacrament of forgiving*".[357] This piece of secular sacramentalism is revealing and one finds it more often than expected in the language of post-exilic ANC. But it shows the resilience of the spiritual content of reconciliation despite the persistent attempt to drastically secularize it.

But what really did we expect? Our commission may have come into being as a legal entity, birthed by an act of Parliament. The call to reconciliation may be enshrined in our secular Constitution, and our reconciliation process may be part of our political agenda as a national project. But we did decide to deliberately depart from the purely secular, legal process of truth seeking and to embark on a process of truth *and* reconciliation. It was not the church, but the President who appointed not a lawyer, a judge, a retired politician or a politically "Eminent Person" as Chairperson, but Archbishop Desmond Tutu, "priest and a father confessor", as we heard from John De Gruchy. The same is true for Dr Alex Boraine, Methodist theologian, who was given the position of Deputy Chairperson. And Parliament endorsed that decision. That was not an emotional or "spiritual" decision. It was the result of Gerwel's "sober, secular, political" reflection by the political powers that be. The politicians reckoned that these decisions would help to convince the millions of South Africans who are Christians and enhance the acceptability of their own political agenda. The complaints about the TRC being "too spiritual" or "too Christian" should not be laid at the door of the Commission or the church. And it was not a case of "excessive spiritualization" *afterwards,* as Gerwel and

---

[357] *Op. cit.*, 49.

others suggest. It was inevitable, I continue to argue, both as a consequence of these political decisions and as a consequence of the very nature of reconciliation itself.

Prof. Piet Meiring, another Christian theologian amongst the commissioners, writes about "the *beruti* among the lawyers".[358] He makes the point of the "natural flow" towards religious leanings in the TRC, especially the determination of Archbishop Tutu to make it so, even in the face of complaints by Commission members who were not Christians. Desmond Tutu himself testifies to this over and over again.[359] Every sitting and meeting was opened with prayer, and prayer seemed to saturate the hearings as well. And when Desmond Tutu prays, he does not indulge in the kind of vague, all-inclusive interfaith intercession with which, say, a Hindu would be comfortable – he prays "through Jesus Christ our Lord". He prays "that the truth may be recognized and brought to light… and that the end may bring about that reconciliation and love for the neighbour *which our Lord himself commanded*".[360] It is this kind of direct Christian testimony that causes the great discomfort. But again, who is to blame here? Certainly not Desmond Tutu. He is known for his Christian convictions. His standing in the Christian community world-wide, his bent towards spirituality, even his emotionality were all carefully weighed and considered as part of his charm, his personality and his armoury, powerful weapons in the effort to persuade South Africans of the integrity of the reconciliation process. He was deliberately chosen. One could almost say, "You should have seen this coming!" The politicians in their sober reflections took a calculated risk, but the idea was that even with this risk the process could be managed.

Here, though, is where the politicians, from the NP and the ANC both, seriously miscalculated. They all consciously or subconsciously accepted FW De Klerk's subliminal text: adding the word "reconciliation" would smooth a process fraught with contradictions, risks and danger, loaded as it was with unspeakable things from the past. The religious twist would help tame it, domesticate it, make it both more pliable and palatable for the broader public. Mr De Klerk did it as much for himself as for the process. It was good strategy to cover the process with an aura of theological respectability that would make it hard for people to oppose. The agony in the Afrikaans church circles regarding the TRC is eloquent testimony to this, as Meiring tells us.[361] It is an agony derived from being crushed between political realism and human resistance, on the one hand, and an inescapable call of the gospel, on the other. It was not just a personal and political crisis, it was a crisis of faith.

The real miscalculation, though, was with the obstinacy of the gospel itself. The ANC had no inkling of this, but the National Party people should have known better. Tutu could not help himself. The radical nature of the Christian faith and the very reality of biblically motivated reconciliation would often push the TRC into deeper waters than it

---

[358] Piet Meiring, *Chronicle of the Truth and Reconciliation Commission* (Bloemfontein: Carpe Diem, 2000), 30.
[359] Cf. his *No Future Without Forgiveness* (Johannesburg: Rider, 1999).
[360] See among the many examples, *op. cit.* 86.
[361] Meiring, *Chronicle, passim.*

wanted, or had planned, or could be allowed to go. Hence the insistence on confession, repentance and forgiveness with the likes of PW Botha and FW De Klerk, openness, transparency and truthfulness in regard to the National Party and the ANC on issues such as violence. Hence also the bent towards the interpretation that the violence of apartheid and the violence of MK merited the same critical understanding and therefore the same critical judgement, an attitude which so enraged the ANC.[362]

One of the central assertions of the Reformation is that Scripture explains itself, it asserts itself. That is true. The same argument that we used vis-à-vis the theology of apartheid is applicable here. The Scriptures will not be ideologized, manipulated or managed to suit our political endeavours, processes or desires. The demands of the Scriptures will always lay a greater claim than these processes are willing to concede. The politicians have allowed themselves to be persuaded that the use of the theological concept would allow for better management and control of the reconciliation process. It did not work. But there might be an even greater problem. It is the theological understanding of reconciliation which has become the expectation of the vast majority of our people, partly because of their instinctive biblical understanding of the word, but partly also because Mr De Klerk's version of it was the political intention. But these masses are now looking at the process with those eyes and are discerning how much is still to be done. Hence the understandable concern from Gerwel, Villa-Vicencio and others about what they consider "unrealistic" demands that are fuelled by a "spiritual" understanding of reconciliation. But the truth is that those expectations are there, and justifiably so. And as Richard Wilson has urged us to remember as he reminds us of the bitter truth how in the amnesty process the word *ubuntu* was used as easily as Christian forgiveness to persuade the victims of apartheid to once again make the sacrifices which we never demanded of the perpetrators, "The *sizwe* will not go away".[363]

But there is another thing that agitates against the argument that our process of political reconciliation and transformation is purely secular and should be purged of all spiritual elements. First of all, Africans are profoundly spiritual people, and whether that spirituality is rooted in African traditional religious experiences or in the Christian tradition, it is undeniable. That alone makes an argument for a strictly secular understanding of such deeply human experiences as the TRC dealt with a singularly strange proposal, deeply alien to the African spirit. To speak of "evil", "suffering", "repentance", "forgiveness" and "symbolically carrying the burden of (an) entire past" – all these terms are used by Gerwel, and such language is likewise employed by Asmal *et al.* – and not to respond at the deepest spiritual level, is not to understand the African soul at all. If this is denied, then all talk of *ubuntu* is either total nonsense or unbearably cynical. As it is, the secularists, with their disparagement of "neighbourly love", have a problem: "*Ubuntu* empowers people to love and respect each other... (it) is a concept of

---

[362] Cf. Asmal *et. al.,* "When the Assassin Cries Foul: The modern just war doctrine", in Villa-Vicencio and Verwoerd, *Looking Back,* 86-98.

[363] Cited in Lyn S Graybill, *Truth and Reconciliation in South Africa* (Boulder CO, USA and London: Lynne Rienier Publishers, 2002) 35.

brotherhood and unity for survival...", writes Prof. Lesiba Teffo, who devotes several pages to the spiritual content of *ubuntu*.[364]

Second, once we concede that in the TRC it *was* about reconciliation at "deeply personal and emotional levels", again quoting Gerwel, the argument for a purely political accommodation becomes decidedly thin. Kwazulu-Natal Roman Catholic theologian Augustine Shulte makes the point:

> The TRC is a model for dealing with the (universal) abuse of political power because it dealt with it at the deepest level, namely the personal... It went below and beyond the merely legal conception of law and punishment... The confrontation was personal and therefore revealed the truth. The truth expressed is thus both confession and judgement and this is the necessary condition for forgiveness and repentance. Full forgiveness without full knowledge is impossible. Repentance without the judgement and acknowledgement that what has been done is evil, is equally so. Forgiveness is reaching beyond the evil deed to the person of the perpetrator, and affirming their humanity as of equal value to one's own. It forgoes the right to punish, grants amnesty for the crime. Repentance is the only adequate response to forgiveness. It expressed itself in the desire to make reparation and restitution for the wrong done. The result: amnesty freely granted together with reparation freely given, is reconciliation.[365]

These are, however, the very "romanticized notions of repentance, forgiveness and restitution" that Charles Villa-Vicencio calls "unhelpful". They are called "unhelpful", not because they are not true or appropriate, or of benefit to the political process, but because they did not happen, or were perhaps not intended to happen. Villa-Vicencio speaks, not out of his hope that the political process *pur sang* will as yet realize these ideals, but out of his calculations that human sinfulness will once again fail us. For me, instead of losing hope in the spiritual necessity of reconciliation and clinging to the slender straws of secular politics, this state of affairs would all the more underline the necessity of the spiritual essence of reconciliation as these are applied to politics. They may be difficult to realize, but for our political reconciliation to work, and for justice to done and be seen to be done, they are imperative.

One reason why these fundamental promises of genuine reconciliation remain unfulfilled, is similar to what Argentinian journalist Horacio Verbotsky has observed in his homeland. "The political discourse of reconciliation", he says, "is profoundly

---

[364] "Moral Renewal and African Experience(s)" in *African Renaissance*, 149-169. *Op. cit.*, 164, See also 165-169.
[365] *Ubuntu, an Ethic for a New South Africa* (Pietermaritzburg: Cluster, 2001), 193-194.

immoral because it denies the reality of what people have experienced".[366] That certainly holds true for South Africa as well. One reason is that, already at the genesis of the reconciliation process, FW De Klerk introduced the concept not for the process to respond to the biblical demand for justice, but precisely in order to undermine that demand. One can legitimately argue that De Klerk's chagrin at the conclusions of the TRC regarding his role in the apartheid disaster and his adamant refusal to acknowledge that guilt had to do also with the fact that *his* expectations of the TRC were fundamentally centred on his reasons for insisting on the inclusion of the word "reconciliation", as a theologically domesticated and politically disempowered concept, which would serve the dual theological and political purpose of anaesthetizing the nation into a simplistic forgetfulness and of taking the sting out of such truth as may emerge. Another reason was the attempt to use the word in order to deny and bury the past. They spoke of reconciliation, John De Gruchy writes, "as though it was coterminous with moral amnesia".[367]

De Klerk's example was a bad one. The whole white political leadership found it impossible to come forward as expected and the disenchantment with De Klerk and this inability was a major issue for both the TRC and the vast majority of South Africans who expected more of him than of PW Botha.[368] Even today he insists that apartheid was conceived and practiced "with good intentions". The business community was loath to make any kind of concession on its own complicity with apartheid, The Agricultural Union of South Africa did not respond well, although economist Prof. Sampie Terreblanche argues that "there can be no doubt that the apartheid system (or more correctly, the system of racial capitalism) was deliberately constructed in a very close *collaboration* (conspiracy?) between white business and white politicians to create a (mainly African) labour repressive system on behalf of white business".[369] And the judges from the old regime who had done so much damage to the people, the integrity of the courts and the credibility of law, and who continue to make dubious judgements even in the new situation, refused to show the remorse for their cohabitation with apartheid which they require from the accused who come before them.

But it is revealed in other ways as well. The white Afrikaans community defended themselves with too much vigour, perhaps understandable in light of the propensity with which South Africa and the world held them solely responsible for apartheid. They were, in the eyes of our (English) media and the world, the "perpetrators". White, English-speaking South Africans acted as if the TRC and the process of reconciliation was entirely an Afrikaner affair.

---

[366] Cited in Priscilla Hayner, *Unspeakable Truths, Facing the Challenge of Truth Commissions* (New York and London: Routledge, 2002), 160 .
[367] *Op. cit.,* 42.
[368] See the discussion in *op. cit.,* Chapter 4.
[369] See Sampie Terreblanche, "Dealing with Systematic Economic Injustice", in Villa-Vicencio and Verwoerd, *Looking Back, Reaching Forward,* 265.

From the start the ANC pleaded for the acceptance of "collective responsibility" as a basic point of departure if the process of reconciliation was to have any lasting affect. "We need", wrote Kader Asmal and his collaborators,

> an accelerated understanding of the full extent of the complicity of the South African privileged in the atrocities of the past, since it is true that most privileged South Africans wilfully insulated themselves from the confounding realities of the apartheid country. There was a day-to-day *cordon sanitaire*, an existential buffer zone...Privileged South Africans lived less under a regime of ignorance than of carefully calculated avoidance.[370]

This cynical denial of complicity is a device white English-speaking South Africans in general have used consistently. In an editorial the Johannesburg English language paper *The Star* asked South Africans to avoid self-serving claims of innocence through ignorance. Then in an amazingly hypocritical twist the editorial ends by urging whites to say, "Forgive us, for we knew what *they* did.[371] The "they" here clearly refers to the "perpetrators" of the "horrors" of apartheid. "They" are to be found amongst the Afrikaans-speaking whites who alone shall bear that cross.

When it became clear that the government was not going to honour its promises and obligations regarding meaningful reparations for the victims of apartheid abuses, and the TRC made a call for business to be taxed once-off to help pay for reparations, it was again an English-language newspaper that rushed to put up that *cordon sanitaire* Asmal speaks of. The call, the paper exclaimed, "is in effect to say that all whites benefited from apartheid". The fact that they did well is not because they were part of an oppressive, exploitative system of racial capitalism, as Terreblanche has pointed out, but because "they realized that life must go on, even within an evil system".[372] It is this continuing blatant denial of an obvious truth, with its attendant *systemic* consequences, not the Christian demand for the love of the neighbour, which stands in the way of genuine reconciliation and transformation of South African society.

But Prof. Mahmood Mamdani made an extremely valid point which we find entirely convincing. He expresses his surprise that in South Africa we continue to speak of "victims" and "perpetrators" in connection with the reconciliation process. This is too narrow a focus. There are some whites who perpetrated the system of apartheid, but *all* of them benefited from it. And this is how we should address the question of guilt, repentance, reparations and restitution. It is galling that this truth is so vehemently denied when it is so devastatingly self-evident. All whites *did* benefit from apartheid: in schools and education, economic opportunities, salaries and job reservation, health care and homes, the chance to build a wealth platform from which successive generations

---

[370] *Reconciliation*, 144.
[371] May 7, 1996.
[372] *The Eastern Cape Herald*, 25 March, 2003.

could be launched; the self-confidence that comes from the easy access to the world of power, nationally and internationally, and in the myriad subtle ways which constitute the self-esteem of human beings. "If reconciliation is to be durable" Mamdani writes, "would it not need to be aimed at society (beneficiaries and victims) and not simply at the fractured elite (perpetrators and victims)? ..." And does not justice then become the demand for systemic reform of society as a whole, so that the "target" is all who benefited, rather than just the personal conversion of "the perpetrator"? [373]

Asmal and his co-authors have shown conclusively what we all know to be historically true, namely that white English-speaking South Africans were and are no less racist, that apartheid in some form or another was always part of their politics from the early days of colonialism, through the reign of the United party to their support and that of the English media for PW Botha's 1983 Constitution. "The grip of white supremacy was not limited to Afrikanerdom", and "not all blame for apartheid can be shifted onto an evil government. The government was expressive of the core values of the privileged electorate... Conformist civil society under apartheid is saturated with responsibility for what was done".[374] I submit that this amazing ability for denial and the concomitant inability to take collective responsibility for the benefits deriving from apartheid while simultaneously blaming others for the creation of "the evil system", remains one of the singular most dangerous blockages standing in the way of true reconciliation and genuine transformation in South Africa. This too places a question mark behind Gerwel's assumptions about "shared nationhood" conditioned by "history".

There is a final point we must raise in this particular discussion. Concerned observers have commented on the paucity of real truth-telling there had been during the Commission's sittings and at amnesty hearings. This quite apart from the fact that the apartheid regime had made doubly sure that the real truth would never emerge. Priscilla Haynor regards the platform for story-telling a "great measure of success", for revealing the truth, for holding the perpetrator accountable, for reparations, remorse and forgiveness.[375] De Gruchy concurs: "What the TRC did was to create space in which victims, perpetrators and benefactors could encounter one another around the truth for the sake of personal and national healing".[376]

We thank God for every genuine act of remorse, repentance, confession and forgiveness that took place. There were not many, and the remarkable thing is that few as they were, they seem to have contributed greatly to the kind of confidence in the reconciliation process, personal and political, that inspired Jakes Gerwel to speak of the "progress" we have made as a nation, despite the difficulties and divisions and problems that still exist. For I have no doubt that it is this that in the final analysis gives political transformation meaningful content and lasting character.

---

[373] Mamdani, "Reconciliation Without Justice".
[374] *Reconciliation through Truth*, 150-162.
[375] *Unspeakable Truths*, 7.
[376] *Op. cit.,* 148.

Still, we must remain sober about these things. The horror stories of torture and abuse of the victims are matched only by the horror stories of abuse of the reconciliation process and of the amnesty on offer. Lyn Graybill tells of one such an instance, and it is chilling.[377] She concludes: "So the vast majority of victims and their families opposed the amnesty of their perpetrators and the vast majority of perpetrators offered little remorse, regret or apology". So De Gruchy's "platform for forgiveness" is small, and Asmal's "sacrament of forgiveness" became the ritual at the sacrifice of the justice that was promised, and hoped for, but never attained. The amnesty was given, anyway, because the politics of accommodation demanded it. The question that haunts us, however, is: where are all these people, these victimized victims of apartheid and the reconciliation of sober politics, in their hearts and in their minds?

We must be careful about the "truth" too. What truth did survive the last months of the apartheid regime was not always told at the TRC. Dumisa Ntsebeza and Terry Bell keep our feet solidly on the ground: at the prospect of a democratic transition, tons of files, microfilm, audio and computer tapes and disks were shredded, wiped and incinerated. "In little more than six months in 1993, while the political parties of the apartheid state negotiated with the representatives of the liberation movements, some 44 metric tons of records from the headquarters of the national Intelligence Service alone were destroyed". A "paper Auschwitz" they call it.[378] What then, is truth after the paper Auschwitz?

And that is not all. Terry Bell writes that in November 1993, as Nelson Mandela and FW De Klerk made their separate ways to Norway to collect their jointly-awarded Nobel Peace Prize, De Klerk was legally implicated in a massacre.[379] Mr De Klerk was cited as a defendant in the Transkei supreme court in a civil action for murder brought by the parents of the five children who had been killed by the apartheid security forces in their sleep "at his admitted behest". In a telling point about the state of our politics as well as our journalistic integrity, Bell adds soberly, "There was no outcry". As a journalist Bell thought it was a "dramatic exposé". He sent the story to local media as well as to newspapers in every capital De Klerk would be visiting. "It was not published". So the conspiracy of silence and lies continues and it does not matter: they were children, they were black, they were of no account, they were dead. They are the broken eggs political realism needs to make the omelette. This is the "imperfect justice" De Lange admits, but apparently does not regret.

---

[377] Captain Jacques Hechter, after showing "remorse" before the Amnesty Committee, said to journalists outside: "Ach, I'm not f*...n' sorry for what I did. I fought for my country, I believed in what I did, and I did a good job... I'll do it again...No man, I'm not really f*...n' sorry for what I did..." (*Op. cit.,* 52). She adds, "FW De Klerk, PW Botha and Mangosuthu Buthelezi did not bother with the charade... denying responsibility, they remain unrepentant."

[378] *Unfinished Business, South Africa, Apartheid and Truth* (Cape Town: RedWorks, 2001), 7.

[379] *Op. cit.,* 2, 3. The authors give example after example of such cases. They probe where "the TRC failed or feared to tread." "The undeniable reality is that many of the principal perpetrators of apartheid were not only never called to account, but all too often remain in positions of power."

Ironically, where the TRC does turn idealistic and naïve is *not* when it stands in the power of true spirituality, but precisely when it plays the game of political realism, when it bows down to the dictates of what is politically palatable and deemed possible. Thus it is that the TRC shows itself most ineffective when it deals with the role of big business in South Africa's past, the refusal of the South African Agricultural Union and the South African judiciary to appear before the Commission and be accountable for their own complicity in apartheid. Regarding the business community, the Commission's recommendations are vague, weak and utterly unconvincing.[380]

The TRC makes an "appeal" to business to play a *voluntary* role in compensating black Africans for the disadvantages of apartheid. The TRC says that business "could and should play an enormously creative role in the development of new reconstruction and development programmes". Sampie Terreblanche's criticism is to the point and absolutely spot on:

> From a moral point of view these kinds of requests have a positive ring to them. What should be remembered, however, is that the exploitation of blacks did not happen voluntarily. It was compulsory and *systemic*. It was based on an economic and political system embedded in a network of compulsory legislation and justified by ideologies that were propagated as self-evident truths. To expect that business will be prepared to compensate the blacks *voluntarily – and to the necessary degree – for the injustices committed towards the majority of them for almost a century is not only too idealistic but also rather naïve. To give business the opportunity to pay off their 'apartheid debt' through 'charity' will boil down to an opportunity to let them off the hook.[381]

But this is exactly *not* positive from a moral point of view, as Terreblanche suggests. The moral point of view can never be to replace justice with charity, as the Commission does here. If the Commission had remained true to the genuine nature of spirituality, it would have demanded that "justice rolls down like waters, and righteousness like a mighty stream". Real spirituality does not find its place alongside the rich and powerful, to formulate a position not "too" challenging, "too" confrontational, "too" discomfiting for the wealthy. It always finds its place alongside of the poor, whose voice it must become.

It is because of this dubious stance that the TRC is able to admit that it knows about "the huge and widening gap" between the rich and the poor, but yet "let big business off the hook". It knows that this gap is "morally reprehensible, politically dangerous and economically unsound", but yet, as Terreblanche rightly argues, it does not take up the challenge of the *causative* role played by the *systems* of white political dominance,

---

[380] Terreblanche, *op. cit.,* 267, 268.
[381] *Op. cit.* 268.

racial capitalism and apartheid over a considerable period of time. It does not face the problem of those systems, in a deliberate and systemic way, "bringing about and sustaining, white wealth and white privileges on the one hand, and black poverty, black deprivation and black humiliation on the other".[382]

This is not just a shortcoming. It is a failure of major proportions. On this point, the Commission did not just fail the poor. It betrayed the radical demands of reconciliation which are in turn bound up in the very nature of the gospel of Jesus Christ, in whose Name the Archbishop opened with prayer, and in whose Name they pledged "to bring about that reconciliation and love for neighbour which our Lord himself commanded". It is unutterably sad to see that on this crucial issue the Commission itself falls into the trap which the politicians had set for it, and which should have turned out to be its strongest weapon against the wiles and vagaries of the powers that be, whether they be political, philosophical, or economic. This business-friendly attitude reflects a theology sensitive to the dilemmas of power, but certainly not sensitive to the needs of the poor, and therefore not sensitive to the heart of God.

Compared, for example, to the merciless hammering of Winnie Madikizela-Mandela to bow down to the judgement and mercy of God and to repent on national television, the Commission's anaemic resolve to seek truth and remorse from big business, i.e. a commitment to justice, with its continued bland denials of guilt is startling. The contrast to its timidity before the political powers represented in the judiciary and the white business establishment leaves one somewhat amazed. In other words, where it *mattered,* the TRC was quite willing to bow down before the altar of Gerwel's "secular pact", and in the process truly following the mystic trail of the Holy Grail, expecting "voluntary" righteousness from hardened capitalists whose first and last concern is always the profit bottom-line. The hammer of God was saved for other occasions, even though one cannot help but wonder how well the Commission understood the *political significance* of their approach and knew too how well it might have served the broader political agenda of the secularist elite at that point.

But the Christian spiritual element remains inescapable. Evidence is that just about every time there was genuine truth-telling, genuine repentance and genuine forgiveness, that process was driven not by the "long-embedded goals" of our political history, nor by a belief in a South African nation already "inherently united", but rather by those persons' faith in Jesus Christ, which demands that genuine repentance should be met with genuine forgiveness.[383] The stories are intensely moving and fairly vibrate with the power of true spirituality. Those involved recognized not only that the truth was told, they acknowledged the truth that sets *both* free, victim and perpetrator, tortured and torturer. They came to understand the claim of Christ on their lives: love for God requires love for the other. And if one can make that true on this most fundamental

---

[382] *Op. cit.,* 267. This remarkable, inverted idealistic and romantic mode holds for other critical issues as well. See Terreblanche, *op. cit.,* 267-268.
[383] See the moving examples in Hayner, *Unspeakable Truths,* 158; also Piet Meiring, *Chronicle:* 56, 121-126 and 169-170 . Also De Gruchy, *Reconciliation,* 175.

of levels in human life, "political reconciliation" is not so unattainable as one might be tempted to think. It is, I think, dishonest and short-sighted in the extreme to write this off as "romantic idealism" that "sows division" and is irrelevant for the "hard, complex realities" of political reconciliation. A persistent secular reading of the reconciliation process also robs the TRC process of the genuine moments of reconciliation that did take place, sometimes against all "sober, political" expectations, opening the curtain on the wondrous work of "the God of surprises".[384] The immense value of these experiences for the country and the process of reconciliation can hardly be overestimated.

That great German philosopher Karl Jaspers is quoted just about everywhere in our growing "reconciliation literature" for his insightful discussion on guilt. And correctly so. But he offers another, equally valuable insight that is hardly ever mentioned. Reflecting on the harsh realities of life and the "challenges for the German soul" after the Nazi period, Jaspers discovered something that is essential for dealing with the enormous question of guilt on a corporate scale, forgiveness, and the strength required to start all over again, such as was the situation in Germany after the war. Writing after the institution of the Nuremberg trials, Jaspers observed that "only a transcendently founded religious or philosophical faith could provide a basis for the new world now waiting to be built".[385] What is at stake, he says, is the search for an answer that would be "decisive for the German soul".

We too, cannot escape that decisive moment. The questions still facing us are of the same frightening enormity, and they cannot simply be answered by secular pacts, contemporized solidarity or the politics of accommodation, however important those in their right place might be. It is about the soul of South Africa, as it ultimately is about the African soul. What is being asked of us is more than we have a historical tradition for, "more than we have within ourselves", to quote Charles Villa-Vicencio's Mozambican woman. Facing the agonies of culpability and forgiveness, breaking "the hold of self-insulating pride" as Jaspers says, is the only way toward political freedom, personal liberation and the opportunity for a new national beginning.[386] And that can only happen if one has something other than historically conditioned compromises or new political slogans, something both higher and deeper than our even stronger conditioned human responses of revenge and retribution. This is something quite different from Gerwel's proposal of a kind of sacral secularism that must replace spirituality and "love for the neighbour" in the self-understanding of the nation and in the shaping of our identity and ultimately our destiny. As Karl Jaspers discovered, standing at the ruins of one of Europe's most advanced nations, it is precisely our modern, complex world that needs more than "conventions of civility" and "respect for contracts" to help us build a new world. Without what Nelson Mandela once called "the RDP of the soul" we shall not be able to build it. Or biblically put, "Unless the LORD builds the house, those who build it labour in vain" (Ps. 127:1).

---

384 See, for example, Meiring, *op. cit.,* 123 ff.
385 Karl Jaspers, *The Question of German Guilt* (New York: The Dial Press, 1947), 59.
386 *Op. cit.,* 112.

"No Future Without Forgiveness"

In choosing these words for the title of his book Archbishop Tutu did not simply choose a title, he expressed his firmly-held belief and conviction. It is a conviction he took with him to the TRC. It is part of those "gospel imperatives" Christians cannot seek to avoid, nor are able to live without. As he sat in those hearings, Desmond Tutu listened with a different ear than the lawyers and politicians did. He wanted to know whether people understood his insistence that "the victims of injustice and oppression must ever be ready to forgive",[387] that without it South Africa has no future. The discussions around concepts such as forgiveness are intense, and not just because of the very nature of the word. In the TRC process "confession" and "remorse", the two inescapable requirements for forgiveness, were not required by law. Nonetheless, the Christian flow of the proceedings made it nearly impossible for forgiveness not to lay claim on those present, not as a response to any heartfelt confession and a plea for forgiveness from apartheid perpetrators, but on its own as a central tenet of the Christian life.

But many are unhappy about this. There is a legitimate debate on whether victims of apartheid abuses were put in an atmosphere where the strong impression was given that forgiveness was the only acceptable response. "Commissioners never missed the opportunity to praise witnesses who did not express any desire for revenge" writes one critical observer.

> The hearings were structured in such a way that any expression of a desire for revenge would seem out of place. Virtues of forgiveness and reconciliation were so loudly applauded that emotions of revenge, hatred and bitterness were rendered unacceptable, an ugly intrusion on a peaceful, healing process.[388]

Some understood this to be an almost calculated kind of emotional blackmail. If you did not forgive your torturer, you were made to feel as if there was something wrong with you. Beforehand, Wilson reports, victims making their statements were purposefully guided toward telling their stories within a framework of forgiveness and reconciliation.[389] Even worse: Audrey Chapman has charged that at the Human Rights Violations hearings over which Tutu presided, more emphasis was placed on eliciting forgiveness from the victims than in securing knowledge of wrongdoing or apologies from the perpetrators. She feels that "reconciliation can best be achieved by integrating the anger, sorrow and trauma rather than subtly repressing them".[390]

---

[387] Desmond Tutu, *The Rainbow People of God* (New York: Doubleday, 1994), 222.
[388] Philip Wilson, quoted in Graybill, *op. cit.*, 50.
[389] *Ibid.*
[390] *Ibid.*.

In this regard a young woman is quoted as saying, "I don't know if I will ever be able to forgive. I carry this ball of anger within me and I don't know where to begin dealing with it. The oppression was bad, but what is much worse, what makes me even angrier, is that they are trying to dictate my forgiveness".[391]

The problem here has several layers. Forgiveness is indeed a "gospel imperative", as Desmond Tutu correctly says. But forgiveness is a *willing response* as an expression of our obedience to the prayer of Christ that we should forgive "as our heavenly Parent forgives us". Forgiveness is always freely given. If it is given in response to a confession which itself is a plea and need for forgiveness that is already remarkable enough. If it is given even where the perpetrator sees nothing that he or she should be forgiven for, and there is no remorse or confession, it is extraordinary and an even greater cause for thanksgiving. But it can never be forced on anyone. People should not be coerced, however subtly, into forgiving. Forgiveness is in itself an act of such sensitivity, such sacrificial self-giving, such enormous love that any attempt to coax it out of people robs it of its intrinsic value. It can never be taken for granted and it is always the prerogative of the victim. Clearly most human beings need help to come to that point. But there is a vast difference between help and subtle pressure, especially in public, especially on national television.

There is a place for rightful anger. And the Commission should have given it that rightful place. It is impossible not be angry at what happened to people under apartheid and it is grossly unfair to act as if that anger is an offence to God. That anger must not be "managed", it must be given respectful hearing. Just as the victim has to hear the truth and the words of contrition, it is necessary for the perpetrator to hear the words of anger. The perpetrator has to *see* and *hear* the consequences of the wrongful deed in order to understand the depth of the wrong that was done, as well as the depth of the forgiveness given. "Only those who are truly angered by injustice can really begin to practice forgiveness or know what it means", says Dr Willa Boezak and he is absolutely right.[392]

Here Jakes Gerwel's remark about "liberal theology" holding sway in the TRC is absolutely correct, even though I suspect he might have meant it differently. Liberal theology could by its very nature never find either the words or the courage that was necessary for the passion to fight apartheid. Likewise in situations like these it cannot find the necessary room for the anger and the passion of the oppressed as for the first time they come face to face with the persecutor outside of the torture chamber. Liberal theology can read Paul far more easily than it can the Psalms. But one must first learn to sing Psalm 94, before one dares to read 2 Corinthians 5. The Bible neither denies nor ignores the magnificence and the frailty of our humanity. It acknowledges it, makes room for it, restores it, redeems it. There is a reason why some of the most moving and

---

[391] *Ibid.* Quoted from Wilhelm Verwoerd: "Forgiving the torturer but not the torture", *Sunday Independent,* December 14, 1998.

[392] Willa Boezak, *God's Wrathful Children* (Grand Rapids: Eerdmans, 1995), 195.

profoundly beautiful words in the Bible are found in Psalm 139, next to some of the most disturbing and discomfiting words one can read anywhere. And there is a reason it ends the way it does, "Search me O God, and know my heart; test me and know my thoughts, see if there is any wicked way in me, and lead me in the way everlasting".

It is because this was so often the case at the TRC that we can come across the gross violations of trust exhibited in the casual, brutal carelessness of a Captain Hechter. I make the point deliberately. What was at stake here was not just the violations of human rights. It was also the violation of trust. And that holds true not just for the TRC – it includes the government, and the whole process of reconciliation. What the Commission seemed to have forgotten is that it is the *right* of the victim to be angry. The celebration of the human spirit does not wait for the effectuation of reconciliation, it begins with the expression of righteous anger. The miracle of God's grace is not that we can manipulate the angry young woman into forgiving by making her feel guilty about her anger, but that she is moved to overcome her anger, to willingly forgive, and as she remembers what has been done to her, she thinks back not in hatred or bitterness or despair, but in gratitude of having been able to reclaim her humanity and in the process that of her torturer also, in order to create both a new humanity and a new beginning for both of them. These are the ongoing miracles in the life of the nation, and *this* is the celebration of the human spirit. Inasmuch as the TRC, for whatever reason, has denied people this, it has denied its own mission. It has subjected victims to the pain and humiliation of the "story-telling" and has victimized them again in that they were denied the freedom of righteous anger and in the process to challenge the perpetrator on the basis of equality. Within the context of apartheid and its aftermath, it is the expression of anger that brings the first level of equality, which then frees us for the equality of love. Only in the freedom of righteous anger can one find the freedom for that anger to be overcome, which can lead to the freedom of forgiveness and the joyful liberation of the way of reconciliation.

One of the TRC's major problems from our point of view is that it was not nearly as insistent with the perpetrators and beneficiaries of apartheid as it was with the victims. In acting thus, it perpetuated the powerlessness of the victims because it exploited both their faith and their powerlessness to exact remorse. The same was not done, or did not succeed, with the powerful. They were both too powerful and too protected by the institutions of power: Parliament, the courts, government, the media, which to a very large extent still boils down to white public opinion. The same is true for the powerful institutions: the media, the judiciary, big business. The TRC chose to make the radical interpretation of reconciliation the litmus test for the victims. Especially those who are Christians. Inasmuch as the TRC failed to apply that test universally, it failed both the victims and the gospel.

If reconciliation is to be for the "common good" as the politicians and the defenders of the "secular pacts" idea constantly argue, then it is to be *all* of reconciliation that is good for the common good, not just part of it. So far, only forgiveness by the victims has been truly realized. All the other elements without which reconciliation cannot be genuine – restitution, reparation, restoration, justice – are left to languish on the ash heap of the stories, told, listened to, not acted upon, and forgotten.

That forgiveness is necessary for the wounds to heal is an assertion made over and over again. But does this not place another unbearable burden on the victims, *on top of everything else?* Why did we not tell the perpetrators and beneficiaries of apartheid that *remorse and confession* are necessary to heal the wounds, instead of using the law to obfuscate that evangelical and obvious truth and to protect them from that healing demand? And why, when the call to "Christian forgiveness" was not so effective, did we then turn to the emotional blackmail of the African tradition and hit them over the head with *ubuntu*?[393] And there is yet another question: if the story-tellers are called "the Kleenex club", if remorse is not required, if forgiveness is not invited, sometimes scorned, if your pain and the reliving of it becomes a joke or a senseless waste, do the wounds really heal? And if the wounds of the single victim are not healed, is the nation healed, at peace with itself? "The wounds of our nation" is in this regard a dishonest, an unworthy, if often heard notion. This is taking the ideology of "collectiveness" too far. Our nation's wounds are in the wounds of the victims: one by one and wound for wound. We are wounded because every single one of them is wounded. We, the rest, can only stand with them, weep with those who weep, and fight for them and side by side with them. It is the woundability of the victims that constitutes the vulnerability of the nation, since it was the courage of those same victims that constituted the strength of the nation in the times when we needed it most. It is the wounds of the single victim that constitute the wounds of the nation. The perpetrators and the powerful beneficiaries of apartheid can, and do, appeal to the law, or to the economy, or to political realism. In their power, they speak to power, over the heads of the powerless. The victims can only appeal to their wounds and our memory.

There are vast, deeply painful areas the TRC was not able to cover and that are virtually ignored by the discussions on reconciliation, perhaps partly explained by our pathological need and unseemly haste to "move on". It is one thing to forgive the one who has always been the enemy, even though that is hard enough. But how does one forgive betrayal? An enemy can be forgiven for the killing of a loved one. We have seen it happen, difficult though it may have been. It becomes harder when the enemy is one of our own. We have always wrestled with the unpalatable experience that in a police attack on our marches or on our students, the black policemen (I use "black" here in the generic sense) always tried to be more cruel than the whites in the riot squads, invariably going for the most vulnerable first. Intellectually we tried to understand: being a policeman was their job; the need to "prove" themselves to the white commanders, to show their loyalty to the regime; the fear that drove them to be even more inhuman than their white counterparts. But the hurt went deeper than the blows from the sjamboks and the clubs. Their question (if it ever was asked) as to how they lived with themselves could never be as painful as the question of how we had to live with *them*.

---

[393] Cf. Richard Wilson, who asserts that "Ubuntu is a current invention", in: Graybill, *op. cit.,* 33-35.

How does one find the mercy and love to face, and forgive, the one from next door who had turned informer? The true friend and comrade who spurred others on to take certain actions, just so he could betray them and fatten his pay packet, even working for bonuses? Have we really worked through that feeling when we had to bury a child, a brother, a sister, a friend who has died after being "fingered" and trapped, by the one we least suspected? And when in our shock, blind anger and hatred for the act of betrayal we put tyres around their necks, set them on fire and "necklaced" them? What about their family? We have been asked to forgive the whites who gave the orders, and the whites who benefited from their deeds, who felt "safer" because of their betrayal. But what about them and us? The violence we then employed obliterated their bodies and rid us of the "political" problem. But what about those scars burned into our own soul? What about the effects of that embittered violence on *us*? Their commanders and political masters are in parliament, or have retired with huge pensions paid for from the taxes on their meagre earnings, or are business partners of the new BEE elites. But what about the smouldering irreconcilables still in their, and our, own hearts and minds? Is the informer a perpetrator, a victim of a system he could not resist, of a lot he could not escape, or is he both? Are those wounds that we even want to acknowledge? We have had healing services with whites, and that is good. But have we reconciled amongst ourselves? Have we given words to that particular pain? Have *we* been able to rebuild a shared memory? Have we met with them, prayed with them, sang *Nkosi sikilel' iAfrika* with them as we did with whites, felt their tears and ours mingle in the sacred ritual of forgiveness, celebrating the joy of God's miracles as keenly in the dusty streets of our townships as it was felt in the hallowed space of the cathedral? Can it be that we have hardly scratched the surface? I suspect that we have more work to do than I can say.

In South Africa, if we are not careful, forgiveness might become an attitude of "let bygones be bygones", "live and let live", "leave the past behind", "forgive and forget". Reconciliation is too easily misunderstood as political wisdom, tactful forgetfulness, the adaptability of power, the tolerance of vicarious understanding, by which I mean that even though the victims do not understand what is still happening to them and why, the rest of us do it *for* them, on their behalf. Much of our discourse on reconciliation and forgiveness is done within the framework of that expressive French adage, *"Tout savoir c'est tout comprendre, tout comprendre c'est tout pardonner"*. (To know all is to understand all; to understand all is to forgive all). Forgiving is possible only where something cannot be forgotten, writes E L Smelik, a Dutch theologian, as he wrestled with the realities of wrongdoing, revenge, retribution, remorse and forgiveness in the midst of the Nazi occupation of Holland during World War II. "Forgiving is eliminating that which cannot be forgotten, after it had been fully exposed. Forgiveness is not a psychological phenomenon, but an ethical deed, an action, not just an understanding".[394] Forgiveness is therefore truly an act of self-sacrificing love, despite what was done. It is the opening

---

[394] Cf. EL Smelik, *Wraak, Vergelding, en Vergeving* ('S Gravenhage: D A Doomens, 1941). Smelik has deeply sensible things to say about forgiveness and remorse, love and justice. "God's forgiveness in Christ does not mean that there is no divine judgement, but that the divine judgement is set aside by God". Hence forgiveness is always a miracle.

of the hands to give what cannot be forced or coaxed, only hoped for. Surely it cannot be the opening of the hands for a repeated crucifixion?

Therefore it is not possible, nor called for, to "forgive" on behalf of the victims. There is no dignity in it. We can only pray that they do, and rejoice when they do, and hope that in their acts of magnanimity and love we too, as a nation, shall be restored and healed. And we will, if we do justice. For that is the only response that is called for and the only response that is appropriate. For if forgiveness is needed "to heal the wounds", then the victim is again left powerless at the mercy of the perpetrator, if the perpetrator does not see the need for remorse and confession. Forgiveness requires the relinquishment of power by the one who asks to be forgiven, for it empowers the victim to accept or reject the repentant. If this is not done, the disempowerment of the victim continues. The only way to rectify this, to empower the victim, then, is to seek the solidarity of justice. Not the "imperfect" justice of the courts, nor the uncertain justice of philosophical definitions, for that is rarely justice, and unsatisfactory at best, but the justice required by God, the justice of human restoration, which is not a romantic notion, but an act of personal, economic, social and political rectitude. Is this "pathologizing" an essentially healthy nation? I think not.

"The least of these ..."

Perhaps it all has to do with where one stands as we talk about these issues. The *Confession of Belhar* adopted by the Dutch Reformed Mission Church in 1986 (now the Uniting Reformed Church in Southern Africa) has as one of its central claims the fact that God is revealed as the One who brings justice and true peace, and that "in a world filled with injustice and enmity God in a special way is the God of the destitute, the poor and the wronged... that the church as God's possession is called to stand where God stands, namely against injustice and with the wronged". This is where the Confession of Belhar helps us, today still, as clearly as the time in which it was first heard, believed and written. It does so in a number of telling ways. It helps us, firstly, to understand that the poor are not poor because of some historical accident or because it is the will of God. The poor are poor because they are the *wronged*. They are the victims not of an act of God, but of deliberate historical, political and economic decisions in which wrong was done to them. In other words, the decision that some should be *enriched* has as its corollary that others should be *impoverished*. In South Africa the abject poverty is one side: extravagant wealth is the other.

Belhar helps us to first *stand up* (and be counted) for the poor and the destitute, and second, to stand where God stands. Not just in front of, in protection, but alongside, in solidarity of struggle. Not in mere sympathy but in *identification with*. The church must do that not because it is obsessed with the poor, but as the *possession of God*, in Whom its grounds of being, its identity is found. *Belhar* helps us to discern the difference between gospel and ideology, between genuine good news and propaganda, between truth-telling and myth-making, between the dictates of political "realism" and the demands of Christian solidarity. In the Bible "standing where God stands" was the guarantee for the prophets to distinguish between the myths of the idols, the demands from the palace, and the "whispers" of the LORD. It is by no means a *safe* place to stand, but it is without doubt the *right* place.

The test of the spiritual quality of our politics is whether we are to be found where God stands. If the truth of the gospel does not possess us, we shall fall victim to the myths of power. It is now years ago that American economist and adviser to President John Kenneth Galbraith, reminded us of the power and the ability of the managerial elite to create, by way of ideological propaganda, an attractive image of themselves other than what was the reality.[395] That warning has more relevance today than ever before. If we ourselves are too charmed by power, too comfortable in its presence, too tempted by its trappings, we will not be able to discern the gap between the *myth* they create and the *reality* they represent. And this is exactly what happened in the TRC's failure to soberly understand and analyse the association of big business with the racialist, capitalist apartheid system, and what had made it succumb to the myth of false innocence that white business created.[396] Standing where God stands, however, sharing the pain and the destitution of the poor, feeling the pain of their exclusion as well as the burning for their right to inclusion, protects one from the luxury of myth-making. It does not prevent the myth from being fabricated, but it protects us from believing it even as it helps us to resist it. It requires us to soberly assess the situation, not from the comfortable seats of power, but from the depths of the pits from where the poor are yearning to be heard. Reconciliation begins truly when the voice from the pit is heard, and when that voice sets the tone. For that is the voice that unmasks the lie, reveals the truth, disempowers the myth, opens the way.

Terreblanche asks the critical questions: "Was the Commission intimidated by the managerial elite who gave testimony before it; was the TRC oversensitive towards the business sector with which the new government had developed such a friendly relationship; was it afraid to antagonise both business and government?" And the answers seem all to be in the affirmative.[397] The kind of "myth creation" Sampie Terreblanche has exposed in the endeavours of big business is immeasurably more dangerous than any "myths" secular prophets see emanating from the Bible.

But myth-making seems to be the staple of South Africa's quest for secularized reconciliation. We are constantly confronted with the criticism that the Christian call for "love for the neighbour" is either a primitive, over-simplistic demand no longer suitable for our "complex" society, or it is a design to run away from the demands for justice and transformation. We have already pointed out that genuine Christian reconciliation, certainly the kind we have always stood for and proclaimed, *is* transformation. Just as

---

[395] See Terreblance, *op. cit.,* 273.
[396] *Ibid.*
[397] Sampie Terreblanche asks a host of questions which the TRC cannot satisfactorily respond to because he is so right, 273-276. His conclusion that "The Commission was unfortunately not vigorous enough in this regard in its findings…" is entirely justified. 276.

consistently, we have pointed out that reconciliation is not possible without justice. True justice, Willa Boezak writes, is "redemptive and reconciling, the exercise of love and power in a way that heals relationships and builds community".[398] De Gruchy himself has devoted several pages to the argument that reconciliation means "restorative justice", that reparation "is restorative justice in action, redistribution of land and wealth, as well as affirmative action with regard to access to resources, education, employment, housing, and health care".[399] The Archbishop of Cape Town, Njongonkulu Ndungane, has virtually filled his pleas for reconciliation with his passion for the poor and those afflicted with HIV/AIDS, and has called for our process of reconciliation to be seen as a challenge, a *kairos* and a *Jubilee,* a God-given moment for conversion and restoration our country cannot let pass by without dire consequences to ourselves.[400] I have already alluded to my own understanding of my participation in the struggle as a consequence of Christian discipleship wherein love, justice and reconciliation are compatible with divine obedience only when they are realised in socio-economic justice, fundamental transformation and meaningful political participation.[401] Why is it so necessary to continue with the myth that the concept of Christian reconciliation is a denial of justice?

Jakes Gerwel is right in his observation that "material inequality is a major source of division in South Africa" and that "as such the alleviation of poverty must be one of government's primary responsibilities".[402] But his bland assertion that "South Africa has a relatively rapid deracialization of capital" gives the game away. We have already shown the alarming and growing gap between the rich and the poor in South Africa. The tensions around this are growing, not abating, and they are exacerbated by the government's inability to keep its promises in terms of job creation. The latest United Nations Population Fund Report informs us that increasing poverty and inequality for a decimated citizenry five million smaller than it is now with a life expectancy of just 30-odd years is the grim scenario South Africa faces in less than fifty years.[403] South Africa is rated by the UN Agency as among the ten most unequal societies. There is also growing evidence that per capita economic growth will be diminished as a result of increasing dependency ratios, increased burdens on health systems, constrained investment in productivity and reduced labour forces, because of, among other things, the impact of AIDS. As if this is not enough, the news tells us that BEE deals for 2003 amounted to

---

[398] In *Gods' Wrathful Children,* cited in De Gruchy, 201.

[399] *Op. cit.,* 201-205.

[400] See his contribution in *Looking Back, Reaching Forward,* and especially his inspiring *A World With a Human Face, A voice from Africa* (Geneva: WCC Publications, 2003). The call for a "Jubilee" refers to the Jubilee Year of the Old Testament, found in Leviticus 25. It is a call for every seventh year to be a year of radical social and economic redistribution, of restoration and forgiveness of debt. It is, in short, a call for justice, social equality, political reform and personal conversion. It is a call Jesus repeats in his first public appearances in the synagogues of Galilee and which causes great upheaval and resistance alongside great joy. Cf. Luke 4:16 ff.

[401] See, for example, *Farewell to Innocence Black and Reformed; If This is Treason, I am Guilty.*

[402] Gerwel, *op. cit.,* 284.

[403] Cf. *Sunday Argus,* October 17, 2004.

over R42 billion. That staggering amount was divided amongst basically the wealthiest and most powerful six BEE groups in South Africa.[404] This is not "deracialisation" of the economy by any stretch of the imagination. All it means is that the tight circle of the new, empowered black elite have joined the white rich and the rich are still getting richer. It is as simple as that. To speak of "deracialistion of capital" as if the poor are actually actively benefiting from this skewed process is pure myth-making.

Let me say it again, the command to love the neighbour is not romantic, spiritual escapism. I follow John Calvin in this, who argues that the love for the neighbour is the recognition of the oneness of the human race, created by God "like members of a body". It is the "fraternal (*sic*) affection which proceeds from the regard that we have when God has joined us together and united us in one body, because He wants each to employ himself for his neighbour, *so that no one is addicted to his own person, but that we serve all in common*".[405] Hence Calvin's conviction that,

> The name 'neighbour' extends indiscriminately to every person, because the whole human race is united by a sacred bond of fellowship... To make any person my neighbour, it is enough that he be a human being.[406]

This view has at least two immediate consequences. First, "any inequality contrary to this arrangement is nothing else than a corruption of nature which proceeds from sin".[407] Second, out of this flows the radical demand for socio-economic justice.

> There will be those who would rather that the wheat spoil in the granary so that it will be eaten by vermin, so that it can be sold when there is want,,, (for they only wish to starve the poor...) ... How true is it that our Lord is mocked by those who want to have much profit.[408]

This is not charity Calvin is speaking of; it is justice, and he is not withholding anything in his attack upon the rich who seek to thwart that justice.

---

[404] Cf. *SakeRapport* October 10, 2004.
[405] *Opera*, 53, 639. *Sermon LIII* on I Timothy 6:17-19 (my emphasis).
[406] *Opera*, 45, 613.
[407] Cf. Calvin's commentary on Genesis 1:28 on the creation of human beings in the image of God.
[408] *Opera*, 21, 432.

> They entertain a firm and deep-seated conviction that the rich are happy, and that there is nothing better than to increase their wealth by every possible method, and to brood jealously over whatever they have acquired, rejecting as foolish paradoxes all the sayings of Christ which have a contrary tendency.[409]

In other words, in their efforts to escape the radical gospel and maintain the status quo, they were creating myths. For Calvin, and hence for all true Calvinists ever since, it was the treatment of the weak and vulnerable in society that really determined the value of a political regime. "A just and well-regulated government" Calvin said in a sermon on Psalm 82:3, "will be distinguished for maintaining the rights of the poor and afflicted". Again, the call is not for "Christian charity" that would leave systemic injustices untouched. What is at stake here are the *rights* of the poor. Calvin is not impressed with outward, superficial morality or political piety of either the wealthy or those in positions of political power – and neither should his spiritual children be. In other words, he is not satisfied with programmes and slogans that keep the poor dancing but leave them hungry. His measure for good governance was *conduct towards the poor*. In other words, a conduct measured by political and economic policies that guaranteed justice and were driven by compassion.

Just to make it abundantly clear. The justice we are speaking of is inextricably linked to the rights of the poor. Justice has to do with rights. A social situation is *just* when the *rights* of people in that situation are honoured, says that eminent North American philosopher, Nicholas Wolterstorff. "When we fail in our obligations, we are guilty. When we fail to enjoy our rights we are morally wounded. So obligations have to do with guilt, and rights have to do with woundedness. I have come to think that these are two irreducible sides of moral life".[410] Neither are we speaking of "justice" as defined by the "imperfect" and fallible bodies of law and court proceedings De Lange has reminded us of. If there is justice there, it comes to the poor and the weak almost accidentally. We are speaking of rights as "ground requirements", as Wolterstorff calls them. These rights not only tell us that they are grounded in the justice and love of God, they mean also that "we are not beggars in life".

Wolterstorff makes us aware of the contrast between philosophical concepts of justice and the biblical understanding of justice. It is helpful for our discussion to follow him on this.

---

[409] *Opera*, 46, 406. Commentary on *Harmony of the Gospels*, Luke 16:14, on the Pharisees, "lovers of money".

[410] Nicholas Wolterstorff, "The Contours of Justice: An Ancient Call for Shalom" in Lisa Barnes Lampman (Ed.), *God and the Victim: Theological Reflections on Evil, Victimization, Justice and Forgiveness* (Grand Rapids: Eerdmans, 1999), 107-130.

It is clear from Plato's *Republic* that for him, the most fundamental indicator and root of injustice in society is people not doing what they are best at doing, and in particular the chain of authority in society not having wise people – philosopher-kings – at the top. For John Locke the most fundamental indicator and root of injustice is the violation of a person's property, in his own body and in the fruits of his labour. By contrast, for the songwriters of the Old Testament, the salient indicator of injustice in society would appear to be the presence of persons in society who lack the material and other goods necessary for flourishing.

In ancient Israel, the groups who were especially vulnerable in that regard were widows, orphans and aliens. Thus I don't think there can be any doubt that there is a 'preferential option for the poor' in the Old Testament. The claim, characteristic of liberation theologians that there is such an option, has enraged a good many writers in North America and Europe; but if one comes to the prophets and song- writers of the Old Testament after reading Plato and John Locke on justice, the presence of such an option slaps one in the face, as it were. (Ps.146:7-9) In all of Plato and Locke, there is nothing remotely similar to this.[411]

This is the justice we are speaking of when we speak of reconciliation. And it is wrong, if not utterly cynical to speak of the Christian concept of reconciliation as if we had not said this for years and proved its meaning in the struggle for justice and freedom in South Africa. I suspect strongly that it is not the "romantic', "idealistic" and "transformation-blocking" possibilities of Christian reconciliation that irk its opponents so much as it is the compelling demands for true justice and genuine transformation that they, with the paucity of "civic solidarity", "secular pacts" and "political realism" cannot hope to fulfil, and that make "political reconciliation" so much harder. But that makes the public responsibility of Christian witness not less, but greater.

Calvin has as much to say with regard to a person's right to have employment. And again, it is striking just how relevant these views are to our situation in South Africa today. Says the Reformer, "If a person is deprived of labour they are also deprived of the necessary means to live". It is "as if one had cut their throat... God has ordained that we should work. But is that work denied someone? Behold, that man's life is

---

[411] *Op. cit.,* 111-112. With "flourishing" Wolterstorff means the same I do when I say "fulfilment of human potential". It is a state of shalom, that "comprehensive mode of flourishing". It is personal, psychological, spiritual and material. It is what Jesus meant when he spoke of "abundant life", and that he has come to "bring good news to the poor" as his first priority in Luke 4:16. It is the right of the poor not to remain poor, not to be perpetually impoverished, but to enjoy the abundance of the grace of God for all of life; to be "uplifted" before the face of God and of society.

stamped out!"[412] And it is not just "getting a job" that matters. It is the quality of work, the conditions of work as well as the mutual benefits for the community at large that should be considered: "It is not enough when we can say, 'Oh I have work, I have my trade, I set the pace!' This is not enough; for one must be concerned whether it is good and profitable to the community and if it is able to serve our neighbours".[413] It is not personal satisfaction only that counts. It is the *systemic* transformation which extends justice *to the other* that helps society to function better.

See here not only how radical is John Calvin's interpretation of the biblical message as he applies it to the political and socio-economic situation of his day, notice also how he radicalizes the notion of the neighbour to undermine selfish, self-centred capitalist tendencies, as well as uncaring politics. And then comes a sentence that shifts not only the paradigm of fighting poverty, but shifts also dramatically the measure of our success in fighting poverty: "It is not enough to know that the poor person has work or receives charity, *it is necessary to know if the poor person is content*". [414]

This is the way in which we have always understood the gospel's demand to love the neighbour, and this is how we have always applied it to the political and socio-economic realities during the struggle. And this is what we mean when we apply it now to the political and socio-economic ramifications of reconciliation as we understand it. It is not when government, or big business, or the media moguls are satisfied that justice has been done and reconciliation has genuinely occurred in our country. It is when the poor, the wounded, the vulnerable are content. To be "content" is to be fulfilled. In body and in spirit. When they have seen with their eyes and experienced in their bodies that justice has been done, then "the poor person is content".

Calvin is correct in demanding that paradigm shift because all the demands of Jesus in the gospel regarding justice, righteousness and humanity are made within the context of reference to the one, single, irrevocable criterion which we find in Matthew 25:40 and 45. "Truly I tell you, just as you did it (or have not done it) to one of the least of these brothers (or sisters) of mine, you did (did not do it) to me". That is the heavenly critique, the final judgement, the ultimate criterion of all piety and politics, *and* of the piety of our politics.

The tradition from which I come has always been unequivocal about this fundamental truth, and it echoes from John Calvin to Abraham Kuyper to Karl Barth and the Confession of Belhar. After one hundred and thirteen years the words of that fiery Dutchman, Abraham Kuyper, still ring like a bell in their uncompromising evangelical fervour:

---

[412] *Commentary,* Deuteronomy 24:6.
[413] Sermon XXXI, in the *Harmony of the Gospels,* Matt.3:11-12.
[414] Sermon CXL on Deut. 24:14-18 (my emphasis).

> When rich and poor stand opposed to each other, Jesus never takes his place with the wealthier, but always stands with the poorer. He is born in a stable; and while foxes have holes and birds have nests, the Son of Man has nowhere to lay his head... Both the Christ, and also just as much his disciples after him as the prophets before him, invariably took sides *against* those who were powerful and living in luxury, and *for* the suffering and oppressed.[415]

This, I submit, is the radical nature and demand of Christian reconciliation, and inasmuch as the TRC had tried to "follow the way of Christ" in this process as Desmond Tutu has confessed, this is the criterion by which its work should be judged and valued. And from a Christian responsibility point of view, this is how we should judge the government's participation in the process of reconciliation. Its response to the poor and the weak of our society, in terms of its laws, economic policies, social and political transformation; it must all be measured through the eye that looks from the pit. If the "least of these" who are the family of Christ,[416] of whom the church must be the uncompromising defender, are "content", in other words, if they have seen and found justice so that *their* human potential stands a chance of fulfilment, then we have succeeded, then we have been obedient.

"Resting in the Womb of God"

With these words Dr Curtiss Paul DeYoung captures the meaning of the penultimate chapter of his passionate, moving book, *Reconciliation, Our Greatest Challenge, Our Only Hope*. We have quoted from this book before. Throughout the book, DeYoung takes us on a journey in which we discover the inescapable demands of true reconciliation, the difficulties and obstacles in our way, the practical problems in a country where racism, sexism and materialism are gods upon whose altars sacrifices are made every day. He lingers long upon Dietrich Bonhoeffer, whose words, life and death testify to the costliness of reconciliation. Now DeYoung says that it is not possible to do all this on our own.

> The process of reconciliation requires that we experience a deep healing of the soul, both as individuals and as a society. Taking responsibility, forgiving, and repairing wrongs are important ingredients in this healing process. Yet there may be a deeper pain that endures. This hurt cannot be completely eased until we discover a way to rest in the womb of God.[417]

---

[415] In his address before the Christian Social Congress in 1891, cited by Nicholas Wolterstorff, *Until Justice and Peace Embrace* (Grand Rapids: Eerdmans, 1983), 73.

[416] By "the family of Christ" I do *not* mean "Christians". I refer to *all* who can be classified as the "weak", "the poor", the "destitute", the "excluded" in society. All who are regarded as "less", whose full human potential for whatever reason cannot be fulfilled.

[417] DeYoung, *op. cit.*, 114.

The title of the book is at once a confession and a firm resolve to make a Christian contribution to the realization of reconciliation in society. What is true for the United States is true for South Africa as well: "Generations to come face dire consequences if we do not embrace a reconciliation that is life-changing, society transforming and long-lasting".[418] We too know those consequences. But it is especially true for South Africa because God has given us a miracle in the face of all odds, and we have become such a beacon of hope for the world that our responsibility to have a process of genuine reconciliation is more important than we sometimes seem to realize.[419] In claiming what we are claiming, South Africa is offering the world not just an example. We are offering a possibility of redemption. I say this with fear and trepidation, but it is nonetheless true.

For that reason we dare not speak of reconciliation without talking full account of the words of Dietrich Bonhoeffer. And we have to let those words sink into our collective consciousness, not just as Christians, but as a nation. Bonhoeffer wrote in 1937, seeing and understanding not only the threat and danger of Nazism, but even more the temptations for the church to "go along", to support unthinkingly and uncritically the "national agenda", to be co-opted by the needs of the nation, to call for, and fall for, "cheap grace". Cheap grace, Bonhoeffer then warned, was "the preaching of forgiveness without requiring repentance… grace without the cross, grace without Jesus Christ, living and incarnate".[420]

Note that Bonhoeffer was not speaking of Jesus as the subject of Dogmatics or Systematic Theology, nor as the central figure in the ongoing theological disputes about the "historical Jesus", nor as someone who held up vague ethical ideals which, according to Jakes Gerwel, we in our modern, complex society can no longer follow. He was speaking of Jesus Christ, *living and incarnate*. The One sent by God, who came to liberate humankind and whose words and deeds, life, death and resurrection are the living inspiration of his church. The Christ incarnate who in turn is embodied by his church in the world. Jesus of Nazareth, whose compassionate politics radically overturned the society of his day and which should be the *leitmotif* of his church today. It is as the *living Christ* that Jesus of Nazareth lays claim upon his church, always and always anew, calls the church forth to a life of prophetic boldness, sacrificial love and costly grace:

> Costly grace is the gospel which must be *sought* again and again, the gift which must be *asked* for, the door at which a man must *knock*. Such grace *costly* because it calls us to follow, and it is *grace* because it calls us

---

[418] *Op. cit.,* xviii.

[419] Forgiveness has become a "growth industry" Desmond Tutu has said, and that is "because of us". Just about every book since 1994 about "reconciliation" or "forgiveness" uses South Africa as the hope of the possible. So does Curtiss DeYoung, and so does Jim Wallis, with whose book we will deal in the last chapter.

[420] Dietrich Bonhoeffer, *The Cost of Discipleship* (1937; New York: Simon and Schuster, 1995), 44, 45.

> to follow *Jesus Christ*. It is costly because it costs a man his life, and it is grace because it gives a man the only true life... Above all, it is *costly* because it cost God the life of his Son: "ye were bought at a price", and what has cost God much cannot be cheap for us. Above all, it is *grace* because God did not reckon his Son too dear a price to pay for our life, but delivered him up for us. Costly grace is the incarnation of God.[421]

It is my contention that whatever the understanding of secular politics, *this* is the dictum we should follow. If Christians are to make a lasting contribution to reconciliation and politics in South Africa, this must be our point of departure. Herein lies our integrity, herein lies our identity within the broader body politic. Whatever the motivations of others, and wherever they may derive their inspiration from, for the Christian the costliness of grace and the claim of the living incarnate Christ is the meaningful fulfilment of our political and civic responsibility in the politics of reconciliation. When Trevor Manuel therefore calls upon the church "to be God incarnate in South Africa today", *this* is what it means, for the church and for *all* of life. And this is what we must answer him: "What has cost God so much cannot be cheap for us". It was true during the struggle, it is true now.

Reconciliation, therefore, is of God, realized in Christ and embodied in his church. It is not cheap. That is the first, most fundamental truth about it. But it is more.[422] The Christian cannot deny it, avoid it, or refuse it. It is not an option – it is a call to obedience. It is not possible without confrontation; of the evil past as well as the evil within ourselves. True reconciliation is self-examination. As the story of Zaccheus in Luke 19 teaches us, reconciliation is not possible without restitution. To make right what has gone wrong, to give back what has been unlawfully taken, to restore to the person and the community that which has been appropriated. That is why Ndungane is right in his insistence that reconciliation is a call for jubilee. Reconciliation is the transformation of the person who then becomes an actor in the transformation of society. It is holistic, persistent in its resolve to transform all relationships. Reconciliation is possible only between equals, so that the remorse exhibited is not "handed down" as charity but offered as a sacrifice, and the forgiveness given is not "handed up" as appeasement to power, but as a gift freely given. This equality is not in the first place equality "before the law", although it is certainly that as well. It is in the first place that equality which is rooted in our common humanity, as persons created by God, as standing before God as sinners and beggars, pleading from God for that mercy which we ourselves do not own but cannot live without.

---

[421] *Op. cit.,* 45.

[422] DeYoung has written convincingly about this, both in this book and in his previous work, *Coming Together, The Bible's Message in an Age of Diversity* (Valley Forge, PA: Judson Press, 1995). Cf. De Gruchy, *op. cit.* Wiersinga, *op. cit.,* offers exceedingly valuable insights.

It is as DeYoung says,

> As ambassadors of reconciliation, we are called to act on behalf of God
> to remove barriers to harmonious relationships. We struggle against
> racism, sexism, classism, homophobia, and all things that produce
> division. We grapple with hatred, prejudice, jealousy, gossip, and the
> like. At the same time we strive for peace, justice, equality, and integrity.
> We practice, and encourage in others, love, joy, hope and faith. It is an
> honour to be involved in the ministry of reconciliation… The road to
> recovering our oneness may be paved with struggle, but as followers
> of Jesus Christ we must respond to the call to take up our cross and
> proclaim reconciliation with our words and actions no matter what the
> cost. God's one-item agenda is our only hope![423]

But working thus, in hope, "no matter what the cost" is a risky undertaking. It takes,
DeYoung reminds us, "the risk of trusting". To learn to trust the *political process*, with
its "civil contracts" and "secular pacts", possibly backed by acts of parliament and due
legal process which will hopefully become reality, is one thing. But to trust the erstwhile
oppressor to become a friend, to trust the erstwhile betrayer that the relationship of
comradeship can be restored? To trust the one who necklaced my brother that that
hatred is understood, and forgiven? To trust now, after all the pain, that the pain will
not be prolonged in the agony of poverty, dejection and exclusion? To trust that the
racism we have fought against will not be brought back under the respectable guise of
"ethnic identity"? To trust that the identity that I am giving up will indeed be celebrated
in a new identity?

Because that, really, is the issue here. It is remarkable just how much our identity is
shaped not just by culture or religion or what we are taught formally as well as informally,
but by our *experience*. Our past is a powerful factor our make-up and shapes us in ways
we sometimes rather would not have. In South Africa much of our lives, sometimes *all*
of our lives, has been shaped by apartheid and the struggle against it. Our identity as
persons and as a people have been indelibly marked by both. That identity is hard to
give up or get rid of. Hence our difficulty of speaking with each other without reference
to the past; hence our unending fixation on race and ethnicity; hence our struggle with
the multiple legacies of apartheid; hence our emotional responses if we think someone
is slighting the struggle or is trying "to make us feel guilty". Hence also the wrenching
experiences of people before the TRC. It has all become part of our identity as South
Africans, individually and collectively. And yet, if we are to become a reconciled people,
that will have to change.

---

[423] *Op. cit.,* 59.

Reconciliation, in order for it to be genuine, demands that we give up our identity as shaped by our past and accept a new identity which can embody our hopes for the future.[424] Giving up that identity as conditioned by our past in order to accept a new one embodying the future can only be done if we, as Christians, do not find our identity within ourselves as shaped by our experiences, but in Christ, as shaped by his love. This does not mean "forgetting" the past, but rather redeeming the past, breaking the hold of our memories on our identity, breaking the chains of self-insulating pride, setting us free to make new memories, not separately, but together. In other words, becoming a new person, as Paul begs us to understand.

This is not easy, and it is part of the cost of reconciliation. How shall we do it? It is possible, van de Beek argues, only if we accept the faith embodied in the question and answer of Lord's Day One of one of the ancient confessions of the Reformed tradition, the *Heidelberg Catechism*.

In 1981, at the beginning of the decade of darkness which would bring unseen and unheard of challenges to our faith as we struggled against apartheid, I fell back upon this same article of faith.[425] I then found in it "prophetic clarity and pastoral comfort", a "powerful statement of faith" that could (and did!) uplift us, held us strong in the midst of the almost indescribable devastation caused by apartheid. Now, more than twenty years hence, the power of this statement in our search for genuine reconciliation again becomes amazingly apparent. This is how it reads. Lord's Day One asks the question: "What is your only comfort in life and in death?" The answer is:

> That I, with body and soul, both in life and in death, am not my own, but belong to my faithful Saviour, Jesus Christ; who with his precious blood has fully satisfied for all my sins, and delivered me from the power of the devil, and so preserves me that without the will of my heavenly father not a hair can fall from my head; yea, that all things must be subservient to my salvation, wherefore by his Holy Spirit he also assures me of eternal life, and makes me heartily willing and ready, henceforth, to live unto him.

How do I become an agent of reconciliation? van de Beek asks. By giving up my identity shaped by my past, to find a new identity in Jesus Christ, to whom I, with body and soul, belong in life and in death. I believe that that is true. If all that has shaped me from my past is submitted to the One who has given all to secure my life, then nothing is as important as my life in obedience to him. Then overcoming my past is possible, forgiveness is possible, a new life together is possible.

---

[424] This was the point made by Prof. A van de Beek from the Free University in Amsterdam, Holland, in his valuable contribution at the Barmen/Belhar Consultation, Stellenbosch, 18-20 October 2004.
[425] See my *Black and Reformed,* 96-99.

Is this excessive spiritualization? I asked in 1981. No, it is not, I answered then. But "it is a revolutionary spirituality without which our being Christian in the world is not complete, and without which the temptations that are part and parcel of the liberation struggle will prove too much for us".[426] Now, as we praise God for what we as a nation have been able to achieve, and as we continue to struggle for economic justice and for genuine reconciliation, I still believe these words. I still believe their power can help us build a democracy that will be a beacon of hope for the world. I still believe they can help us to stand where God stands and to find our measure for justice in the justice done to the least of the family of Christ. I still believe they can help us withstand the temptations that come with power. They can help us distinguish between the myths of power and the "good news for the poor". They can help us build a vision, transform our future so that that "mounting rage" Thabo Mbeki warns of, if our people's dreams of justice and humanity are endlessly deferred, can be overturned and our people's future can be secured. A vision without which "the people will perish"; a vision we can both write *and* run with.[427]

Knowing, and in knowing believing this, and in believing striving for its fulfilment, is "resting in the womb of God".

---

[426] *Op. cit.,* 97.
[427] Mbeki, *Africa,* 63, and 81, quoting from Proverbs 29:18 and Habakkuk 2:2.

CHAPTER SEVEN

THE TENDERNESS OF CONSCIENCE
A Paradigm for a Spirituality of Politics

"The Dark Ages Are Upon Us ..."

> *"Calvinism understood that the world was not to be saved by ethical philosophizing, but only by the restoration of the tenderness of conscience".*[428]

When Abraham Kuyper spoke these words in his *Stone Lectures* at Princeton University, he could not have dreamed how relevant they would become for post-apartheid South Africa more than 100 years later. Despite arguments that religious conservatism "has the future" in terms of a public political and legal platform, I am in firm agreement with Dutch historian Hans-Martien ten Napel that historical Protestantism, and specifically as it expresses itself in its Calvinistic form, has a major contribution to make to the building of a modern, pluralistic democracy in today's globalizing world.[429]

Throughout this book we have argued for the indispensability of religious faith during the struggle as well as in our national project of democracy, transformation and nation building. I find Kuyper's conclusion true, and truly inspiring, and this final chapter I shall endeavour to show how a fresh understanding of this return to tenderness of

---

[428] Abraham Kuyper, *Six Stone Lectures* (Grand Rapids: Eerdmans, 1931), 123. These lectures are at times unbearably triumphalistic, and Kuyper does not escape the religious chauvinism of his times, nor has he been able to overcome the benighted racial bigotry which characterized so much of European intellectual expression. Nonetheless one cannot but have appreciation for the universality and timelessness of the insights he espouses here on this particular issue.

[429] Hans-Martien ten Napel, *Protestantism, Globalization and the Democratic Constitutional State,* paper read at the Congress on the Occasion of the 150th Anniversary of the Kampen Theological University, 'Reshaping Protestantism in Global Context', Kampen, the Netherlands, 1-4 September 2004. This contra Alister E McGrath, cited in ten Napel. McGrath refers to "evangelical Protestantism, Roman Catholicism and Eastern Orthodoxy." Besides the fact that I discern major problems with McGrath's statement that "a comprehensive Protestant political and legal platform, faithful to the cardinal convictions of historical Protestantism and responsive to the needs of an intensely pluralistic modern polity did not emerge in the twentieth century", cognizance must be taken of the fact that, for example, "Evangelical Protestantism" covers a very broad spectrum in which a coherent, comprehensive public platform is by no means clear or clearly articulated. Moreover, the question is not just whether "a platform" could be found to which the future supposedly belongs. The question is rather what *kind* of public theology is being expressed by these conservative groups and whether the future of both the church and the world should be entrusted to such a theological-political platform. James Skillen, quoted by ten Napel in the same paper, is right when he asserts that "If individualism, collectivism, and secularism are all misleading in one direction or another, then the need for a God-centred, pluralist social vision [as articulated by Kuyper for the Dutch society of his day, AB] will remain strong throughout the world".

conscience can be crucial in the shaping of our South African democratic ideal, as has already become apparent right through this book.

In that lecture, Kuyper speaks of the "overflowing mass of ethical essays and treatises and learned expositions" being churned out by philosophers and theologians, a "never-ending search" for a new morality. There is something that all this host of learned scholars have not been able to do: they have not been able "to restore moral firmness to the enfeebled public conscience".[430] Kuyper then makes the remark that Calvinism, in its attempt to change the world, has put its trust not in "ethical philosophizing", but in "the restoration of the tenderness of conscience".

For Kuyper it is clear that this conscience is not a privatized, inner sense of right or wrong. It is right or wrong within what he considers the "universal character" of religion, and its "complete universal application".[431] He reminds us that for Calvinism the dominating principle was not, soteriologically, justification by faith, as with Lutheranism, but in the widest sense *cosmological,* the sovereignty of the triune God over the whole cosmos, "in all its spheres and kingdoms, visible and invisible".[432] Hence, "a religion confined to the closet, the cell or the church is abhorrent. God is present in all life in which God shall be praised, that every *labora* shall be permeated with its *ora* in fervent and ceaseless prayer".[433] This is a religious experience and theological expression that appealed directly to the soul and placed it "face to face" with the living God, "so that the heart trembled at his holy majesty, and in that majesty discovered the glory of his love".[434] This discovery sends us out to seek the glory of God and the Lordship of Jesus Christ in all areas of life. It is not a closeted piety, it is a worldly holiness, a world-engaging and world-transforming faith. It is in *this* spirituality that the tender conscience is embedded.

Kuyper understood John Calvin well. When Calvin discusses the concept of *conscientia,* he does so not in the context of moral philosophizing, but in the context of political duty. A person has a conscience "when they have a sense of divine justice, as an additional witness" (apart from the Word of God). "For it is a kind of medium between God and man, because it does not suffer a man to suppress what he knows within himself, but pursues him until it brings him to conviction".[435] Doing what is just and right does not come automatically, or "naturally". We have to be pursued and persuaded. A good conscience, in other words a tender conscience, "is no other than integrity of heart". And its outpouring is always in the acts of justice and compassion.

Likewise, the impetus for transformation in South Africa and the shaping of our democratic identity cannot be the enormous amount of discussion, debates and

---

[430] Kuyper, *op. cit.,* 122-123.
[431] *Op. cit.,* 88
[432] *Op. cit.,* 126.
[433] *Op. cit.,* 88.
[434] Op. cit., 123-124.
[435] John Calvin, *On God and Political Duty,* (ed: John McNeill) in: The Library of Liberal Arts, (Bobbs-Merrill Educational Publishing, Indianapolis, 1956) 42.

sloganeering that our democratic efforts, or Thabo Mbeki's dream of an African renaissance, have generated during the last decade. It is my view that that impetus lies in the restoration of the tenderness of conscience, of the refusal to live with injustice, poverty and inhumanity, of the political articulation of the conviction, in the face of injustice, that "this must not be", grounded firmly in the spirituality that has always been the life-giving source of meaningful African existence.

But we have to take cognizance of the general observation from many quarters that there seems to be a growing understanding among thoughtful and concerned Christian citizens that in our politics, local and global, all is not well.

"The world isn't working". This is the sober reflection of that keen observer of politics and advocate for radical Christian participation in public life, Jim Wallis.[436] He agonizes about the state of affairs in the United States and the state of politics world-wide, and despairs as he watches the opening up of new cracks in American society.

> Our most basic virtues of civility, responsibility, justice and integrity seem to be collapsing. We appear to be losing the ethics derived from personal commitment, social purpose and spiritual meaning. The triumph of materialism is hardly questioned now... We are divided along the lines of race, ethnicity, class, gender, religion, culture and tribe... Our intuition tells us the depth of the crisis we face demands more than politics as usual. An illness of the spirit has spread across the land...[437]

Wallis knows that "something has been lost": the simple but yet fundamental things that make politics and society human, "respect for each other, for the earth, and for the kind of values that could hold us together". What is required is not just better political systems or more efficient delivery of services. The requirement is for "a change of our hearts and our minds", but then a change that "will demand a new kind of politics – a politics with spiritual values".[438]

Wallis is seeking a "new vision" of politics, but a vision that "clarifies the essential moral issues at stake in any political discussion. Spiritual values must enter the public square". The spiritual values Wallis is speaking of are not the conservative, neo-fascist political agenda espoused by the far religious right in the United States, who have claimed credit for the victory of George W Bush in the US elections just completed as we write this last chapter of this book.[439] Wallis has other values in mind: "We must learn to judge our social and economic choices by whether they empower the powerless, protect the earth, and foster true democracy".[440] Wallis is certain that without values of moral conscience,

---

[436] Jim Wallis, *The Soul of Politics* (New York: The New Press; Maryknoll: Orbis, 1994), xv.
[437] *Ibid.*
[438] *Op. cit.,* xvii
[439] Cf. Jerry Falwell, leader of the "Moral Majority" in an interview on SABC's *PM Live,* Friday 5 November 2004.
[440] Wallis, *op. cit.,* xxii-xxiii.

"our political life quickly degenerates into public corruption, cultural confusion and social injustice".[441]

Central to any new politics will be a new spirituality, Wallis says, "indeed, a renewal of some of our oldest spirituality – creating a moral sensitivity that refuses to separate ideas from their consequences for human beings and for the rest of creation".[442] This last is an immensely important insight, the notion that the awakening of a political moral conscience is not merely the articulation of moral ideas, but the awareness that political choices and decisions have consequences, sometimes dire, for the weakest in society and for the earth. These decisions and choices are never made in a vacuum, and should not be taken without full cognizance of their ramifications for human society and the rest of creation. The true moral character of such decisions is not determined by the mere claim that they are "moral", but by the political, economic and social consequences they have for human society and the earth.

In these concerns Jim Wallis is not alone. "We must seek a politics of conversion", writes African-American scholar Cornel West,[443] and political commentator Michael Lerner speaks of the need for a "politics of meaning", which is "to reject the ethos of selfishness and materialism, to seek an ethos of compassion and caring".[444] Wallis agrees, but makes it clear that changes in consciousness will not be enough, "without a consciousness that changes the world". The change, in other words, must be more than personal; it must transform society and the world. The life-transforming journey inward must result in the world-transforming journey *outward*.

But even earlier than Jim Wallis it was moral philosopher Alasdair MacIntyre who discerned certain parallels between late-twentieth century Europe and North America, and the era which saw the Roman Empire descend into what he calls the "dark ages".[445] What was important in those times was the fact that people who strove for the moral good stopped identifying the continued existence of the empire with a moral community. They then constructed new forms of community within which civility and morality could be maintained in the midst of the attacks of barbarism and darkness. MacIntyre sees an analogous situation for North America and Europe, and warns of the dark ages that "are already upon us".[446] We do not intend to engage MacIntyre on his solution to this problem, namely the construction of "local forms of identity within which civility and the intellectual and moral life can be sustained...", for that would cause us to stray too far from the central argument of this chapter. We do, however, want to make grateful use of his observation which points to the heart of the matter and which Wallis and others have subsequently recognized.

---

[441] *Op. cit.,* xvii.
[442] *Op. cit.,* xix.
[443] Cornel West, *Race Matters* (Boston: Beacon Press, 1993), 18.
[444] Michael Lerner, *The Politics of Meaning: Restoring Hope and Possibility in an Age of Cynicism,* cited by Wallis, *op. cit.,* 35.
[445] Alasdair MacIntyre, *After Virtue* (Notre Dame: Notre Dame University Press, 1984)
[446] *Op. cit.,* 263.

> This time, however, the barbarians are not waiting beyond the frontiers;
> they have already been governing us for some time. And it is our lack of
> consciousness of this that constitutes part of our predicament.[447]

The important point here is not only that we are "already governed by the barbarians". That in itself is bad enough. Worse is that we are not even aware of it. Our insensitivity to political, social and economic realities and our inability to discern the nature of our own times is a serious problem. If we are unaware of the dangers already engulfing our society, undermining the moral integrity of our politics, how are we going to be able to take responsible ethical decisions to combat the problem? What does this say about responsible participation of Christians in our democratic life? It points to a dangerous political naïveté, an unrecognized passivity that paralyzes and disempowers. No wonder Jim Wallis warns that "a reawakening to a politics of renewed moral conscience will shake us to our very foundations". [448]

Wallis's recognition of the power of a genuine faith commitment in renewing American politics is supported by no less an eminent figure from the left than Eugene Genovese, and Z Magazine, realizing that "only a religiously based radicalism" can succeed in mobilising a major sector of the American people's sympathy, editorializes that

> The American people will not sacrifice their lives for a secular utopia that
> does not fulfil their emotional and spiritual needs. The American people
> do know what they want, what Jesus wanted, a universal community of
> peace, love and justice sustained by the existence of a loving God.[449]

It is not only in the United States that there is the realization that something fundamental is amiss in politics. In Europe, too, concerned citizens have begun to understand the corrosive effects of careless politics on the life of the nation. From Germany Dorothee Sölle has pleaded for a new political spirituality by keeping open "the window of vulnerability".[450] It is a window that opens towards the world so that the cries of pain and anguish of the wronged and helpless could be heard, so that we are made vulnerable through their vulnerability; and it is open towards the future, not yet tangible but which can be seen and believed, even though that faith makes us vulnerable, leaves us open

---

[447] *Ibid.* Seeing the impact of globalization and the uni-polar realities of global politics, what MacIntyre fears for North America and Western Europe is now true for the whole world.

[448] Wallis, *Soul of Politics,* xxiii.

[449] *Z Magazine,* 7, No. 1, January 1994. Cited in Wallis, *op. cit.,* 38. That the American people have now chosen George W Bush by such a solid margin is yet another reality shock America is giving the world, but it does not nullify the point *Z Magazine* wishes to make: that the American people in their political choices clearly do not know what Jesus wanted and are therefore even more confused about what they need, gives Wallis's concerns more substance and his arguments even greater urgency.

[450] In a fascinating little book of the same title (Minneapolis: Fortress Press, 1990). She continues to plead and work for a renewed spirituality of politics, understanding mysticism *as* resistance. Cf. Sölle, *Mystik und Widerstand, "Du stilles Geschrei"* (Hamburg: Hoffmann und Campe, 1999), especially Part III, "Mystik ist Widerstand".

to be wounded, to be hurt. It is a vision, Wallis writes, which depends on seeing what cannot be seen in the present, and indeed, the capacity to picture that new reality.[451]

World-wide, the consensus for a radical change in our politics is growing. Thabo Mbeki, quoting from Proverbs 29:18, ("Where there is no vision, the people perish…) has also recognized the fact that having a vision is crucial for the people's future. Wallis knows that "when politics loses its vision, religion loses its faith, and culture loses its soul; life becomes confused, cheap and endangered. Nothing less than a restoration of the shattered covenant will save us". By that he means a transformation that stands at the core of what he calls "prophetic religion", "a change of heart, a revolution of the spirit, a conversion of the soul that issues forth in new personal and social behaviour".[452]

> Such a prophetic perspective sees racism and sexism as spiritual as well as social sins and calls for repentance. In foreign relations, it puts human rights over national self-interest and seeks alternatives to war as the familiar solution to the inevitable conflicts between nations.[453]

South Africa, too, has not escaped the moral *malaise* that seems to have gripped us despite the extraordinary hopes of so many people both from within and without.[454] Under the heading "The faces of the moral crisis"[455], two young theologians begin their chapter on South Africa's own moral disorientation with WB Yeats's haunting and spellbinding *The Second Coming*:

> *Things fall apart; the centre cannot hold;*
> *mere anarchy is loosed upon the world…*
>
> *The best lack all conviction, while the worst*
> *are full of passionate intensity.*

For them, the moral fibre of our young democracy is under threat; there is a "vacuum" that needs to addressed and filled, and they hear a clear call for "urgent attention" to this problem. They seek to give "faces" to this crisis involving, among other things, the ascendancy of crime, violence and vandalism; poverty and unemployment; the rapid spread of the dreaded AIDS virus; the culture of corruption and dishonesty; feelings of despair and helplessness in people who feel there is no support for them in their efforts to make difficult moral decisions every day; and a growing social apathy in many

---

[451] *Soul of Politics*, 41.
[452] *Ibid.*
[453] *Op. cit.*, 43.
[454] Wallis, *op. cit.* calls the events in South Africa "salvation events" because they are happenings "filled with the pregnant promise of freedom, justice, liberation, peace and reconciliation… They testify to God's purposes and will for the earth". In these events is "hope for the world, the doorway to change…" 236.
[455] Nico Koopman and Robert Vosloo, *Die Ligtheid van die Lig, Morele oriëntasie in 'n postmoderne tyd* (Wellington: Lux Verbi, 2002),15.

who are loath to become involved with the needs of others and in matters of public importance.[456]

The crisis in our country is an identity crisis, a "people crisis", for it is not just a matter of finding better laws or rules (South Africa has taken enormous strides in the creation of more just laws and the instruments that serve as watchdogs over their implementation); it is essentially a question of *better people*. "People must be changed".[457]

What distresses Koopman and Vosloo is that South Africans seem to be caught in a veritable bind of confusion. What has happened in our country in the last ten years is so positive that many are moved to speak of a "miracle", despite warnings from some sides that we be more temperate in our optimism. Wallis's choice of words may indeed be embarrassing to those South Africans who fear that we are not nearly close to fulfilling those lofty promises, let alone offer "salvation" to the world. At the same time, however, for too many, in fact the vast majority, nothing has changed. Koopman and Vosloo see a "pendulum movement" between the "experiences of hope and despair". These two authors are wary of sounding negative and they want to make sure we understand that they do not believe that there are some South Africans who are "hopeful and optimistic" and others who are "disillusioned and despairing". The pendulum swings "in *all* our hearts". Yet, even in their efforts to be positively even-handed in their judgment, they cannot help but themselves give voice to their own despair and painful confusion about our South African realities. They see dark parallels with Charles Dickens's *A Tale of Two Cities*:[458]

> It was the best of times, it was the worst of times, it was the age of wisdom, it was the age of foolishness, it was the epoch of belief, it was the epoch of incredulity, it was the season of Light, it was the season of Darkness, it was the spring of hope, it was the winter of despair, we had everything before us, we had nothing before us…

These writers are not the only South Africans writhing in this vortex of pain-filled contradictions. No less a figure than the "father of the nation", Nelson Mandela, has been forced to give voice to this paradox in South African life, the feeling of great gratitude for so much achieved and simultaneously of great perplexity at so much gone wrong as he reflects on the road travelled in ten years of democracy:

> We South Africans have succeeded quite admirably in putting in place policies, structures, processes and implementation procedures for the transformation and development of our country. We are widely recognised and praised for having one of the most progressive constitutions in the world.

---

[456] *Op. cit.*, 16.
[457] *Op. cit.*, 17.
[458] *Op. cit.*, 19.

The solidity of our democratic order, with all of its democracy-supporting structures and institutions, is beyond doubt. Our economic framework is sound and we are steadily making progress in bringing basic services to more and more of our people. It is at the level of what we once referred to as the RDP of the soul that we as a nation and people might have crucially fallen behind since the attainment of democracy. The values of human solidarity that once drove our quest for a humane society seem to have been replaced, or are being threatened, by a crass materialism and pursuit of social goals of instant gratification. One of the challenges of our time, without being pietistic or moralistic, is to re-instil in the consciousness of our people that sense of human solidarity, of being in the world for one another and because of and through others. It is, as Biko did at that particular moment in history, to excite the consciousness of people with the humane possibilities of change… To bestow on South Africa the greatest possible gift – a more human face.[459]

We have done much, says Nelson Mandela, but we still miss much. On the outside, we can point to the products of our work: the Constitution, a new body of laws, our development. But on the inside the desert is growing, and woe to the one, warned Friedrich Nietzsche, "in whom the deserts hide". We have fought a long, valiant and noble struggle for freedom and dignity for all our people. We have wrested our future from the stranglehold of racism and naked oppression. We are no longer dwelling aimlessly in the desert. The danger is that the desert may be growing inside us. We are in need of what Mandela longs for, "the RDP of the soul", so that we can bestow on South Africa that "greatest gift" of a more human face.

This underscores two more very important issues. First, what we have is obviously something to be proud of. But we need more. We have a progressive Constitution, a body of good laws, economic soundness (however that is measured), social development – all these are laudable and undeniably good. But without moral values, without an authentic vision-driven politics we devalue ourselves, and the paucity of our spirituality undermines our democratic integrity. Second, Nelson Mandela is saying that with all of our achievements, our greatest gift is still not realized: a more human face. We have still not succeeded in undoing what apartheid has done, stripping from all of us our full human potential. Even more: what we have allowed to grow – greed, crass materialism, instant gratification, the loss of human solidarity – has prevented us from giving and accepting that gift. Our not having that human face is a sure sign of the desertification of our souls.

---

[459] *Biko Lecture,* September 10, 2004.

The God Crisis

Thus, despite our memorable achievements, there is a discernable lack in South African politics, and that lack has been identified. What we are lacking is the spiritual values all these commentators are talking about, and what the people are longing for. I say this with utter conviction: just as we had a spirituality of struggle, so South Africa needs a spirituality of politics. What we are facing is not just a crisis of identity, it is a "God crisis" as Jürgen Moltmann correctly suggests.[460] Our social and political frigidity towards the disadvantaged, the poor and the humiliated is an expression of our frigidity towards God. The cynicism of modern political and economic manipulators is an expression of our contempt for God. "We have lost God, and God has left us, so we are bothered neither by the suffering of others which we have caused, nor by the debts we are leaving behind for coming generations". [461]

In our inner life as in our politics, we need to rediscover God. And we cannot discover God in whatever images *we* can find ourselves reflected in. God is not the mirror of our deepest desires. Neither can we discover God as a distant stranger, a neutral Observer of human actions and therefore of human suffering and misery, aloof from and untouched by human pain. God is not the Silent Other who leaves us to our own devices in order to preserve the "maturity" of our mind, to respect the "integrity" of our human reason – postmodernism's reward for our "independence" from God. We need to discover God in the consequences of our decisions and choices. We must learn, in the words of Moltmann, to discover and "revere" God in the "victims of our own violence", as the victim of human greed for world domination.[462] It is not in withdrawing into ourselves that we find God. It is in reaching out to the wounded other that God reveals himself to us. Therein lies the tenderness of conscience I am pleading for. It is not simply an "inner voice" which leads us to deeds of charity. It is the presence of love that demands justice, that cannot rejoice in the lie and that creates havoc within ourselves until justice is done. It is the piety that is subversive towards complacency within and tolerance of wrongs without.

Tenderness of conscience means that piety and politics belong together, intrinsically and inseparably. It is the kind of piety, writes American theologian Paul Lehmann, that is the combination of reverence and thankfulness that forms and transforms the reciprocity between creaturehood and creativity, in privacy and in society, into the possibility and the power of fulfilling human freedom and joy. Thus understood, politics is the compound of justice, ordination and order that shapes, sustains and gives structure to a social matrix for the human practice of privacy and for the practice of humanness in community.[463]

---

[460] Moltmann, *God for a Secular Society*, 16.
[461] Moltmann, *op. cit.,* 16.
[462] Moltmann, *op. cit.,* 20.
[463] Paul Lehmann, *The Transfiguration of Politics, Jesus Christ and the Question of Revolution* (London: SCM Press, 1975) 233.

"So piety apart from politics loses its integrity and converts into apostasy; whereas politics without piety subverts its divine ordination and its ordering of humanness, perverts justice, and converts into idolatry".[464] Hence, to read and understand the Bible *politically* and to understand and practice politics *biblically* is to discern in, with and under the concrete course of human events the presence and power of God at work, giving shape to human life.[465]

This is how we speak of a spirituality of politics. It is a tenderness that leaves us open to the woundedness of others, that makes us take the risk of vulnerability ourselves. It is a spirituality that infuses politics with the sensitivity that knows that we should not wish for wounds to be healed too quickly and for tears to dry too soon. It behoves us to weep with those who weep so that we can more authentically rejoice when they rejoice. Drying their tears without having first cried with them is denying their right to tears. It is an unholy impatience with the consequences of suffering caused by injustice.

"Politics is an eschatological sensitivity", maintains Prof. G Ter Schegget in an entirely convincing essay, "Of fantasy and conscience".[466] He does not speak of conscience "as the alibi of the unscrupulous", but of the conscience we do not possess but that is awakened in us by the promises of God, the conscience that calls upon those promises for God's sake. It is the conscience vulnerable to those who suffer and who are most easily wounded. It is not just knowing about right and wrong, it is being touched and moved by things we normally are inured to – not just the suffering of others, but their hunger for justice, by which Ter Schegget understands that they have had their fill of humiliation and dejection. It is what we meant when we spoke of the *right* of the poor no longer to be poor, the right to say "no" to their ongoing impoverishment, the right to claim the riches of God's blessings upon God's earth.

It is this openness to the woundability of others that saves the conscience from becoming no more than culturally determined morality, no more than just the tyranny of public pseudo-morality determined by the dominant culture, by whatever happens to be the morality fixation of the day. When it is this "window of vulnerability", it can no longer be a quest for privatized morality, a subjective dependence on an uncontrollable, utterly flexible personal opinion which so quickly freezes into sterile moral immobility.

The relationship between intimacy with God and solidarity with suffering humanity is inextricable. This is an intimacy not with the God of dogmatic formulae or orthodox "correctness", but with the crucified God, the incarnate God in Jesus of Nazareth. The tenderness of conscience means allowing ourselves to be seduced by the dream of God for the world: justice, peace, humanity, solidarity. This double appeal, from the wounded other and the crucified God, from the dream of God and the hopes of humanity, from

---

[464] *Ibid.*
[465] *Op. cit.,* 234.
[466] *Het Geheim van de Mens* (Baarn: Wereldvenster, 1972), 131-144

the pain of the poor and the afflictions of the suffering Servant, allows us to wax to our full humanity. This is how we live *coram Deo* and *coram publico.*

It releases us from our compulsive revolutionary fervour that binds us more to the dictates of revolution than to the daily care for the lives of people. It frees us from the stifling rules of the revolution and from the bureaucratization of the mind, and opens us up to the liberating possibilities of fantasy and sensitivity in our obedience to God. It liberates us from the stranglehold of historical predetermination and sensitizes us to the dream of eschatological possibilities as protest against empirical reality. It helps us understand the freedom of not just fighting for power, but wresting power from the hands of the powerful and sharing it with those who have none. It helps us to make the transition from self-righteous justification because we happen to benefit, to that holy rage at the injustice which makes us benefit. In short, it blesses us with the freedom of humanizing love.

This conscience is a consciousness of the closeness of the other and of God. It means not only sharing the pain of the other, but also sharing the rage of God against injustice and inhumanity. The fantasy we spoke of is not empty, without meaning or content, but a reasoned and reasonable account of the hope that is within us (1 Pet. 3:15). It allows the powerless to call us to account on account of that hope, for us as well as for them, and it allows the powerless to present us with the authority with which that hope endows them. When we speak of our politics as "people-driven", this is what we mean. People have *authority* even when they have no power, because of the incarnation of God and the hope for the promises of God that God has awakened, and kept alive within them.

John Calvin understood this well:

> Tyrants and their cruelty cannot be endured without great weariness and sorrow... Hence almost the whole world sounds forth these words, How long, How long? When anyone disturbs the whole world by his ambition and avarice, or everywhere commits plunders, or oppresses miserable nations, when he distresses the innocent, all cry out, How long? And this cry, proceeding as it does from the feeling of nature and the dictate of justice, is at length heard by the Lord...[The oppressed] know that this confusion of order and justice is not to be endured. *And this feeling, is it not implanted in us by the Lord? It is then the same as though God heard Himself, when he hears the cries and groaning of those who cannot bear injustice.*[467]

One would almost think that John Calvin was writing in our age of globalization, as if he knows about the devastation caused by superpower foolishness in Central America,

---

[467] *Commentaries on the Twelve Minor Prophets,* Habakkuk 2:6, vol. 4, 93-94 (emphasis added).

Afghanistan, Kosovo, Iraq. But this just by the way. Notice how Calvin characterizes injustice as the "confusion of order and justice". For Calvin, "order" is not the enforced state of confusion when the law and violence are used to keep the poor impoverished and subjugated, which is then called in that often lethal but always abusive combination, "law and order". "Order" prevails when justice is done and there is no confusion about right and wrong in society. Hence Paul Lehmann's conclusion that "freedom is the presupposition and the condition of order: order is not the presupposition and the condition of freedom. Justice is the foundation and criterion of law: law is not the foundation and the criterion of justice. These are the proper priorities of politics".[468]

Furthermore, the point is not just that the rage against injustice as well as the longing for justice is "planted in us by the Lord". That in itself is as utterly important as it is amazing. We have become far too used to understanding the "image of God" with which human beings are blessed as the "power to have dominion", which quickly in our peculiar bent towards perversion becomes the power to dominate, rule and exploit. Our truest reflection of the image of God is our capacity to cry for justice, to love justice in our love for the other and for God.

The point really is God's identification with the wronged and the destitute: it is as if we are hearing God crying in the cries of the poor, says Calvin. Even more: God is hearing Himself when he hears the cries of those who cannot bear injustice. God is not just "the God of the poor", God *is* the poor. "Those who cannot bear injustice" can be read another way still. God hears Himself not just in the cries of those to whom injustice is done, but God hears Himself in the cries of those who cry out on behalf of the wronged, those who for God's sake and for the sake of the poor cannot "bear injustice", and therefore cry out to God and therefore do what is right. It is vitally important that we cling to both these meanings in these explosive words. But it is only the tender conscience that hears the voice of God in the voice of the powerless and it is only the tender conscience that responds by doing justice.

Shepherd Servanthood: a Paradigm for Leadership

We cannot do justice without love or humility or the deepest sense of servanthood. But it is always good, as we reflect on these things, to take seriously the gentle protest of Njongonkulu Ndungane to the uncritical use of the words "servant of God" and "servant of the people", as he chides unthinking Western Christianity that has loaded these words with their own master/servant, white/black, madam/maid relationship. It is easy to romanticize the notion, he warns, but it is also "painful" as well as "dangerous", because it is used by people in power to keep others in a place of subservience.[469]

---

[468] Lehmann, *op. cit.*, 235.
[469] Ndungane, *op. cit.*, 95ff. See also the way I have dealt with power as power "over others" as against power "shared with others". *Farewell to Innocence*, Ch. 3.

How dare we then speak of servanthood today? he asks. Only if we ourselves become servants of the One who made himself a servant for us, Jesus of Nazareth. He willingly gives away his power, which he was free to hold onto. He washes feet. He makes room for others. He redefines servanthood by challenging and overturning the paradigm of domination and power, and doing precisely what he is *not* required to do, but does anyway, out of love. Jesus does not ask others to be his servants. He invites them to be his friends, and then he serves *them,* feeds them with his own body and blood, his life. And this is how Jesus relates to people, not as a ruler, but as a friend and a servant.[470]

This is what the tenderness of conscience calls us to. Understanding this is experiencing the "trembling of the soul" Kuyper spoke of. It is a paradigm for leadership we are called to make our own, if leadership is to be worthy of following, if the power invested in us by the people is to have legitimacy. It is understanding that Moses was called to lead God's people, to challenge the might of Egypt, to provoke awe from Egypt's magician-priests and call forth obedience, however reluctant, from the Pharaoh, *not* as a magician, not matching power with power, but as a *shepherd,* with only what he had "in his hand", namely his shepherd's staff. And as a shepherd he became the leader. It was Moses the shepherd who stood in awe before the burning bush of God's presence, and it was Moses the shepherd who led God's people out of the bondage of Egypt. It is the shepherd who receives the Ten Words of life and promise, and it is the shepherd who intercedes with God on behalf of the people. It is therefore entirely fitting that in this tradition the kings of Israel are called "shepherds" and it is entirely fitting that Jesus calls himself "the good shepherd".

We must resist the easy temptation to turn this around as if this were an injury to our human dignity, an undermining of our political independence, an insult to our intelligence. The biblical intention is not to treat human beings as "stupid sheep", whose herd instincts render us mindless at the sound of some divine bell, easily prodded, easily manipulated, easily misled. In the Bible the image of the shepherd is not one of intellectual paternalism or aristocratic condescension, and therefore of immature, autocratic high-mindedness. It is rather an image of justice and compassion, of love and caring, of measurement and judgement (Ezek. 34). It is a metaphor for just government, for legitimate leadership, for democratic uprightness, for the authority of true servanthood.

The words with which the prophet Ezekiel ends that stirring and powerful chapter come from God not as a paternalistic autocrat, the one-eyed king in the land of the blind, but as a loving, compassionate care-giver and dispenser of justice.

> *"You are my sheep, the sheep of my pasture, and I am your God, says the LORD".*

---

[470] Ndungane, *op. cit.,* 97.

God says this to a scattered, hungered, bewildered people, from whom justice has been withheld, who have become the victims of the carelessness, the avarice and greed of leaders who in their concupiscence for wealth and power have forgotten what they had been called to be: shepherds. Yahweh speaks of leaders who, instead of feeding the sheep, have been feeding themselves. Not only that: after they have fed themselves they "trample" and "muddy" with their feet and leave *that* for the poor to eat and drink. (verse 19) And always the criterion is what they have done for the weak, the defenceless, the "least of these". So they stand condemned, because they have not "strengthened the weak, healed the sick, bound up the injured, brought back the strayed, or sought the lost". Rather they have ruled with "force and harshness", they have made their people "a prey" on whom they themselves have preyed. Their failure to be shepherds is their failure of compassionate justice. And in their failure to do justice they have failed the people; they have failed God. "Thus says the LORD GOD, I am *against* the shepherds, and I will *demand* my sheep at their hand… I will *rescue* my sheep from their mouths…" (verse10). This is the inescapable build-up of divine justice as it is with divine liberation: God sees, God condemns, God demands, God rescues. Because God cares.

And what does this Liberator-God consider as justice, what is the measurement of leadership? Ezekiel tells us: to "rescue" the people "from all the places to which they have been scattered"; to "bring them to their own land" and "feed them with good pasture"; to "seek and bring back the strayed", to "bind the injured, strengthen the weak, and to destroy the fat and the strong". What it all comes down to, says Yahweh, is *"I will feed them with justice"* (verse 16).

As it is measurement for the shepherds, it is likewise measurement for the sheep. The people have lost the meaning of togetherness, they have thrown away the solidarity of humanbeingness. They speak glibly of *ubuntu,* but they live lives of self-centred individualism. They call upon "the spirit of the ancestors", but they exude the spirit of postmodernist cynicism. They quote the Holy Scriptures, but it is to "manage" and to use them, not to be captivated by them. What should have been the language of life-giving hope and shared solidarity has instead become the empty prattle of useless after-dinner talk, the conscience-salving piety of vain political discourse, the self-serving sermonizing of media pieces. They feed the poor slogans instead of food, while they fatten themselves on the hopes and trust of the poor. Instead of giving glory to God, they gloat on self-aggrandizement. They lack, Madiba would have said, the RDP of the soul.

The strong among them (the "fat sheep" Ezekiel calls them) have in their greed and carelessness deliberately "fouled up the water" for the weak (the "lean sheep"), thereby depriving them of the means to life and dignity. They have "pushed with the flank and the shoulder, and butted at all the weak animals with your horns until you scattered them far and wide". (verse 21) This is how the Bible always sees any form of injustice: as violence not only against the defenceless, but essentially against God.

So now God takes a stand. The corrupt leaders he shall destroy, the opportunistic, uncaring elites he shall judge, but with the poor and dejected, the excluded and the destitute, the deprived and the scattered, God "shall make a covenant of peace" (verse 25) Yahweh shall make them a "blessing", and the rains he will send down shall be "showers of blessing"; the trees shall yield their fruit, the earth shall yield its increase, and the people shall be "secure". This God shall not brook injustice and oppression, and will "break the bars of their yoke, and save them from those who enslaved them". They shall hunger no more, and neither shall they "suffer the insults of nations", in other words, they shall be given the respect that is their due. They shall live in safety, "and no one shall make them afraid", for everyone shall know that "I, the LORD, am with them, and that they are my people". This how the Bible defines "security": the people have peace, they have food, they enjoy freedom, they have dignity, they have justice; and they know that the LORD is with them. Then and only then, come the closing words, and they are a blessing, a promise and a pledge formed in love and sealed with justice: "You are my sheep, the sheep of my pasture, and I am your God, says the LORD GOD". (verse 31)

To know this, is to know the trembling of the soul. This is the tenderness of conscience.

It is no wonder that Israel's expectations of royal rule were so different from those of the surrounding nations. Deuteronomy 17:14-20 is singularly instructive on this matter, and it will be worth our while to spend some time on this portion of Scripture. When the time comes that Israel shall desire a king to rule over them, it will be a desire to be "like all the nations that are around me". But that is exactly what kingship should *not* be, the Deuteronomist warns.[471] At the very moment the people tend to lay down criteria for the monarchy that would have it resemble kingly rule in the surrounding nations, Yahweh cuts it off at the root. In Israel, the rule of the king expressly should not imitate "the other nations". It should reflect the rule of God.

The first rule laid down by Yahweh has to do with military power, since that is invariably the first thing earthly rulers think of. "He shall not acquire many horses for himself…" (verse 16) Horses, like chariots, were weapons of war. The numbers of horses, chariots and "men who drew the sword", were the signs of the king's strength, measurement of the respect of others for him, of his ability to make war and of what was considered to be the security of the nation. But already here the biblical understanding is that the security of the nation does not lie in its ability to make war, or to acquire weapons of war. It lies, rather, in the faithful trusting in the protection of Yahweh, in the faithful keeping of his commandments, in doing justice to the poor and the needy. Yahweh

---

[471] We are for the moment setting aside the very important issue which is raised in 1 Samuel 8, namely just how much the prophetic presence in Israel resisted the idea of Israel having a king, "just like the other nations". Yahweh gives in only after much "pressure" by the people, and lets them have their way, but with dire warnings of just how much the monarchy will change the nation's life in terms of its self-understanding, its political and socio-economic life, and the fundamental shift from an egalitarian to a class society.

knows the temptation of rulers to establish their "strength" and seek their security in violence and war. Yahweh knows that these weapons are not just to be used against the enemy from outside, but all too soon and all too frequently to subjugate and dominate the people to shore up their own position. All too soon the "security of the nation" becomes first synonymous with, and then subjected to, the security of the throne.

Yahweh knows that this hankering for weapons is a hankering for war, and in the hankering for war is a hankering for personal glory, and on this list of priorities the needs of the people and the longing for the security of justice are simply not to be found. Yahweh knows that in the evil cycle of violence and war and glory there is no place for the consideration of the "little people". They are merely considered as fodder for the war that must end with victory and therefore never stops. Dependence on arms leads to the indispensability of arms, which leads to the deification of arms. So when Thabo Mbeki quotes Nelson Mandela in his plea that "we must fight against and defeat the deification of arms, the seemingly entrenched view that to kill another person is a natural way of advancing one's cause or an obviously correct manner by which to solve disputes"[472], he is, if he really means what he says, much closer to the deuteronomistic ideal of a ruler than he knows. It is a closeness that edifies as well as admonishes, for it brings us back to the fundamental questions we have raised regarding South Africa's weapons producing and procurement programmes, and hence also about the integrity of such pronouncements.

Then comes the second rule. He shall not "return the people to Egypt in order to acquire more horses..." This could be understood in several ways. First, and quite practically, the king would need to send emissaries to Egypt, to negotiate the price of horses, to bargain and to buy. But that physical return to the land of their slavery is not acceptable. "Stay away", Yahweh seems to say, "don't even go there". Second, "returning" to Egypt, superpower of the day, means turning to Egypt for help, thereby giving Egypt recognition it should not have, honour it does not deserve. It also takes Israel into the circle of worldly power by which the status of these nations is measured, but which is in total contradiction to Israel's belonging to the LORD. Buying weapons of war from Egypt, placing themselves at Egypt's mercy, depending on Egypt for its very existence instead of on the power of Yahweh is a political mistake Israel will regret, a wrong turn Israel will have to correct, a sin Israel needs to repent of.

But the logic of the deuteronomist takes us yet one step further. "Returning" to Egypt, placing oneself at Egypt's mercy and therefore also at its beck and call; "buying into" the skewed logic of superpower politics, accepting their definition of "security", adopting for themselves that fundamentally flawed notion of what makes a nation "great"; choosing not Yahweh but Egypt, not justice but weapons; replacing faith with the crippled certitude of *Realpolitik;* preparing for peace by making war, *that* is returning to the slave mentality Yahweh has liberated Israel from. It is putting the people back into an *Egypt mindset* that is the articulated sin here. Living in the promised land with their

---

[472] In his *Prologue* to *African Renaissance,* xv.

minds in Egypt: that is an enslavement the people do not deserve, and that Yahweh will not tolerate. Giving up the hard-won freedom for a new, albeit gilded, slavery from which only the privileged will benefit; exchanging the liberating torah which secured the rights of the poor for the subtle entanglements of the Egypt consensus, that is what the Bible cannot understand and what Deuteronomy urgently warns against. Time and time again the prophets of Israel and the protest singers of the psalms would rail against this temptation Israel seemed not to have been able to resist. "Some put their trust (and take pride in) chariots and some in horses, but our trust is in the name of the LORD our God", is the affirmation, the confession and the plea of Psalm 20:7.

"And he must not acquire many wives…" Deuteronomy goes on to say. That has nothing to do with sex; it has to do with pride. It is not just lust, but it is the lust for *acquisition.* It is not just pride or acquisition, but it has to do with *alliances.* And alliances have to do with one's understanding of power and of politics. For the sake of the acquisition of power, the king's heart "would be turned away". It is not the women who would mislead, or seduce, or lure with their sexual wiles the king "away from Yahweh"; it is the lust for power that would do so. It is for this reason that the failure of Solomon's rule is not simply sought and found in his many wives, but also in the way he treated his people, in his creation of forced labour, forcing upon them a new kind of slavery akin to that of the nations around him. In other words, he "returned the people to Egypt" (1 Kings 4:6; 5:13-18)[473]

Then the preacher of Deuteronomy turns to the heart of the matter. What shall protect the king from vainglory, insulated pride and heartlessness? What shall make him understand justice, withstand the insidious power of power? What shall keep him sensitive to the cries, the needs, the humanity of the poor and the weak? The law. The law that demands that before the king speaks, he should listen: *"Shema, Yisrael!"* The law that reminds him that there is no other god than Yahweh; that it is this God, and no other, that brought Israel out of slavery, that defeated the powers of oppression, that gave Israel a name and a sense of belonging, a future and a sense of being. The law that proclaims that God alone is God; that no human being, however powerful, however iconised by the people, however mighty in his own eyes, can take the place of God. Other kings did just that. The Pharaoh was a divine being. In Israel it should not be so. There is only one God, and before this God *all* shall bow.

The law that guarantees freedom as it demands honour for the elders and love for the neighbour and respect for creation. The law that calls for responsible personhood so that society may be a safe place. The law that serves as a constant reminder of where the people have come from, where they are going and who they are: "Remember that you were a slave in the land of Egypt, and the LORD your God brought you out from there with a mighty hand and an outstretched arm…" (Deut. 5:15) The law does not remind them of their slavery, it reminds them of their liberation *from* slavery. This is

---

[473] While Chronicles only has praise for Solomon, it is surprising how the 1st Book of Kings, even in an obvious piece of "royal theology", twice makes this crucial point of criticism.

the God who freed them from slavery and this is the God who stands between them and a new slavery. This is the God the king must fear, and all this has to do with good government.

The fear of the LORD shall save him from the fear of others, even of superpowers such as Egypt. It shall save him from greed, the hunger for power and the thirst for blood. It shall save him from estrangement from Yahweh and from his people. It shall save him from losing himself, his destiny and his people's lives in the pursuit of vainglory. It shall save him from squandering the dream of God for the people and from plundering the hopes for the people for profit. It shall make him love justice and prevent him from defending the unjust. The fear of the LORD shall give him wisdom and discernment: he will know that those who deem themselves great, who claim for themselves grand titles, "gods", "sons of the Most High" (as rulers of those days were indeed wont to call themselves), the "icons" of the times, are no more than "mere men" and that they shall die – "like mere men, they will fall". But he, if he holds on to the torah, will "defend the cause of the weak and fatherless; maintain the rights of the poor and oppressed, rescue the weak and needy; and deliver them from the hand of the wicked" (Ps. 82). In this he is the true king, for he is the true reflection of the kingly rule of Yahweh. The king defends the cause of the weak and needy because *God* "upholds the cause of the oppressed and gives food to the hungry" (Ps. 146:7).

Even here love for God and love for the neighbour, the fear of the LORD and the respect for the other, humbling oneself before the glory of God and losing oneself in the love for the other and therefore finding oneself in the humanity of the other go together, inseparably linked, inextricably intertwined. Verse 20 exhorts the king to hold onto the precious principle of the equality of all human beings before the face of the LORD. He should be king, but as one amongst his own. "Neither exalting himself above other members of the community nor turning away from the commandment" is the guarantee of good rule, of long life and the measurement of the proper use of power. This does not call for that false, post-apartheid egalitarianism that seems to be our affliction, where respect for either the office or the person holding the office is avoided with a single-minded rudeness that leaves all civility behind. And, no, respect for the office and the person, and for the gifts of leadership well-displayed does not mean slavish acceptance of everything said and done.

The tradition I come from has understood this: the equality of all human beings is grounded both in our having been created in the image of God and in our state as sinners before God. Our entire life is placed before God, and therefore all men and women, rich or poor, weak or strong, talented or not so talented, "have no claim whatsoever to lord it over one another, (but) we stand as equals before God, and consequently equal as man to man (and woman to woman)".[474] The right to "rule over" is never given, argues the Reformed tradition, since such right immediately and of necessity "becomes the right of the strongest", and in any case, all sovereignty in heaven and on earth belongs

---

[474] Kuyper, *Lectures,* 52-53.

to God, and it is within that sovereignty that rulers must find their place. Abraham Kuyper wastes not a single word: "As a man I stand, free and bold, over against the most powerful of my fellow men… in the sphere of the state I do not yield or bow to anyone who is a man, as I am…"[475]

That is a consequence not of disrespect for the king, but of respect for the value and worth of the human race as a whole, of whom the king is a part and apart from whom he has no existence. Deuteronomy understood the crucial truth of these words. The honour does not come from the people, who have made him king. The honour derives from God, who has made him a human being. It is not the kingship that affirms his worth; it is his humanity, as displayed in the way he rules, that affirms his kingship. The king as shepherd, the king as neighbour, the king as equal partner for the sake of the kingdom of God. Kingship as servanthood. It is here that the principle of equality should first be honoured: at the "top". And it remains central in any discussion of values of what the 2004 UNDP Report calls "global ethics". Underlining what we have strongly argued until now, the Report tells us that the "principal source of global ethics is the idea of human vulnerability and the desire to alleviate the suffering of every individual to the extent possible". Another source is the belief in the basic moral equality of all human beings:

> Recognizing the equality of all individuals regardless of class, race, gender, community or generation is the ethos of universal values. Equity also envelops the need to preserve the environment and natural resources that can be used by future generations. [476]

It is vital for modern democracies where, inspired by the victory rhetoric emanating from the United States, the ideal of equality, since the collapse of socialism, has been scornfully pushed out of our political discourse. Without equality there is no freedom or a "free world". "Equality", Moltmann emphasizes, "is not collectivism. It means equal conditions for living, and equal chances for living for everyone. As a social concept, equality means *justice*. As a humanitarian concept, equality means *solidarity*. As a Christian concept, equality means *love*. Either we shall create a world of social justice, human solidarity and Christian love, or this world will perish through the oppression of people by people, through a-social egotism, and through the destruction of the future in the interest of short-term, present-day profits". [477]

The king, and hence the people, shall live by the fear of the LORD. To fear the LORD is to know the LORD. Knowing the LORD is knowing the true measure of kingly rule.

---

[475] *Op. cit.,* 130-131.
[476] *UNDP Report 2004* (New York: United Nations, 2004) 90.
[477] Moltmann, *op. cit.,* 69.

Woe to him who builds his house by unrighteousness
And his upper rooms by injustice…
Do you think you are a king
because you compete in cedar?
Did not your father eat and drink
and do justice and righteousness?
then it was well with him.
He judged the cause of the poor and needy;
then it was well.
Is this not to know me?
says the LORD.

This is what Jeremiah tells king Jehoiakim, (Jer. 22:13, 15-16) and this is the message of all those fiery, 8th century prophets of social justice. This is what good governance will be judged by.

In the New Testament it is no different. Even with all the wild contestation around the words of Paul in Romans 13, the point we have been trying to make right through this section remains abundantly clear. Government is an agent of God "for your good". The government is there for the good of the subject, even more precisely, for the good of the neighbour, which is the whole point of the tension we find in Romans 13.[478] Paul underscores the point by using not civil or political categories to describe governmental authority, but by employing the language of the liturgy. Government is God's *leitourgos,* God's liturgical servant for the good of the people. For him the exercise of governmental authority is a liturgical function.

Therefore, for the prophets as well as for the people of Israel as expressed by the deuteronomist, the criterion for true kingship, for responsible rule, was not military might, diplomatic victories or the accumulation of wealth, but rather the way in which the image of Yahweh was seen in the rule of the king. Proper rule is just rule. True government is servanthood.

Walking Humbly with God

Let me say it again: a true spirituality of politics finds its deepest source in Kuyper's "trembling of the soul" before God. In the humble walk with God. It is in the awe-filled silence before the glory of God that we find the courage to speak boldly in and to the world. Our souls tremble before God so that our knees won't have to tremble before kings. We are awed by the presence of the Living One so that we need not be over-awed in the presence of earthly power. It is in the rest in God's mercy that we feed the restlessness within ourselves for the sake of justice.

---

[478] We do not intend to repeat our arguments here. The point has been thoroughly discussed before. Cf. Allan A Boesak, *Comfort and Protest, The Apocalypse from a South African Perspective* (Philadelphia: The Westminster Press, 1987), 97ff.

A spirituality of politics means walking humbly with God. It is not a closeted, albeit pious, immobility. It is a *walk,* a way of life[479] guided by strategy, but sustained by faith, made possible by policy, but nurtured by prayer. It is a private and public acknowledgement of our utter dependence upon God, of our openness to be called upon by the authority of the poor. We are engaged in politics, not simply to "help" others, but because we are compelled by justice; not because we believe that the poor need help, but because we believe they deserve justice. For us this justice is not a philosophical concept or a legal definition or an ideologically adapted and approved slogan. It is, as the prophet Micha has taught us, the act of humbly walking with God.

This "humbly walking with God" is not simply "an attitude of adoration and humility", as some have suggested, though it certainly is that as well. Neither is it an admonition to "know our place", wretched sinners and worthless humans before an omnipotent, omniscient, omnivorous God. It is, rather, an act of learning to understand what Yahweh requires. That, after all, is the explicit invitation of the prophet. It means to listen attentively, to be careful in knowing the ways of God, and to be diligent in walking the way, that is, in *doing* what Yahweh requires, which is "to do justice, and to love mercy" which is to "walk humbly with your God" (Micha 6:8). It is learning to read the heart of God.

"Walking with God" is much less mystical than we have sometimes made it sound. It means just what it says. It is walking with God through Egypt, *seeing* both the oppressive, heartless might of the Pharaoh *and* the pain and suffering of God's people (Ex. 3:7). It is standing in the midst of the slaves, counting the blows, bending under the weight, feeling the pain. It is understanding the power of the Pharaoh and the mercilessness of his slave drivers, and it is "to come down" to rescue, to liberate, to end the violence and the suffering. Walking with God is walking from the brick-making yards through the palace gates to the throne, telling the Pharaoh, "*Let my people go!*" It is breaking down the wall of resistance between the will of Pharaoh and the longing of the people, between the power of the Pharaoh and the cry for freedom. It is knowing the difference between making bricks for the Pharaoh and building the walls of Jerusalem.

Walking with God is walking hand in hand with Jeremiah through the beleaguered city, seeing the helplessness of the people and crying out in anguish at the coming disaster: "Oh my insides! My insides! I writhe in pain! Oh the walls of my heart!" (Jer. 4:19). Most translators have it that it is Jeremiah who cries out here. But it is *Yahweh* who cries, whose "heart is beating wildly", whose pain is that of a woman in child-birth. For that is the image of the Hebrew: the compassion of God is the tearing of the womb in giving birth. God's anguish is not a low, gritted-teeth growl, tight with pain but manly, controlled. It is an unadorned, atavistic feminine shriek. Jeremiah is merely echoing the pain-filled words of God, simultaneously shattering the image of a male, patriarchal God.

---

[479] It is best expressed in the meaningful Afrikaans word, *lewenswandel.*

Walking with God is listening with God to the righteous anger of Habakkuk, "How long, LORD, must I call for help, and you do not listen? Or cry out to you, 'Violence!' but you do not save? Why do you make me look at injustice, and why do you tolerate wrong?" It is responding with God,

> *Write the vision,*
> *Make it plain on tablets,*
> *So that a runner may read it.*
> *For there is still a vision for the appointed time,*
> *It speaks of the end, it does not lie.*
> *If it seems to tarry, wait for it;*
> *It will surely come, it will not delay...* (Hab. 2:2-3)

It is knowing with God and Habakkuk, that the vision lives. Even though evil seems to prosper and the law is paralysed so that justice never prevails, the vision lives. Even though the righteous are trapped, "hemmed in", have nowhere to turn to and justice is "perverted", the vision lives. It is, like Habakkuk, not to run away, or to hide in fear, but to take our turn at the watch tower, to station ourselves on the ramparts, and not move one inch until the LORD hears and responds.

Walking with God is walking with Jesus, restoring life to the bodies of children and thereby restoring life to the hearts of their parents. It is walking with Jesus, making the wounded whole, healing the sick, liberating those in prison, touching the untouchables and overturning the thrones of the Untouchables. Giving women their rightful place, weeping with those who mourn, releasing the life-giving power of the law, challenging and confronting the powerful on the issues of justice and mercy, in their temples and their palaces, giving notice that the kingdom of God has come.

Walking with God is to stand where God stands, and to fight for whom God fights: the poor, the weak, the powerless and the defenceless. It is to have the courage to know that trepidation before the might of the powerful is overturned by the fear of the LORD. It is to understand, without doubt or equivocation, that justice is what Yahweh requires. Not seeks or asks, or requests, or hopes to eventually coax from our unwilling hearts, but *requires*. The biblical metaphor is truer than we might think.

This is the spirituality we are speaking of. It is to be done with silly, romantic notions about poverty, whether or not covered with some biblical gravy, like the so often-quoted words of Jesus, "The poor you will have with you always". As if Jesus had simply reminded us of a God-ordained, unchangeable fact to which he, and we, should meekly resign ourselves. So now we can wash our hands, both in innocence and of the poor. In truth, this quotation from Deuteronomy 15 is a sharp, angry reminder of the words with which that chapter begins: "There shall be no poor among you!" (15:4) *That* is God's desire. And there shall be no one in need among you, "if only you will obey the LORD your God by diligently observing his entire commandment..." The poor are poor and *there* not because God wills it so, but because of human greed and avarice, of heartlessness and disobedience. In other words, because of hardness of conscience. So instead of lulling us to sleep, it is a wake-up call; a scathing criticism of the way in which we run the world, of the way we allow things to be and remain. Jesus highlights not the irreversible lot of the poor, but our insistent, rebellious disobedience, our deviance from the way God has called us to walk.

John Calvin has preached on this text. There is no such thing as "the poor masses", faceless crowds for whom some relief must be sought through grants or charity. *The poor* do not exist, Calvin says in this sermon, "They are *your* poor, *your* brother, *your* poor, *your* needy". That is what the Hebrew text says.[480]

The spirituality we are seeking is one that shuns empty political chatter about poverty and confronts politicians with the human face of the poor. The issue is not "poverty" as if it were some vaguely disturbing, slightly distasteful, but nonetheless unchangeable condition, inescapable not because of the poor, but because of its political correctness. The issue is *the poor,* not faceless masses, but human beings made in the image of God, victims not of the will of a cruel, capricious God, but of human predatory greed; whose assaulted and battered humanity deserves to be defended with more passion than we are currently able to bring forth.

It is a spirituality both tender-hearted and tough-minded. It knows that poverty is an enemy of humanity in the widest sense of that word, but it is no longer an unbeatable enemy. It is no longer inevitable as we have argued earlier. It knows that poverty is still with us, not because God wills it so, but because of political unwillingness and inhuman economic policies. It exists because we sacrifice to neo-liberal capitalist gods who place profits over people.[481] It affirms with the UNDP Report that eradicating absolute poverty in the first decades of the 21st century is feasible, affordable and a moral imperative. It is a practical possibility. Therefore we shall brook no more excuses, no more inversion of priorities, no more empty promises.

Again, it is a spirituality that is infused with the love of Christ.[482] The love, as Paul says, that compels us. We must confess that quite openly and shamelessly in a time in our country where there is a shameful eagerness to forget the role faith played in our lives during the struggle for liberation. Hence many, as we have already seen, will find this embarrassing or irritating, and somewhat foolish. We hear the word love and immediately we are warned off: it is useless sentimentality, dangerous spiritualization, irrelevant primitiveness that has no role to play in our complex world except for "pathologizing" the nation.

---

[480] Cf. Boerma, *op. cit.* at 26.

[481] Cf. Noam Chomsky, *Profit Over People, Neoliberalism and Global Order* (New York: Seven Stories Press, 1999).

[482] I have worked this out in sermon form, in an effort to broaden the participation in these discussions among "ordinary" church-going Christians. Cf. Allan Boesak, "The Heart of the Matter", in *The Fire Within, Sermons from the Edge of Exile* (Cape Town: New World Foundation, 2004) 145-157.

Talk of love replaces reason and logic, suspends clear-headed thinking and scientific analysis. Or so we think. It demands that we think and act as if we were not in the real world. Or so we think. We claim that we have come of age, we know too much, have seen too much, been lied to too often, experienced too much. We have indeed learned our lessons and that makes us weary of life, wary of each other, suspicious of God. Keeping our level-headed distance is a sign of our adulthood. We do not want our maturity to be tampered with. We do not want to be treated like children who don't know better; who cannot see the woods for the butterflies.

But that is exactly what love does *not* do, Paul argues in 1 Corinthians 13. Learning to love is precisely to "put away childish ways". To love is to know true wisdom, to speak words of truth and value. Not being able to love is to speak like a child, think like a child, reason like a child. What we think of as childish foolishness: to be patient, kind, not envious or boastful or arrogant; not to insist on our own ways, not to "stand on our rights"; not to be irritable or rude or resentful; not to rejoice in evil but to rejoice with the truth: now *that*, says Paul, is the hallmark of adulthood, of genuine humanbeingness. And is it not indeed these very qualities we admire so much in those "stalwarts of the movement", who endured so much, held onto the vision for so long on behalf of so many, and who, having missed so much of their own productive lives, time with family and dear ones, have now emerged as symbols of reconciliation and forgiveness, of an all-embracing love, setting examples of genuine *ubuntu* for generations to follow?

This love is not sentimental nor distant. It is a love that makes choices: for rejoicing with the truth rather than to profit from evil. To expose the foolishness of the world by becoming fools for Christ. To spurn what the world considers "wisdom" – that only which can be calculated, measured beforehand – and choose for the risk of trust in reconciliation, for justice and peace without guaranteed outcomes. To seek our strength in the imitation of Christ and to resist emulating the world. To seek to do what is right, rather than what is popular. To find, in the defencelessness of the cross, the strength to love; to stand up for the weak and helpless, the excluded and the marginalized. To love is to share the dream of God for this world, and to claim the realization of that dream in our pursuit of justice.

This love reflects genuine maturity, of personhood and of community. It is not some vague romantic notion. It is the unmissable deepening of true adulthood. To love thus is to explore the open spaces beyond our own limitations, to surrender to the power of our wider imagining, to discover the vistas of what is possible beyond the foothills of our stunted fantasy. It is to discover in the other the best that we ourselves want to be, to offer the other more than we have allowed ourselves to be. This is the only way, I am convinced, through which we will be enabled to take up the task ahead of us, to face and confront the challenges that will otherwise daunt and slay us. Only through this love will we have find the courage to unlearn what we must, to learn what we should, to renew both our minds, our politics and our land.

This is what African people have long since discovered and experienced: this vision for themselves and their children, enabling them to dream God's dream for themselves and their children. In dark and lean years, through veils of tears and suffering, in the most appalling situations of the most fearsome adversity, they drank from this well, and out of all this they fashioned a spirituality that infused their struggles from colonial times, turned their weaknesses into strengths and their fears into courage, their despair into a wellspring of hope.

It is the hope of which that other son of Africa, St Augustine, spoke. Hope, Augustine said, has two daughters: Anger and Courage. The anger of hope means that one refuses to accept what is wrong, to put up with what is driving one to despair. The courage of hope means to have the firm resolve to pull oneself to one's feet and attack injustice, even though one has to pay the price for doing so.[483]

In this new phase of struggle and nation building, of seeking reconciliation and finding a way through the wilderness of globalized politics, of resisting the temptations of power as well as the abdication of national responsibility to faceless trans-national entities dedicated to other things than justice and the wellbeing of the little people of God, this struggle will ask as much of us a nation as did the struggle against the far more visible gods of yesterday's Canaan. Besides, there are enough of our own new rulers who brook no critique, who can hear no voice but their own, who see no vistas except from their own lofty places. In our present political climate the epithet "counter-revolutionary" is as ideologically loaded and politically effective as the word "communist" had been in apartheid South Africa. Still, we shall have to as truthful in these things as we can, and what the LORD whispers into our ears, shall have to be shouted from the rooftops (Matt. 10:26).

To Name God

It is perhaps good to return to a reminder from Argentina, as anguished and tortured a land as our own had been. The voice is that of liberation theologian José Miguez Bonino, as relevant and powerful today as it was when we first began to see the challenges of global politics for our Christian witness in the world today. Christians became involved in politics, Bonino writes, even though at first it was a strange, new world for us. We became involved because of the growing conviction that this was the call of the gospel. We must move into that arena, we decided, crudely ambiguous and dirty though it may be, to "courageously assume our position as believers, and dare to name God, to confess him from within the womb of politics, from within the very heart of commitment". [484]

---

[483] For this insight I am grateful to Coenraad Boerma, *op. cit.,* 127.
[484] Bonino, *op. cit.,* 8.

But what does it mean to "name God"? It means to "denounce and condemn all the new idolatries, all claims ideologies and systems make to being perfect and absolute... to stake one's life with and for the poor... those of unimpressive proportions, those whom the revolutionary movements tend to undervalue and even annihilate".[485]

There are some who think that Christians should be engaged in political struggles solely in order to "call the devil by its name". There certainly is something of that in our politics too. Not to shy away from pointing to what is wrong, to call our attention to the festering sores within our society, although I am hoping that Christians will also learn to tend the wounds of society *before* they become festering sores. It is well worth remembering: every festering sore in our body politic is a wound that we have not tended, nor bound, nor healed. As I am writing today, the most recent statistics regarding rape, woman and child abuse have been released.[486] South Africa, we hear, has the world's highest incidence of rape, and of women and child abuse. One woman is raped every minute in our country, and every fourth woman is abused by her male partner. I find this shattering, and it should be named. For the sake of all the women and children surely, but also for the sake of men, and most of all, for the sake of our nation as a whole. If the renaissance is about saving the African soul, here is where it must begin. Without the safety of women and children there will be no salvation. The silent suffering of the abused (for we are not nearly loud enough about this evil) is a loud cry for a tenderness of conscience we still do not allow to possess us.

But "naming the devil" is only a small part. "Naming the devil" is merely recognizing that evil exists and that, while it exists, it is creating havoc amongst the most vulnerable in our society. There may be shock value in "naming the devil", and it may even be a handy vote-catcher, but there is power in naming God. Naming the devil is pointing to the problem; naming God is allowing God to lay claim on us, empowering us to do what is right; to enable us to rise to our feet and right the wrong. One can name the devil and still, out of a sense of shock or distaste, unbelief or helplessness, stand aloof, remain untouched, run away. Naming God means neutrality is lost, aloofness is not an option, distance is not possible. Naming God means having to "denounce all idolatries", especially those who try to convince us that we, in the face of the horrendousness of it all, the vastness of the problem, the sheer evil of its expression, are helpless, too small, too powerless.

It is idolatry to act as if the gods of evil are more powerful than the God of love. It is idolatry to believe that the women who are being raped, battered and killed are of such small worth that we cannot "stake our lives with and for them". It is idolatry to believe that the children who are the victims are of no account, so far on the margins of our own lives that we can afford to stand aloof, follow from afar what others do. It is idolatry in the face of such inhumanity in the heart of South Africa's hopeful

---

[485] *Ibid.*
[486] According to the Unilever Institute at the University of Cape Town, SABC's *Midday Live,* 15 November 2004.

democracy to convince ourselves, or be convinced by others, that our contribution cannot matter, cannot change things, cannot make a difference. Naming God in politics means naming the hope that never dies, the future that still exists, that is waiting to be claimed by all of us on behalf of all of us, the love that will not let us go. Naming God means standing where God stands, fighting for whom God fights – the children, the women, the undefended; weeping with them the tears of Rachel who, for the sake of her wounded and abused and murdered children, will not be consoled until the Judge of heaven and earth rises up with her and they do what is just.

And this is what we must do, in our local and national politics and on a global level. The world belongs to God; it is the whole world that is the theatre of his glory. We shall do it because we ourselves have been redeemed, called and empowered by the One who himself took on "unimpressive proportions" for our sake. He is the suffering Servant whose willingness to lose, to give up all forms of majesty, to become acquainted with grief, to become a man of sorrows, is our salvation.

He was despised and rejected by those who thought him a danger to their positions of power and privilege within the status quo, *and* by those who found him not pliable enough, as well as not hard enough, to fit into the predetermined mould of their revolutionary zeal. They knew, as we do, that the unimpressiveness of his incarnation was not the absence of his glory, but the heavenly solidarity with the poor and the lowly. Those who found him offensive would not look at him because looking at him means looking at the human face of the poor. They hid their faces from him because they could not bring themselves to look upon the misery their greed had visited upon the helpless. They held him of no account because the powerless do not feature in their reckoning except as sacrifices on the altar of political expedience. They held him cursed because he carried in his body the afflictions they brought upon the wounded by keeping them outside the gate, outside the circle of protection. They crucified him because he was the tender conscience that would not let go of their hardened hearts. But because God awakens in the hearts of the poor the longing for freedom, justice and contentment, they are doomed to hear his voice as long as the poor cry out. They shall see him as long as the poor have a face. They shall have to face him as long as the poor have hope. The suffering God, like the hopeful *sizwe,* will not go away.

But those who accepted him saw in him the power that can change the world. They knew that the incarnation is the key to understanding all God's dealings with human history. They know the incarnation is not just the presence of Jesus of Nazareth in the world, it is the *difference* that presence makes *in* the human story in the world. That presence constantly asserts itself, presses itself upon history, inviting us to conversion, and in converting, to transform the world. It is as Rubem Alves of Brazil has said: "What drives us is not the belief in the possibility of a perfect society, but rather the belief in the non-necessity of *this* imperfect order".[487]

---

[487] Bonino, *op. cit.,* 90.

So we dream with Thabo Mbeki the dreams of the prophet Habakkuk and with him we see the vision with which we, because we believe, are prepared to run. But the vision of the prophets is indivisible and the dreams of the prophets are all the one dream of God, and Thabo Mbeki needs to know this. The Bible is not there for convenient quotations in order to play to the proper audience. It is to be taken seriously for our life and our work. If we want to use it, we should first be overwhelmed by it. To accept Habakkuk's vision is to long for Isaiah's vision of peace and justice. If we dream, with Amos, of a day when "they will plant vineyards, and drink their wine; (and) make gardens, and eat their fruit", and that the people "shall never again be uprooted"; then we must heed his call that justice should roll down like waters and righteousness like a mighty stream. If we call upon Habakkuk, we cannot ignore the dream of Hannah, of the bows that shall be broken, that the day shall come that all the world shall understand that "not by might shall one prevail". Then we cannot reject the dream of the swords that shall be turned into plough shares, and the cessation of war "to the ends of the earth". One cannot claim Jeremiah and reject Hannah, or lean on Amos but turn one's back on Mary of the Magnificat. The dream is the dream of God, and it is planted in the hearts of God's people. The vision is the vision of God, and it comes forth out of the hearts of God's people.

Those who scoff at South Africa's miracle are wrong. What happened with us ten years ago is a miracle, because it went utterly beyond our wildest imagination, beyond our abilities to project or control. That we did not wade through rivers of blood, as so many had expected and even more had feared, was more than we could have planned. It was not a miracle that fell out of thin air, as if God as *Deus ex machina* lifted a finger from outside our history to create something out of nothing. The miracle, in a very real sense, is the fruit of the struggle. It is the fruit of faith, sometimes wavering, always under attack, but never diminished, of a believing people who with sacrificial love, an amazing endurance and a God-given gift for forgiveness refused to give up hope. They recognized within themselves that hope which God had implanted in them, and with that hope cried their cries for freedom and justice. And it was as if the LORD heard himself when he heard their cries.

Those who scoff at our achievements in ten years of democracy, who act as if nothing has changed, who propagate and believe the lie that under apartheid things were "better", are wrong also. They speak the language of the foreign country that was yesterday. We have just begun the walk toward genuine democracy and we have a long way to go still. But we are walking! If we honestly recognize our mistakes, rectify them before they become fatalities, we will reach our goal. And as a country and a people we must not just reach our goals – we must reach our destiny. But we must not make the imperfect our yardstick, nor the mediocre our consolation. We must not measure our progress by the comfort of the rich, but by the contentment of the poor. Judgement on how we walk must not be taken from the privileged, the family of the powerful, but from the powerless, the least of the family of Jesus. The authority with which we rule must not be derived from the approval of the mighty and the boastful, but from the ones of unimpressive proportions, in whom the living God has invested the hope for life, and where our hope for life is to be found.

Our strength should not be found in weapons made by hand in order to destroy and maim and kill. It should be found in the power that only the love of justice can bring. The health of our nation can never be found in the determinations of the Washington consensus, but in the security of our people, the safety of women and children, the integrity of our laws, the inclusiveness of our democratic life. Our true confidence should not be sought in the indexes that measure our compliance with rules not our own; it should be found in the faith of our people who continue to dream the dreams their parents, their siblings, and their children had fought and died for. And who are ready to trust us with those dreams, again and again. Our impetus for transformation should not come from the wealthy who fill our coffers with what moth and rust destroy, and who can only promise us life after politics. It should come from the One who embodies the weak and helpless, who appeals to the tenderness of our conscience and promises us life after death.

What Thabo Mbeki is offering South Africa, Africa and the world in his dream of an African renaissance is beyond price. It is, I believe, a dream from the heart of God. It is not his dream alone. All of us must claim ownership. For this reason it should be nurtured and grown with all the love and care we can muster. For this reason our defence of it should be robust, our hopes vested in it girded with passion. But it is a dream, therefore it is fragile. It is a dream, and therein lies its power. In that fragile power lies its fulfilment, because it is the dream of God, implanted in the heart of God's people. It is a tree planted in African soil as well as in African hearts, and the only nourishment it needs is hope, love, passion, faith and the determination to make it come true.

We are not there yet. We have a long walk ahead of us. But it is a dream so authentic we cannot dismiss it. It is a vision so truthful we cannot deny it. As with Habakkuk, when I heard it, "my heart pounded, my lips quivered at the sound…" And as with Habakkuk, we shall not be deterred by the struggle that lies ahead to realize it. We shall not be discouraged by the voices of nay-sayers. We shall not be diverted by rivers that seem too deep or mountains that seem too high. Our faith shall be like a cloud by day and a pillar of fire by night. Like Moses, we may only be allowed to see it from afar, but like Moses, we shall nevertheless walk as if we will reach it tomorrow. For we too, like Habakkuk, know the joy of seeing what God sees, and to let our people lead us in their faith that it shall be fulfilled. So with Habakkuk we too, shall sing:

> *Though the fig tree does not blossom*
> *and no fruit is on the vines;*
> *though the olive crop fails*
> *and the fields yield no food;*
> *though the flock is cut off*
> *from the fold*
> *and no herd is in the stalls,*

> *yet I will rejoice in the LORD;*
> *I will exult in the God of my salvation*
> *God, the LORD, is my strength;*
> *He makes my feet like the feet*
> *of a deer,*
> *and makes me tread upon the heights.* (Hab. 3:17-19)

And then, exquisitely, Habakkuk ends, not with the clouded doom of uncertainty, neither with the hollow arrogance of power, but with the joyful certitude of song: *"For the director of music: on my stringed instruments."*

Wild Goose Publications, the publishing house of the Iona Community established in the Celtic Christian tradition of St Columba, produces books, CDs and digital downloads on:

- holistic spirituality
- social justice
- political and peace issues
- healing
- innovative approaches to worship
- song in worship, including the work of the Wild Goose Resource Group
- material for meditation and reflection

For more information, please contact:

Wild Goose Publications
4th Floor, Savoy House, 140 Sauchiehall Street, Glasgow G2 3DH, UK

Tel. +44 (0)141 332 6292
Fax +44 (0)141 332 1090
e-mail: admin@ionabooks.com

or visit our website at
www.ionabooks.com
for details of all our products and online sales